"After reading Robin Hutton's stirring, heartfelt saga of the courageous, intelligent Sgt. Reckless, you wonder why she wasn't promoted to general. Robin's account evokes echoes of *War Horse* but this story of a great equine Marine is true. Make sure you have a comfortable chair and a box of tissues because traveling the road with Sgt. Reckless will take you to places you've never been before. Both Robin and her inspiration are to be commended."

—Michael Blowen, former arts and film critic for the *Boston Globe* and founder and president of Old Friends Thoroughbred Retirement

"The Korean War is often referred to as 'the forgotten war,' but, among Marines, the memories of that bloody and frozen conflict are strewn with the names of heroes, brave actions, and incredible sacrifices. Robin's new book about one of those forgotten warriors—one with four legs and a quirky appetite—adds detail, drama, and color to the documentation of the Korean War. Her research has brought new information and depth to the story. Bravo!"

—Lin Ezell, director, National Museum of the Marine Corps

SGT.
RECKLESS

SGT. RECKLESS

AMERICA'S WAR HORSE

ROBIN HUTTON

REGNERY
HISTORY

Library of Congress Cataloging-in-Publication data

Hutton, Robin L.
  Sgt. Reckless : America's war horse / Robin Hutton.
     pages cm
  Includes bibliographical references and index.
  ISBN 978-1-62157-263-3 (alk. paper)
  1. Sergeant Reckless (War horse), approximately 1948-1968. 2. Korean War, 1950-1953--Campaigns. 3. War horses--United States--History--20th century. 4. United States. Marine Corps. Marine Regiment, 5th--Biography. 5. Korean War, 1950-1953--Artillery operations. 6. War horses--Korea (South)--History--20th century. 7. United States. Marine Corps--History--20th century. I. Title. II. Title: Sergeant Reckless, America's war horse.
  DS919.H88 2014
  951.904'2450929--dc23
                                          2014019750

Published in the United States by
Regnery History
An imprint of Regnery Publishing
A Salem Communications Company
300 New Jersey Avenue NW
Washington, DC 20001
www.RegnerHistory.com

Manufactured in the United States of America

10 9 8 7 6 5 4 3 2 1

Books are available in quantity for promotional or premium use. For information on discounts and terms, please visit our website: www.Regnery.com.

Distributed to the trade by
Perseus Distribution
250 West 57th Street
New York, NY 10107

Fugue For Tinhorns, from GUYS AND DOLLS, By Frank Loesser
© 1950 (Renewed) FRANK MUSIC CORP.
All Rights Reserved
Reprinted by Permission of Hal Leonard Corporation

Official Marine Corps Photos provided by Camp Pendleton Archives; Command Museum, Marine Corps Recruit Depot, San Diego; *Leatherneck* Magazine; National Archives; Kathy Reesey; San Diego History Center; USMC History Division, Quantico, VA.

To Reckless, for just being ... Reckless!
To her Marines that loved and cared for her and kept
her spirit alive in their hearts all these years;
To everyone who shared a little piece of her with me ...
I am eternally humbled, blessed, and grateful.
You have forever changed my life.
This book is for you.

CONTENTS

*A*s commanding officer of the 5th Marine Regiment, I had the honor of conducting the ceremony promoting Sgt. Reckless to staff sergeant upon her return to Camp Pendleton from Korea with the 5th Marine Regiment in 1957.

This story is a fitting tribute to a dedicated, faithful Marine—"Reckless"—then a symbol of courage to those who served with the 5th Marine Regiment in the 1950s. Now she is a legend of Marine Corps history.

—**Colonel Richard Rothwell, USMC (Ret.)**
One of just five surviving infantry battalion commanders
(among eighteen) at World War II's Battle of Iwo Jima.
After the Korean War he served as commanding officer,
5th Marine Regiment.

REMEMBERING SERGEANT RECKLESS

All horses have a majestic quality, at least in my eyes. One image in particular keeps passing through my mind. Sometimes it comes by a sharp clap of thunder and lightning; at others, it is a full moon shining on one of my horses—and then always at the end of the month of March.

It is the image of a little sorrel mare loaded with 75 mm rounds on March 27, 1953, during our battle to secure Outpost Vegas in Korea. The image never seems to change—her head hangs low for balance as she struggles up the ridge, bringing ammo to the recoilless rifles of our 5th Marines.

She was a critical lifeline to the guns firing in support of us. They were depending on her. I was raised on a ranch/farm in the 1930s and 1940s where we depended on our horses and mules to help work our fields; but they were far more than tillers, horses were a loving part of our lives. We considered it a tragedy if one got hurt while skidding logs or mowing hay.

When I looked back toward the Main Line of Resistance (MLR) from the lower finger of Outpost Reno the night of March 27, I could hardly believe my eyes! There she was, Reckless, barely visible in the flare light, like the ghost of a horse packing 75s up to the guns! She faded in and out of sight and was gone as we continued with the stretchers.

My thoughts went back to our horses at home. I was so thankful that they were not here. They were well-trained ranch horses and used to all kinds of working noises and rifle shots during hunting season. But to withstand all the incoming rounds falling around Vegas? I don't think so.

Reckless was a very special horse and undoubtedly bonded through a spiritual connection of love with her Marines. The noise and waves of concussion can't be described, but she endured it all. I believe an angel had to be riding Reckless, since she was alone and without a Marine to lead her.

I have always cherished my horses. But after watching and learning more about that little mare of the Reckless Rifles, mine are even more special because I know they have the same Creator.

—Sgt. Harold E. Wadley, USMC (Ret.)

INTRODUCTION

I n 1997, *Life* magazine's special collector's edition, "Celebrating our Heroes," recognized the usual statesmen and inspirational figures children learn about in school. The list included presidents Thomas Jefferson, Abraham Lincoln, and George Washington. First Lady Eleanor Roosevelt made the cut, as did civil rights leader the Reverend Martin Luther King Jr. and Catholic missionary Mother Teresa. For good measure, *Life* even included a movie star, John Wayne. But there was another, very surprising entry in the special issue: a small, red Mongolian mare of modest origins who had emerged as the greatest war horse hero in American history.

She was Reckless—not exactly a name you'd associate with valor and selflessness. She first stirred American hearts in April 1954, when Marine Lieutenant Colonel Andrew C. Geer detailed her Korean War exploits in the *Saturday Evening Post*. The feats of heroism were so great that Reckless was eventually promoted to the rank of staff sergeant in the U.S. Marine Corps. She was no mascot. Reckless was the real deal—an actual combat Marine.

After the war, there was a national call to bring her to American soil. When Reckless finally arrived at the docks of San Francisco in November 1954, hundreds turned out, providing a true hero's welcome. A seasoned newsman covering the event remarked that this equine Marine drew more cameras and reporters than had then-Vice President Richard Nixon on a recent visit to town.

But Reckless's fame transcended her wartime heroism. Indeed, she became a uniquely popular personality in the national consciousness.

Beloved not only by Marines but people of all ages, Reckless was an icon in the 1950s, honored and celebrated by the most influential Americans in government and the popular culture.

To the public, her dramatic true story placed Reckless in the company of America's best-loved equine heroes—including Seabiscuit, Misty of Chincoteague, Dan Patch, Man O' War, and Secretariat. But by the start of the twenty-first century, her renown had faded. Today, few Marines know of Reckless—even those stationed at Camp Pendleton in Southern California, where she spent the last fourteen years of her life and is buried in an unmarked grave.

Reckless's remarkable journey with the Marines began in October 1952, amid the raging Korean War. Purchased for $250 from a young Korean man with valiant motives of his own, she trained as an ammunitions carrier for the Anti-Tank Division of the 5th Marines. The soldiers named her Reckless because the gun for which she carried ammunition—the recoilless rifle—was so dangerous it was nicknamed the "reckless" rifle. Like many of her fellow Marines, Reckless endured the worst of battle conditions, including freezing cold winters and regular missions hauling ammunition across impossibly treacherous, rugged mountain terrain.

Reckless was all alone when she joined the Marines. Because horses are "herd" animals, the Marines became *her* herd. She bonded so deeply with them that Reckless would go anywhere and do anything to help her adopted family. Rarely has a fully documented relationship between a horse and humans been more extraordinary.

Bred as a racehorse, Reckless was both tough and smart. When the Marines put her through "hoof" camp, they found the mare a fast study. She only needed instruction on a task once or twice—anything from scrambling into a bunker to avoid incoming shells to side-stepping communication and barbed wires. Once she understood something, Reckless never needed coaching again.

Reckless routinely was led from the ammunition supply point across open rice paddies and up precarious mountains to the guns on the front line. Even more impressive: she frequently made the trip by herself.

One of Reckless's finest hours came in March 1953 during the Battle of Outpost Vegas, described at the time as among the most savage battles in Marine Corps history. Her accomplishments in the battle not only earned Reckless the respect of all who served with her, but the unprecedented recognition of being officially promoted to the rank of sergeant.

Never, before or since, has such an honor been bestowed upon an animal.

Such heroic efforts alone make the story of Reckless a compelling one. But there was more to this remarkable horse than bravery. She had the tenacity to survive. Known for a spitfire personality that charmed all, Reckless, as you will see, also exuded a near-human sense of humor.

There simply has never been a horse like Reckless. Her inspiring, heartwarming story must be preserved and shared with this and future generations.

After all, she wasn't a horse—she was a Marine!

—Robin L. Hutton

PART I

KOREA

The Korean War began in 1950, when Communist North Korea invaded South Korea. It was a battlefield test of the Cold War—a time when the Cold War turned hot. Nowadays, the Korean War is often called the Forgotten War, mainly because it was sandwiched between the massive devastation of World War II and the searing controversy of the decade-long Vietnam War. It has been referred to as a "police action" or "conflict" rather than a war because it was fought under the auspices of the United Nations without Congress issuing a formal declaration of war, even though the vast majority of the troops were American and the UN forces were led by an American general (first Douglas MacArthur and then Matthew Ridgway). They faced off against the armed forces of the fanatical North Koreans, supported by the Soviet Union, and eventually the massed might of the Communist Chinese.

To those who fought in Korea, and the 36,914 who died there, this war will never be "forgotten." Neither should a little sorrel mare the Anti-Tank Company of the 5th Marines affectionately called "Reckless."

CHAPTER 1

BEFORE RECKLESS
BECAME RECKLESS

*The first time I saw her, I thought, "For crying out loud,
where did those guys find that horse?"*
—Sergeant Harold E. Wadley, Demolition Sapper,
Able Company, 1st Marines

"Reckless! Let's call her Reckless!" a voice cried out from the crowd of Marines gathered around their newest recruit. The name might have seemed ill-suited for a small, chestnut-colored horse with a blaze down her forehead and three white stockings. But to the Recoilless Rifle Platoon of the 5th Marines, the moniker was perfect—it was their radio call sign and captured the toss-caution-to-the-wind attitude of men who relied on the "reckless" rifle.

The little Mongolian mare bred for the racetrack officially joined the Marines on October 26, 1952. The commander of the Recoilless Rifle Platoon, Eric Pedersen, had bought the horse for $250—a princely sum to a Marine lieutenant in 1952—not as a mascot, but because his unit desperately needed help hauling heavy guns and artillery over Korea's rugged terrain. Trucks simply couldn't negotiate the steep, rutted mountains, especially in frigid, icy conditions. Pedersen realized a horse would make the ideal ammunitions carrier. So he asked permission to buy one. Fate would lead him to a horse known as Ah-Chim-Hai (Flame-of-the-Morning) and owned by a boy known as Kim Huk Moon.

• • •

From the moment he met her, Andy Geer, an accomplished, bestselling author, knew he would write about this remarkable little red horse. In Korea, Andy was more formally known as Lieutenant Colonel Andrew C. Geer, commander of the 2nd Battalion, 5th Marine Regiment. He met Reckless right after her greatest battle heroics in March 1953. As he noted in *Reckless: Pride of the Marines*, published in October 1955, "Some war stories are dated, but in the case of Reckless there was no such worry. Her story is as timeless as that of Black Beauty."[1]

Geer dedicated the first half of his book to the Korean youth he called Kim Huk Moon. At eight, Kim saw his first horse run at a Seoul racetrack—a moment that changed his life. That horse was the acclaimed Japanese racehorse Ah-Chim-Hai, or Flame-of-the-Morning. Ah-Chim-Hai was also Reckless's mother.

Geer spent long hours working with Kim, trying to learn everything he could about Reckless's background. But the effort was seriously hampered by unreliable interpreters and by Kim's desire for anonymity. At Kim's request "certain shadings and alterations to the story were made,"[2] including changing his name (Kim Huk Moon is a pseudonym).

Nevertheless, Andy Geer's book is the only substantive source of Reckless's life before she became a Marine, when she belonged to a boy with romantic ambitions of horse-racing greatness.

Kim Huk Moon became a very successful jockey and trainer during Japan's occupation of Korea before World War II. He rode the older Flame, Reckless's mother, to many victories. Kim loved the horse, and his greatest joy was spending time with her. He dreamed of the day he might own her.

At the end of World War II, Kim's greatest wish came true. During the war, Kim and Flame had been assigned to work at a Japanese prisoner of war camp, and Kim had saved the lives of many American POWs by sneaking food to them. When Japan surrendered and the camp was liberated, Kim's reward for his acts of bravery and kindness was Flame's ownership papers.

Kim returned to his family in Seoul. He lived with his older sister Chung Soon, their mother, his young niece Nam Soon, and his young nephew Yon. Their home, a shabby wattle-and-mud hut in the shape of an L, mirrored a hundred others lining the crooked streets along the Han River. The walls were baked mud, and the roof, fashioned of rice straw, was darkened by mildew. One part of the house was used to store firewood and hang meat or fish—whenever the family could afford such luxuries. The other part, the living quarters, was barely big enough for a small stove and sleeping mats for the five of them. In the winter, window coverings of rice straw were the only defense against the bitter cold.

Chung Soon toiled in the rice fields—back-breaking work lasting from daylight to dark that didn't produce enough money to feed one person, let alone five. As it was, most of the family's meals consisted

of a small bowl of rice with many cups of hot water. They felt lucky
to have even that.

Kim bred Flame to another racehorse, a stallion from Pusan: the
result was Reckless, born at Seoul's Sinseol-dong racetrack in June
1948. The sentimental Kim named her Ah-Chim-Hai—Flame-of-
Morning—to honor her famous dam. It was a day of celebration,
but followed swiftly by tragedy. Within a week, her mother was
dead, dying in the young jockey's arms, stricken by a fever. The
devastated Kim blamed himself, thinking his desire for another racehorse had killed his championship mare and beloved friend. He no
longer could bear to look at young Flame.

Kim's friends at the track tried to help. One, fellow jockey Choi
Chang Ju, offered to take the newborn filly so it could be raised by
one of his own mares—one who had dropped a foal three days earlier. She was big, strong, and could feed two as easily as one. Kim
took Flame to her new foster mother at Sinseol-dong and left quickly;
the racetrack was now a place of painful memories.

Months later, when the winter racing season began in November
1948, the family's gnawing poverty drew the reluctant Kim back to
the sport. That first day back at Sinseol-dong, Kim won three races.
Despite his understandable exhilaration, Kim couldn't bring himself
to visit young Flame in her stable. Another year passed before their
lives intersected.

That impromptu, unplanned reunion came in November 1949.
Entering the racetrack, Kim saw a playful Flame, goofing around
with the other young horses. The twenty-two-year-old jockey
watched with barely suppressed glee as Flame broke from the group
and spun in a fluid, free-spirited prance. In Kim's eyes, it was as if
Flame's namesake, her mother, had returned. All the painful feelings
Kim held against the little horse evaporated.

Kim's joy at seeing the prancing young Flame was suddenly replaced by terror when three massive, snarling dogs streaked across the field and attacked her. Shrieking in horror, Kim leapt over the railing. His screams distracted the dogs momentarily, and Flame broke free. She sprinted toward Kim, the dogs baying after her. Kim threw himself between Flame and the dogs, kicking one of them away, which had them cowering and then finally backing off.

The trembling Flame nuzzled Kim while he stroked the frightened animal, calming her down. He put her in her mother's old stall, and the young Flame became the center of Kim's life.

Flame was now almost two years old. Kim held high aspirations for her as a racehorse and set about training her. He quickly realized Flame had more native intelligence than most horses, a curiosity making her seem almost human. Flame was so eager to learn that training seemed effortless. She only needed to be shown something once, twice at the most, and she had it down. Kim had to admit the horse had qualities and abilities even her famous mother never demonstrated.

It's difficult to determine Flame's precise pedigree. She was "bred to be a racehorse," but that's a very general description and sheds no light on her breed. Even Andy Geer skirted the subject. Mention "Thoroughbred" and most people think of racehorses. But Thoroughbreds generally average sixteen hands high, with one hand measuring four inches. That makes most Thoroughbreds sixty-four inches at their withers—where the neck meets the shoulder. Flame stood a good dozen inches shorter at thirteen hands, making her more of a pony size-wise. She was also sometimes referred to as a "Mongolian" mare, but only on account of her size, for she bore little other resemblance to the breed, which is much stockier, with a heavy head, short neck, wide body, and thicker mane, tail, and leg hair. This may also be more of a regional reference than one of actual bloodline, as the Mongols introduced horses to the region at the time of Genghis Khan in the thirteenth century.

Most likely Flame was a taller than average (by two hands) Cheju (Jeju) pony (which gets its name from its native Cheju Island off the southern tip of South Korea) or possibly a Hanna horse—a crossbred Cheju pony and Thoroughbred. Both the Cheju pony and the Hanna horse were used for racing. Aside from her height, Flame's other features were consistent with the Cheju. Cheju ponies often have long legs with horse-like proportions, rather than the stubbier legs ponies are known for. They are resistant to disease and ticks and are extremely strong, capable of carrying loads up to 230 pounds, which, for Flame, would prove very useful in her military career.[3]

Climbing astride Flame for the first time was magical for Kim. He couldn't wait for their first race. Weeks of rigorous training boosted the horse's speed, agility, and concentration. In practice races, she routinely swept past other horses to victory, prancing in pride afterward in a sort of victory dance.

The summer racing season approached in late June 1950. Kim worked feverishly, preparing the young filly for her professional debut. He was confident of her talent and spirit, but events would take Flame in a different direction.

War

At 4:00 a.m. on Sunday, June 25, 1950, North Korea invaded South Korea. The attack came thirty miles north of Seoul, and many South Koreans who heard about it initially dismissed it as just another border skirmish with the antagonistic Communist regime. Race day was in full swing at Sinseol-dong, and thousands had poured through the turnstiles by 11:00 a.m., post time for the first race.

The seventh race was set aside for one of the biggest track events of the year—to honor Shin Ik Hee, a resistance fighter against Japanese colonial rule and considered a "founding father" of the Republic of Korea. During the fourth race, a plane circled overhead, dropping hundreds of leaflets. They cascaded from the sky, a white storm of propaganda raining down on the spectators. The flyers announced that an invasion—or "liberation" as the pamphlets declared—had just begun. Military jeeps sped to the track, their loudspeakers blaring a demand for all soldiers on leave to return immediately to their divisions.

Yet racing continued without incident through the day, with the Shin Ik Hee race running as scheduled. By day's end, however, it was clear that South Korea's very existence was at threat. All racing was suspended, as the country fought for its life, and thousands of South Korean civilians fled from the capital city of Seoul away from the sound of thundering guns. Flame's racing career was not to be.

Kim gathered his own family, preparing to make a two-hundred-mile journey south to the comparative safety of Pusan. Kim improvised a harness and hitched Flame to an abandoned cart. He hurriedly loaded sleeping mats and food and seated his mother and the children—his niece Nam Soon and nephew Yon—atop the rickety cart, which smelled of excrement and refuse. Flame took all this in stride as Kim took the lead rope and walked ahead alongside his sister Chung Soon.

Heading out of town, Kim heard the cries of an old blind woman who had given him grief since he was a boy. Kim stopped, gathered up the old woman, and placed her alongside his mother. At midnight, they arrived at a ferry crossing point on the Han River. They found thousands of frantic refugees waiting ahead of them.

Kim turned the cart and headed downstream to try to find a place where they could swim across. It took hours, but when they found it, Kim unhitched Flame from the cart and led her to the river's edge. She intuited what he wanted her to do. She gave a loud snort and then waded slowly into the cold, dark water, Kim clutching her mane and Chung Soon holding fast to her tail. Once they safely reached the other side, Kim selected a spot to make camp and then swam back with Flame to help the others cross. One by one, Flame carried Yon, Nam Soon, and Kim's mother on separate, increasingly wearying crossings. The poor horse was exhausted, her head hanging and flanks heaving. Kim and Flame swam back one last time—for the old woman. Flame rested at the water's edge as Kim went to find her.

She was gone. Kim called out frantically and searched up and down the riverbank. No trace of her. Finally, Kim had no choice but to bundle the rice, sleeping mats, and clothing for the final crossing with Flame, which left the horse trembling, struggling for breath, and near collapse.

In a cruel twist of fate, Kim's mother came down with a chill and died a few days later on the way to Pusan. Her dutiful son laid her to rest on a hillside overlooking the Naktong River.

A New Life in Pusan

It took two weeks to reach Pusan. There, Kim and his family stayed at the home of a friend whose horse had sired young Flame. Kim and Flame went to work unloading American ships at the docks. They hauled military supplies to huge dumps, even as the enemy, having overrun most of South Korea, besieged the southern port city.

The siege of the Pusan Perimeter was finally broken in September 1950, but it was two years before Kim and his family felt it was safe enough to return home to Seoul.

Sad Homecoming

In the spring of 1952, Kim hitched Flame to a cart and the family trudged north, bound for Seoul. The Seoul that Kim's family found on their return was a ghost of its former vibrant self; in fact, much of the city lay in ruins. Their own modest home was damaged but still standing.

Kim went looking for work at the racetrack, only to discover that the grounds had been converted to a landing field for the American Army. Kim was, however, still able to board Flame there, alongside other racehorses converted to wartime beasts of burden.

Kim and Flame began hauling rice from the fields to a government warehouse. Kim developed a "walking stick" trick that allowed him to steal extra rice for the family. The stick actually was a bamboo shaft with a cap. When no one was watching, Kim would plunge the shaft into a bag of rice, fill it, then cap the shaft. But Flame also had to eat. Because her grain was in short supply, the children pitched in, spending days pulling grass for her in the hills.

One day, Kim's old jockey friend Choi Chang Ju returned to the track. He had been in the Korean Army, in a battalion attached to the American Army 2nd Division. He had, however, lost an arm in the fighting and his military career was apparently over. Choi had a certificate from an American doctor authorizing him to receive a prosthetic arm from any American military hospital once his stump healed. Choi considered himself lucky—not only was he eligible for a new arm, but, as a disabled vet, he was entitled to government rice rations. He would never go hungry. He agreed to help Kim as much as he could because Kim's family was struggling to get by.

Chung Soon worked in the rice paddies, which offered steady but dangerous work, because the paddies were littered with landmines. One day, a worker next to her in the fields stepped on one. He was killed instantly, along with three others, and the blast mangled Chung Soon's left leg.

Yon and Nam Soon were at home when Chung was carried into the house, hysterical from pain and fear. A doctor arrived soon thereafter. Her wounds were so severe that he decided he had to amputate her leg. Yon ran screaming from the house, looking for Kim.

Kim, Choi, and Flame were returning from work when the sobbing Yon came racing up the middle of the street. Kim picked up the frantic little boy, placed him in the cart, and rushed home to see what was happening. Kim discovered his sister on a sleeping pad on the floor, writhing in pain, one leg missing. The doctor told Kim he did not have the drugs he needed to alleviate Chung Soon's pain and protect her from infection. Choi stepped up, telling the doctor to write down what was needed—that he would find a way to get it.

Kim stroked Chung's damp forehead until she fell asleep, then slipped outside to an astonishing sight: Choi was beating his stump with a stick. Kim pleaded with his friend to stop, but Choi explained that now he could go to the hospital for treatment—and get the drugs for Chung. Kim was beyond grateful for Choi's selflessness.

The next day at the hospital, Kim was amazed to see Korean soldiers walking on new artificial legs. He vowed that somehow he would get one for his sister. Choi, in the meantime, slipped Kim the medications that Chung Soon needed.

A few days later, Choi left the hospital and visited Kim and Chung Soon. With him was the same American doctor who had removed Choi's arm a year earlier, after the Battle of Wonju. The doctor brought medicine and crutches for Chung Soon, as well as food for the entire family.

When the doctor left, an emotional Kim turned to Choi. He was adamant: Chung Soon needed an artificial leg. Somehow, some way, he would get his sister the prosthetic. Choi, however, knew how expensive they were for civilians.

• • •

Weeks passed. On a cool day in October 1952, Kim and Choi finished work early and headed to the track to gallop Flame. This was the filly's favorite part of the day—the chance to sprint free, joyfully, and without care. American troops gathered to watch. When Flame noticed them, she began prancing, spinning, showing off for the crowd. How could Kim not love that spirit? He'd never lost the dream of racing her on that same track before thousands of adoring fans. Later, when they were about to leave the stables, four American soldiers bounced up in a jeep with a trailer attached. Flame's life was about to change.

CHAPTER 2

THE "RECKLESS" RIFLE PLATOON

*With the velocity of the round going out the barrel
and the back blast of the round...nobody
could stand behind it. It would cook a person.*
—Private John Newsom, 5th Marine Division,
Recoilless Rifle Platoon

I t's often said all's fair in love and war. Nevertheless, there were "rules" that ostensibly governed the Korean War. When the village of Panmunjom was chosen as the site for the United Nations truce talks, the peace negotiators drew a circle around a map of the "truce village." This was a no-fire zone. The no-fire zone was extended to cover a road (known as Freedom Road) for UN personnel to get to and from the peace talks. As Lieutenant Colonel Andrew Geer explained, "A larger circle with a two-mile radius was established and aircraft were not allowed to fly over this territory. Other lines were drawn, among them the Corps' No Fire Line, a No Voice Broadcast Line, a No Aircraft West of This Line and a No Leaflet

Dropping Line. These lines of prohibition were drawn by the United Nations command as insurance no overt act would be committed to give the enemy cause for anger."[1]

Operation Dig

Command Outpost No. 2 (COP2), manned by nearly three hundred Marines, was situated six-tenths of a mile east of the Panmunjom Circle. The Communists wanted it because if they could take it, they could threaten the entire Main Line of Resistance (MLR) of the United Nations forces.

The Marines attached nicknames to the various hills and outposts they held. Often the names were not-so-sly references to glamorous movie stars; other times, the monikers reflected how areas appeared on the map. For instance, this particular area was home to Hedy, Ingrid, and Ginger. Kate was nearby, but she was hardly a Hepburn hill, having been named for a Marine's girlfriend. Then there was Marilyn. Because of her height, Marilyn could support, if needed, both Outpost Kate to the east and Command Outpost 2 to the west.

Then there was Toothache and Molar, names the Marines used interchangeably for a hill situated between Command Outpost 2 and the restricted area around Panmunjom. On the map, Molar really did resemble an extracted tooth. But Toothache aptly described problems associated with its location—smack between Command Outpost 2 and the restricted area of Panmunjom.

The Chinese called their plan to isolate Command Outpost 2 "Operation Dig." In this so-called "creeping offensive," they would literally excavate around the outpost, thus cutting the road stretching from it to the restricted corridor. If the Marines were unable to

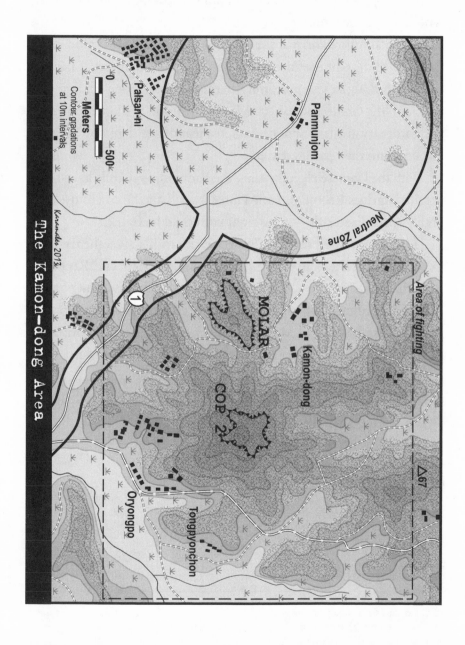

The Kamon-dong Area

receive supplies of food, water, and ammunition, the outpost surely would fall to the Chinese.

A trench was begun just south of the tiny village of Kamon-dong, from which the Chinese often fired on Command Outpost 2. Because of Kamon-dong's close proximity to the restricted zone circling Panmunjom, the Chinese knew the Marines wouldn't risk returning fire with ordinary artillery and mortars, for fear of accidentally dropping a round into the restricted area.

With the Chinese cleverly using the Panmunjom Circle as a shield, the 5th Marines Recoilless Rifle Platoon was called upon to use their highly specialized rifle—if the right site could be found.

Lieutenant William E. Riley Jr. wrote to his sweetheart Patty O'Leary about the role of the Anti-Tank Company and Recoilless Rifle Platoon. "We have one platoon of five tanks and one platoon of six 75s. Primarily we are an Anti-Tank company but the Koreans and Chinese haven't used any tanks in a few years and probably never will, so our primary job is assisting the infantry platoons in

PFC Roman Prauty, a gunner with 31st RCT (crouching foreground), with the assistance of his gun crew, fires a 75 mm recoilless rifle, near Oetlook-tong, Korea, June 9, 1951. *Corbis*

knocking out enemy bunkers, weapons and troops.... It's not a big, behind-the-lines weapon like it sounds. The 75 recoilless rifle is a small, potent weapon designed for front line use to assist the rifle platoons. We go on patrols and raids once in awhile to give added power to a unit."[2]

Because it had no wheels and sat on a tripod, the recoilless was awkward and challenging to carry; moving it in the field usually required three and at times four men, though sometimes two could manage. It could throw a 75 mm shell several thousand yards with extreme precision.

The Anti-Tank gun was a real handful in other ways, according to John Newsom, a Marine private from Woodland, California, who served with the Recoilless Platoon. It was six feet, ten inches in length, weighed nearly 115 pounds, and "was just a tube with a breach and it sat on a tripod."

"With the velocity of the round going out the barrel," Newsom recalled, "and the back blast of the round, the gun just sits there when it was fired. You would have to kneel down alongside of it when fired—nobody could stand behind it. It would *cook* a person."

Newsom said during target practice, Marines would stack old wooden crates and boxes sometimes ten feet behind the powerful gun. When the gun was fired, "the boxes and stuff would disintegrate, so you can imagine what it would do to a person."

"One person would load the gun, look back to make sure nobody was behind, and yell 'Gun up!' and the gunner would pull the trigger and away the shell went.... It made an incredible amount of noise,"[3] Newsom added.

With its ferocious back blast, the rifle's firing position couldn't be concealed from the enemy. At most, four or five rounds could be fired from one spot before the weapon had to be carried to another location, so the enemy couldn't pinpoint the firing site and retaliate.

A Deadly Game of Leapfrog

Sgt. Willard "Ray" Berry from Hazelwood, Missouri, was a scout sergeant for the Recoilless Rifle Platoon. Berry described the strategy in which multiple Recoilless units covered each other in battle. "What happens with a 75 recoilless," Berry explained, "is you set them up in a series of two or more guns, depending on the size of the mission, and you have a primary position and a secondary position for each of the guns.

"Gun One will fire a few rounds and then they grab the gun and disassemble it and run out and go over to another (secondary) position—because you have so much backblast, the enemy can see it and they start throwing mortars and direct fire and everything in there.

"Then…while they are tearing that gun down to make that move, to draw attention away, the other gun (Gun Two) opens up and they fire from another position. It's called *leapfrogging*. And then when Gun One hits their secondary position and opens fire from there…that was the technique that you used so if (the enemy) had a broader field of fire, they couldn't lay in that much concentrated fire on you because you might have five hundred yards between the two guns."[4]

If all really is fair in love and war, you'd think anyone named Gentleman would be out of his element. That, however, wasn't the case with battle-tested Lieutenant Colonel Alexander Gentleman. As commander of the 1st Battalion, 5th Marines (1/5), Gentleman's task was to thwart the creeping Chinese offensive. Gentleman was on COP2 and set up the mission for the recoilless rifle to come in, and sought help from Lieutenant Eric Pedersen who'd taken command of the Recoilless Rifle Platoon only a month earlier. Pedersen and Berry set out on a reconnaissance mission to scout location sites for the recoilless rifle.

"Pedersen and I were like two peas in a pod," Berry recalled, "We lived together in the same bunker and we did all the scouting missions for where we were going to set up our guns and so forth…we would scout out the areas where we could set up and fire our missions and get the heck out of there.

"We tried to get as close to the peace circle there, and there was a road called Freedom Road, and you couldn't fire through that zone a hundred meters on either side of the road. So we tried to get as close to that line as we could to fire from, because they couldn't fire back at us."[5]

Berry and Pedersen found a site atop Molar. The position provided the Marines a dead aim onto Kamon-dong, *and* the Chinese would be unable to fire back without risk of hitting the restricted area around Panmunjom. If the Chinese tried to capture the rifle platoon by force, the platoon could simply retreat to the restricted corridor, just a few yards away.

Yet something happened on that scouting mission. "We got spotted when we were out there and we got a call on our walkie talkie," Berry remembered. "And they said, 'Bug out, you got a platoon coming after you.' And as we started going back to the lines, there was a hill we had to run up. And a sniper opened up—and you could just hear the bullets zinging in and we're running up the hill—and Pedersen went down. And I was only a sergeant, and so I always referred to him as Mr. Pedersen or Sir. But I was always with him, with all the high command officers, when we'd be…finding out what mission they wanted us to go scout, and they always called him Pete, his nickname for Pedersen.

Soldiers of the 2nd Infantry Division and laborers of the Korean Service Corps struggle with a 75 mm recoilless rifle to get it into firing position up the hilly terrain of Korea.

"So as he's running up the hill, he went down and I was off to the side of him, behind him, and I said, 'Are you hit, Pete?' because I didn't have time to say Mr. Pedersen. And we ran up and got up on top of the hill, and there were some sniper rounds coming in pretty dang close. And we got up there and we hit the deck because mortars started coming.

"I swear to you this is true: He crawled over and put his body on top of mine, and I said, 'What are you doing?' and I joked, 'What is this, a love affair or what?' And he said, 'No damn it, he spotted me. It's my fault and if anybody gets hit, it's going to be me.' That's the kind of guy he was...he was *fearless*."[6]

Returning to camp, Lt. Pedersen and Sgt. Berry immediately readied the squad for the firing mission. Pedersen was known as a straight arrow who put the needs of his men first, something that inspired loyalty. Those under his command would do literally anything for him.

Lt. Eric Pedersen and two unidentified members of the Recoilless Rife Platoon demonstrate how to carry, use, and dismantle the recoilless rifle. *Command Museum, Marine Corps Recruit Depot, San Diego*

Drawings by Don Ricks when he was in Korea, (L) showing Marines carrying the recoilless rifle and ammunition, and (R) then firing the weapon.

Pictures courtesy of Jeremy C. McCamic, Korea Revisited *(Taylormade Printing Services, Wheeling, WV), 35–36.*

The immediate challenge would be moving the cumbersome recoilless rifle and its ammunition, without going through the restricted area, which was barred for transporting weapons. The hilly terrain further complicated matters, because the route from the ammunition supply point (ASP) to Molar was impassable for a jeep. The rifle—and its supply of ammunition—would have to be hauled by men on foot. There also was the certainty of, and dangers posed by, repeat runs to the supply point to replenish the ammunition.

The best way to carry the recoilless rifle was two men walking side by side, with a third carrying the tripod. Transporting it over rice paddy levees posed special problems because space didn't allow for the carriers' usual positions. A single man had to bear the burden of the entire rifle on the narrow levees. While the ammunition shells were manageable in size, their weight became a factor over long distances.

Depending on the magnitude of the mission and the number of rifles to be used, generally two or more Marines at a time carried ammunition. Each round weighed about twenty-four pounds, which included the cardboard canister it was encased in. The rounds used were either WP (white phosphorus smoke), used to generate smoke screens; HEAT (high explosive, anti-tank), that gave a range of 7,000 yards in ideal conditions and armor penetration up to 4 inches; or HE (high explosive), used for countering soft targets and infantry. The canisters were roughly 4 ¾ inches in diameter and 29 inches long. Generally, each man carried two rounds strapped horizontally to a hard plastic pack board that was carried like a backpack across the back shoulders of the carrier. There were slots in the board used to tie down the canisters. While two rounds was the standard load, at times, depending on the mission and the size and adrenaline of the carrier, three rounds could be carried in this fashion, along with the other gear, which made for a heavy and dangerous load when crossing rice paddy dikes or running up steep hills while dodging enemy fire.

"These were live rounds, ready for firing," Colonel Walt Ford, publisher and editor of *Leatherneck* Magazine told me. "There is no firing pin associated with the round itself—the firing pin is part of the rifle. The RR fires a fixed round with a firing plug at the base of the round and a primer rod filled with an igniter explosive running up through the canister. The primer rod is surrounded by more explosive propellant inside the canister.

"The round is inserted in the breech end of the recoilless rifle and a vented 'door' is closed over the breech, thereby covering the base of the round; it's called 'closing the breech.' A sharp blow or strike by the firing pin on the firing plug at the base of the round fires the primer rod, which ignites the propelling powder. In handling rounds, care must be taken to prevent dropping so that the firing plug does not set off the primer rod prematurely."[7]

The distance from the ammunition supply point to the firing site was slightly more than a half mile. It was a treacherous trip, forcing carriers to pass under wire, traverse a rice paddy dike, cross a seven-foot ditch, and then make the steep climb to the ridge—all in full, perilous view of the enemy. Pedersen chose Sergeant William Cox's rifle team for the mission. Generally, five men were assigned to a team—two or three men carried the rifle, one of whom was the forward observer who would direct the rifle's fire. Two men were designated ammunition carriers. When the rifle went into action, the ammunition carriers were constantly in motion between the ammunition supply point and the firing site. Cox put the rifle into action right away, firing as many as three rounds a minute at Kamon-dong, about 1,600 feet away, leveling every mud hut in his sight from right to left. He finally hit pay dirt, an ammunition dump, setting off a huge explosion that covered the village with smoke and debris.

Before the air cleared, the crew broke down the weapon and pulled it into the protected corridor. Their work was done for the day—they'd leveled one of the enemy's supply bases.

The men were exhausted on the drive back to base camp outside the village of Changdan—especially the ammunition carriers, privates Monroe Coleman and Jose Cordova, who had made several trips each from the ammunition supply point to the firing site. Their exhaustion gave Lieutenant Pedersen an idea: why not find a horse or mule to carry the ammunition; a horse, after all, could carry six to eight rounds faster than a man could carry two or three. He ran the idea up the chain of command and with final approval given by regimental commander Colonel Eustace P. Smoak, and Lieutenant Colonel Gentleman's offer to lend Pedersen a one-ton trailer to transport the horse, he set about finding his packhorse. "Most people couldn't conceive of what Mr. Pedersen conceived," recalled Berry. "See, he saw that he wouldn't have to put his men in jeopardy there and a horse would be able to carry more rounds a lot faster, and that was his whole idea."[8]

A "Can Do" Packhorse

October 26, 1952, seemed like a perfectly ordinary Sunday. That afternoon at New York's 46th Street Theatre, a rotund man in a funny suit stepped onstage and, playing a comic gambler named Nicely-Nicely, belted out a tune he'd performed about six hundred times in two years. The performer was Stubby Kaye, the show was the Tony-winning *Guys and Dolls* and the song was "Fugue for Tinhorns." Audiences knew it better by its bouncy lyrics:

> I got the horse right here
> The name is Paul Revere
> And here's a guy that says that the weather's clear
> Can do, can do, this guy says the horse can do
> If he says the horse can do, can do, can do

Nearly seven thousand miles away, U.S. Marine Lt. Eric Pedersen was also looking for a "can do" horse. But unlike Damon Runyon's fictional Nicely, Pedersen couldn't afford to gamble on just any horse; the lieutenant knew he needed *exactly* the right animal.

Corporal Philip Carter drove Pedersen and Scout Sergeant Ray Berry into Seoul, with the borrowed one-ton trailer hitched to their jeep. "We had the trailer all rigged up," explained Berry. "We put side stakes up so the horse wouldn't fall over the top of it, because it was kind of shallow."[9]

They were looking for a "can-do" horse that could haul ammunition for the Marines over tough terrain and possibly through enemy fire.

According to an October 28, 1952, letter received by Lieutenant J. C. McCamic from J. H. Rinyak while in Korea, the three men stopped at the camp of the 7th Marines to advise them of their plans to buy a horse. "A buddy of mine, Sgt. Berry...and Lt. Pedersen of AT CO, 5th Marines, just stopped off back here on their way to Seoul to purchase either a horse, pony or mule for use as a packhorse for carrying the 75 MM Rifle thru rice paddies and other obstacles. The idea sounds good. Because I'm very much interested, Sgt. Berry has promised to let me know the results of their experience.

"Lt. Pedersen mentioned that he spoke to you of the idea and I was just wondering what you thought of it; I'm interested in hearing all the pros & cons on the subject."[10]

Lt. McCamic didn't have a copy of his reply, but he did remember taking it up with his platoon, and "there was some laughter and such questions as: 'Are we going to get six horses—one for each squad or just one up for grabs? Who is going to take care of the animal? Who will feed it, curry it, wash it down, see to its hooves etc., etc.?' Then some real in-company humor—let Sgt. Moyers (company scrounger and sometimes forward observer) or Cpl. Nau (company jeep driver) do it. Since...the rice paddies were not in use and were dry, we concluded it was not worth the trouble of getting the horse, our weapons carriers could continue doing their good job."[11]

The three Marines then made their way to the headquarters of the Army Purchasing Mission. While they found no horses or mules for sale there, the lieutenant in charge suggested they try the race-track, just on the other side of town. According to Berry, they picked up an interpreter at the PX who would help them negotiate the sale before leaving for the racetrack.[12]

Kim and Choi had just given Flame a rubdown and feed after finishing an exhilarating run on the overgrown, weedy track, when Pedersen, Carter, Berry, and the interpreter approached and told them they need a horse to carry ammunition. Choi understood English, and the interpreter translated for Kim, whose first instinct was to hide Flame, who was in her stall. But it was too late; Choi was already leading the Americans to the horses in their stalls; Pedersen had said he was willing to pay for a horse in American cash.

Eric Pedersen loved horses. He'd spent most of his life around them, having grown up in Jackson Hole, Wyoming, and Prescott, Arizona. The lieutenant had a good eye for equines and knew instinctively the traits required for the unusual job he had in mind. In the first stall, Pedersen saw a thin, straggly horse with scabs from harness sores. The next three horses were in better shape—but not what he was looking for. The last horse he saw, the fifth horse, was the ticket. Here was a well-groomed filly that possessed "an intelligent eye and fine head." She reminded him of a horse he had as a boy in Arizona—only this one, he soon realized, was much more impressive.

The American approached the horse and put out his hand. To his surprise, Flame wasn't afraid. In fact, she began moving toward *him*. Pedersen checked her teeth for any problems, then asked the horse's age. Choi told him four years, three months.

Pedersen thought he had his horse; now it was all a matter of price. When the Marine lieutenant asked how much, Choi responded with a question of his own: how much was he was willing to pay?

Pedersen held up a forefinger and bent it. "One-hundred-and-fifty dollars."

Choi was insulted and said so. He called Flame "the best horse in Chosin" and gave him an angry lecture on the horse's fine blood lines and history. Pedersen didn't haggle. "Pete said, 'Look, I've got limited funds, this is all I'll pay,'"[13] recalled Berry. Pedersen declared that $250 was his final offer. *That* figure was more to Choi's liking. Kim was sickened at the thought of losing Flame; he wanted the men to leave. But when Choi told him the American would pay 250 *American dollars* for Flame, Kim could barely speak. He finally managed to choke out a question: "Will that buy a leg for Chung?"

Yes, said Choi, $250 would buy a beautiful leg for Chung Soon. Kim agreed to the sale, but asked to be alone with Flame to say goodbye.

Kim stepped inside the stall and closed the door. Flame pushed her head into his chest as he held her close, one last time. He fought back tears. He helped load his beloved horse into the trailer, watched as she was driven away, then walked into Flame's empty stall and collapsed in tears.[14]

CHAPTER 3

FROM FLAME
TO RECKLESS

*Everybody wondered what the hell was a horse
doing here and we soon found out.*
—Sergeant Chuck Batherson,
Anti-Tank Company, 5th Marines

I n just a few hours, Flame had left her old life behind and, as Reckless, began a new one.

"As we drove into camp the MPs said, 'What are you going to do, eat that horse?' They couldn't figure out what we were doing with a horse," Sergeant Ray Berry recalled. "They thought we were going to take it back and eat it!"[1]

Sergeant Chuck Batherson was playing softball when the platoon's newest recruit arrived and the men erupted in cheers. "Everybody wondered what the hell was a horse doing here and we soon found out. To this day, I can see them pulling into camp."[2]

"When we saw he had bought a horse, I think we all just kinda wondered if he [Pedersen] was okay," recalled Sgt. Ralph Sherman, one of the gun crew leaders of the platoon, "because we couldn't imagine how that would fit in with whatever we were doing. But then of course, as he explained the purpose behind it, to allow the horse to carry ammunition and how it could carry much more and much faster than we could, all that made a lot of sense."[3]

Reckless represented a military secret to be kept not just from the enemy, but from many of her new American comrades. "At first we had to hide her," Berry said, "because there wasn't all that much authority with everybody knowing what was going on ...

"In our unit people were really interested in this horse, but it was not known among other units ... [Pedersen] had gotten clearance from up above, but he said to just keep everything mute until we got things all worked out."[4]

The drive back had given Lt. Pedersen time to figure out who would be Reckless's companion. He zeroed in on Private First Class Monroe Coleman, reasoning that being raised on a ranch in Utah and having a love of horses made Coleman the perfect choice. Pedersen also called on Technical Sergeant Joe Latham to help Reckless become acclimated to camp.

Pedersen ordered that no one was to ride Reckless, issued instructions for building her a bunker and getting her feed, and assigned Latham (who had trained horses) and Private Coleman to look after her. Latham was to be her drill instructor. Pedersen told him to put the horse through boot camp.

Latham didn't miss a beat: "Shouldn't it be hoof camp, lieutenant?"[5]

By popular acclamation, the men christened her Reckless, and subsequently led her to the mess tent for her first meal as a Marine: a loaf of bread and uncooked oatmeal.

She liked it just fine.

However, not everybody was excited to see a horse in camp. "The last thing I wanted to do was take care of a horse when I was trying to stay alive,"[6] remembered Julian Kitral, who was a corporal. But most of the Marines saw Reckless as a great mascot, if nothing else.

The next day was spent familiarizing the newest Marine recruit with camp life and providing for her needs. Batherson remembered that "they took up a collection" for her feed and other needs, "I threw in about $5 or $10."[7] Pedersen also approached the camp's shoe company—the guys who did leatherwork and repaired the men's boots—to fashion a packsaddle matching specifications the lieutenant drew up.

The men built Reckless's bunker and fenced in a small pasture for her. The horse's new home was built to standard bunker specifications, with a minimum of four feet of sandbags stacked atop a crossbeam-supported roof. The division engineers believed the design provided the best protection from Chinese shells.

As Latham headed south to forage for feed, Coleman stayed in camp to work Reckless over with an old shoe brush, the closest thing he had to a curry comb or dandy brush. When he finished, Coleman stepped back to admire her glistening coat, as shiny as a spit-and-polished boot.

Reckless took to her new life with gusto: she loved the Marines' attention, and she relished something most servicemen never miss a chance to mock—the chow. Not only was there a lot of it, but her diet was surprisingly varied—from her first apple to her first carrot to her first Hershey bar to the ground cover in her new enclosure, where, to the delight of the Marines, she pranced like a show horse until two dogs ventured innocently into the pasture. Reckless pinned her ears back and charged, chasing them away. Navy Corpsman

George "Doc" Mitchell thought Reckless acted "like she was scared as a kid by a dog. Has a psychosis probably."[8] From then on, standing orders barred all canines from her vicinity—for their own sakes.

Latham returned with an overloaded trailer of barley, sorghum, and rice straw, all paid for by Platoon donations. "I'd buy it from local Korean farmers," Latham recalled. "The men would pitch in money when they could."[9]

Latham put down a nice straw bed for her and gave the new horse soldier a green Marine blanket to warm her at night. Reckless had never known so many wonderful comforts. Latham even volunteered that on freezing winter nights, "I'll take her into my tent and let her sleep by my stove."[10]

Korean winters were notoriously frigid between December and February, with night temperatures often plummeting below zero degrees Fahrenheit. "The Marines who made the first winter in the 'Frozen Chosin' without any cold weather training," Sergeant Harold Wadley recalled, "are the ones that really suffered." The Marine Corps had attempted to address the issue a year earlier. In 1951, after the war's bitter first winter, Pickel Meadows in the Sierra Nevada Mountains south of Lake Tahoe was established to prepare Marines for the cold Korean weather. While training in the rugged area—elevations ranged up to eleven thousand feet—helped immeasurably, conditions were considerably windier and colder on the Korean peninsula.

Wadley described it best: "The clear, starry winter nights impressed me. Seemed like at twenty below, I could hear the stars rattle like ice cubes. When it was quiet at night, sound carried a long ways, making the frozen crunch of a step seem like they were right next to you. The bolt of all weapons had to be worked regularly to be sure they would function when fired.... Once my field jacket got frozen into the mud while laying in ambush for three hours and (they) had to yank me free. A bit scary at the time."[11] The Marines knew what Korean cold was like—and were keen to protect Reckless from its rigors.

Reckless settled into her surroundings, but not without a few early mishaps. "She got cut up quite a bit from the barbed wire because she was not accustomed to it," Berry recalled. "The barbed wire was strung around to hold her in. We made a little corral for her and she would run into it when we first got her and she got all cut up. She didn't know what it was. So Doc Mitchell would go ahead and fix the cuts…but she was pretty scared of everybody at first."[12]

That fear didn't last very long as Reckless soon relished her new life, exploring every inch of her pasture and, after boredom set in, venturing out on her own, as she was given free rein of the camp like every other Marine.

Latham turns Reckless out to feed. On cold nights she slept in his tent. *Nancy Latham Parkin*

Naturally, her favorite stop was the galley tent. One morning, new recruit PFC Billy Jones offered to share his scrambled eggs with Reckless. She shocked the young Marine by not only scarfing down all the eggs, but then washing them down with coffee. "Wait'll Reckless finds out you've been feedin' her powdered eggs," Cordova warned him. "She'll chase you over the hill like she did those dogs."[13]

Pedersen picked up the packsaddle from the shoe company. "It wasn't worth a damn," Berry said. "It was sliding around and Pete looked at it and said, 'This is Mickey Mouse...this ain't gonna work.' And so he contacted his wife. He drew up plans with what he wanted and sent it to her right away to have it made and sent to him. That's where they came up with the bag they used."[14]

Increasingly, Reckless stayed with her newfound friends—they were becoming her herd. Sixty years later, a leading veterinary horse behavioral expert described these bonds as only natural. "Reckless's relationship with the troops is understandable when you realize that horses are a herd animal. They are meant to live in groups," explained Dr. Robert M. Miller, the Thousand Oaks, California, veterinarian, author, and creator of the innovative foal training technique called imprint training. "Most domestic animals, the cat being the exception, in the wild live in groups—all the time, always. Not occasionally, not when they're breeding, or not when they have youngsters—but all the time. Sheep, goats, cattle, and people, of course; we are a group creature."

Miller says creatures normally living in groups but separated by circumstance from their own kind "will quickly accept what's called a surrogate—it's called surrogate bonding. If you go to the racetrack, many times you'll see a goat in with a horse, or a pony, or a burro, or even a chicken in a cage. They need some living creature, otherwise they feel desperately alone. And they're not meant to be alone."

So, Miller reasoned, when Reckless joined an otherwise horseless Marine Corps platoon, "there are all these guys who give her little treats and pet her and stroke her and become very fond of her. And she's perfectly happy with that. And it means a lot to her."[15]

That's just what happened with Reckless. She'd venture into her friends' tents on cold or rainy nights or when she didn't want to sleep alone. The men would always make room for her, usually by the warm stove.

"Hoof Camp" Begins

When it was time to start "hoof camp," Lieutenant Colonel Gentleman had the battalion surgeon examine Reckless, who certified her as "physically fit and capable of performing the duties of a Marine of her age and rank."[16]

Latham began his "hoof camp," working with her daily. He taught her to come when he whistled[17] and how to get in and out of her trailer. Since the trailer was just 36 inches by 72 inches, she had to learn some adjustments. "We had a little deck where she walked up and she was up on the thing," Berry explained, "and she walked into the trailer. She resisted trailers and all that at first. Latham worked with her a whole lot with that."[18]

Finally, Latham's work paid off. "She'd jump in the trailer and go in catty-cornered, and I'd tie her down,"[19] Latham explained. He took her on long walks through the hills, showing her how to surmount barbed wire, which also made her extra cautious around the security fencing. When she was nervous, a shrill whistling sound came from Reckless's nostrils—as if she were "smelling out the danger."[20] When she was sizing up new challenges, she would lower her head, as if in careful reflection and then, if

Latham works with Reckless, getting in and out of her trailer. *National Archives*

Doc Mitchell lends a hand in helping Reckless manage the trailer. *USMC History Division, Quantico, VA*

Latham puts Reckless through "hoof camp." Here she learns to step over wire. Leatherneck *Magazine*

Latham taught Reckless to "hit the deck" when under enemy fire. *Nancy Latham Parkin*

she felt comfortable, move ahead. Reckless would go anywhere with anyone she trusted.

Once Latham and his charge had established a close bond and mutual trust, the training got more involved, especially around the recoilless rifle. "I had to get her to calm down," Latham recalled. "I had to train her not to go behind the guns. It will knock you down, front and back."[21]

He taught Reckless to lie down, even kneel, in case there was no cover and she needed to crawl into a shallow bunker for protection from incoming fire. "I trained her to get down—hit the deck," said Latham. "I'd just tap her on the front of the leg and she'd get down. It took a lot of training."[22]

Latham also trained Reckless to head for the bunker when shells hit near camp. "Reckless was no dummy," Latham said. "She had her own bunker...when incoming started, we'd scramble into ours and she'd head for hers, although there were a few times when she thought ours was more convenient. Nobody complained."[23]

"All I had to yell," Latham added later, "was 'Incoming! Incoming!' and she'd go."[24]

Berry backed up Latham's descriptions of Reckless as a remarkable, intelligent, and resourceful foot soldier. "She actually got to the point that he [Latham] could use arm and hand signals and get her to kneel down," he recalled, "and her little ears, you'd see them move when mortar was fired. And she would duck down on the deck and then, after the mortar went off, she would head for that bunker. It was pretty incredible to watch."[25]

Sgt. Ralph Sherman also had an interesting take on the incoming fire. "Whenever we were with the horse, that automatically triggered action from the North Koreans. And it was always the opportunity for them to kill the horse, that's the impression that I got. And luckily that didn't happen. I just think they watched us as much as we watched them, the North Koreans and the Chinese, and I think when they saw the horse that just prompted them to want to try to kill the horse, destroy the horse, whatever, and so it did bring in some incoming on occasions when it wasn't expected. I think it was because if they killed the horse, they would have food, because they ate horsemeat over there."[26]

Somewhat of a prankster, Latham taught Reckless a trick to play on Doc Mitchell and the platoon. He'd flick her right front leg with a switch, and she'd suddenly limp as if in pain. Mitchell almost sent her to the hospital ship USS *Repose* for an x-ray before the ruse was exposed.

According to Latham, Reckless didn't like people to tease her. She could be aggressive when provoked and almost pushed one Marine

Latham takes a ride on his favorite recruit. *Nancy Latham Parkin*

into a barbed wire fence.[27] She developed, however, a few playful pranks of her own—mostly at Latham's expense. Sometimes she'd pretend to eat, knowing Latham was sneaking up on her. When he got close, Reckless would teasingly run away. Prancing around the gunnery sergeant, the horse then squared off and charged him, ears back and teeth bared in a show of deadly menace. But at the last second, she'd stop, rear, then run off in the other direction. Once she grew bored with these antics, Reckless would nonchalantly amble up and nuzzle Latham for a piece of candy—something he always had handy.

The day came when Latham proudly announced to Pedersen, "Tell her what you want and let her look the situation over an' she'll do it, if she's with someone she trusts."[28] Never in his fourteen years in the Corps had Latham worked so hard with, or been so proud of, any recruit.

Word of Reckless Spreads along the Line

Word of the four-legged newcomer spread fast among different units along the line. While some were jealous they didn't have her, others tried to undermine Reckless before she could prove herself in action.

There was concern among aides to Major General Edwin Pollock, commander of the Marine 1st Division, that Reckless might react badly to the ferocious back blast from the recoilless rifle. The rifle released such violent force that even seasoned Marines often jumped, and horses generally don't like loud noises and commotion. Pollock's aides feared Reckless would bolt after the first shell was fired. Latham tried to reassure them that Reckless was different from other horses, but one officer wasn't buying it, chiding the gunnery sergeant, "Just wait'll she's on the line someday and little China-boy starts dropping incoming. Your horse will be outgoing."[29] That kind of talk was brushed aside within her own platoon, but Latham made sure that Reckless was as familiar with the recoilless rifle as any horse could be, short of actual combat.

Major General Pollock decided to see Reckless for himself. He wanted to meet the celebrity recruit everyone was talking about. The day of Pollock's visit, the platoon made sure Reckless was ready; Coleman had given her a good brushing and she shined like a freshly minted penny.

General Pollock was an experienced horseman, and in a thorough inspection he found that—except for Reckless's need of new shoes—the level of the new recruit's fitness for battle was impressive. Pollock offered to help find a blacksmith, and Pedersen took him up on the offer.

The next day, Reckless lumbered onto the trailer, and Latham drove her to the blacksmith in a neighboring village. As Latham unloaded Reckless from her trailer, the blacksmith spoke to her in

Korean. While Reckless seemed to understand his words, she did not like his manner; the stranger was rough and curt as he led her and Latham into his hut.

He tied Reckless to the center pole and tried to examine her hooves, but she wanted no part of this. When the man yanked her head, Latham yelled at him to take it easy. But when the blacksmith brought out a chain to tie her down, that was enough. Reckless reared and kicked—and finally chased the man out of his own hut. As Latham rushed to calm her, the center pole gave way, knocking him to the ground, and Reckless broke free and rushed outside. The gunnery sergeant crawled out from under the collapsed hut to find the blacksmith tending to his bruises. When Reckless saw Latham, she walked over to him, ready to leave. He loaded her in the trailer and drove away.

Back at camp, Reckless's friends roared over how she kicked the man out of his own hut. They loved her independent spirit, praying she would display the same determination under fire. Since the shoe shopping expedition had failed, Latham trimmed Reckless's hooves himself, then tightened her existing shoes as best he could. This would have to do until he could take her back to the racetrack in Seoul, where someone she knew and trusted could handle the job.

Serious Work Begins

When the packsaddle arrived from Kay Pederson, the serious training finally began. A veterinarian and old friend, Dr. A. P. Immenschuh, designed packsaddles and had donated one, which Kay sent via the Navy because the post office wouldn't handle the forty-pound package to Korea.[30] The first time Sergeant Harold Wadley saw Reckless was with the packsaddle. "I thought, 'For crying out loud, where

Left, Reckless with 75 mm recoilless rifle and pack saddle. Right, Reckless on hill with gun crew. *USMC History Division, Quantico, VA*

Reckless being loaded with a round of recoilless rifle ammunition. Each round weighed twenty-four pounds. Leatherneck *Magazine*

Marines lace the canisters of ammunition onto Reckless's pack. *Command Museum, Marine Corps Recruit Depot, San Diego*

did those guys find that horse?'" the sergeant recalled. "The first thing they were trying to do was adjust the packsaddle and harness on her. And of course, me being a ranch kid, and even in the pictures, it's the most fouled-up adjustment of pack rigging you could find. It's a

Latham leads Reckless out in the field with her squad. Notice the rounds of ammunition out of the canisters and sticking directly out of her pack. *Nancy Latham Parkin*

sawbuck they had on her, and everything was super loose on her and there was no way the guys didn't have a leather punch to adjust the buckles through the britch and strap on her. My first impression was you could stick a bale of hay between her hindquarters and the britch. But they were intent. I just commented to the Marine that, 'If that mare gets in a hurry, all that's going to fall off from her.'"[31]

After much experimentation, the platoon found Reckless could safely and easily carry six rounds of recoilless rifle ammunition in canisters without much trouble. Yet in the heat of battle, they found she could tote eight to ten rounds, if necessary.

Many surviving photos depict Reckless bearing only four rounds. "They packed her high when she was carrying just the four rounds shown in the pictures," Wadley recalled. "At least someone in the gun crew knew to keep the load on top of the rib cage, where the strength is, and not on the extended rib cage to hammer the breath out of her."[32]

Sometimes, the rounds would be taken out of the canisters and stuck directly in her pack. This, however, was a needlessly dangerous way to transport the rounds, which were highly explosive.

Lt. Eric Pedersen leads Reckless up and down the Korean hills to get her accustomed to the terrain. *Camp Pendleton Archives*

Lt. Wayne Gouty (L) serves Reckless her first beer. Also pictured are Lt. William Hoffman (C) and Lt. Col. Andrew Geer (R). Leatherneck *Magazine*

Latham and Coleman walked the hills with Reckless to get her used to the load—which she carried effortlessly. On occasion, Pedersen walked her, too. Reckless seemed to enjoy the forays with her friends—and they knew it. It's been said that sometimes, when an ordinary animal looks at you, all you see in the eyes is an animal. But when the men of the Recoilless Rifle Platoon gazed into Reckless's eyes, they sensed a person was looking back at them.

Latham's "hoof camp" instruction included self-defense training for Reckless. On one outing, he wrote privately that Reckless killed a wildcat near 76 Alley, near outposts Vegas, Carson, and Reno, "by rearing up and crashing down on the cat with her front feet and bellowing at the same time."[33] After one of her workouts, Latham poured a Coca-Cola into his helmet and offered it to her. She sucked it up and wanted more. From then on, Reckless shared a Coke with her friends almost daily. (Doc Mitchell advised no more than a couple bottles a day, concerned over damage the carbonated water might do to her kidneys.)

But Coke wasn't the only new drink she took a shine to. One night, Reckless moseyed over to the officers' mess tent, swaggered in like Duke Wayne and bellied up to the small bar at the back. Another Wayne—Lieutenant Wayne Gouty—was bartending. For fun, he offered the four-legged barfly a brewski. Gouty poured a can of beer into a bucket and Reckless eagerly slurped it up. "That's the first horse's head I ever served here," said the stunned lieutenant.[34]

From then on, Reckless was known to imbibe on many occasions.

Baptism by Fire

The day of Reckless's long-awaited "baptism by fire" finally arrived in late November 1952. The intended firing line was the colorfully nicknamed "Hedy's Crotch," a valley between outposts Ingrid to the south and Hedy to the north, in the center sector of the Jamestown Line. (The Jamestown Line was a series of defensive positions occupied by UN forces stretching about 35 miles from the Imjim River near Munsan-ni, to a point east of Kumhwa, South Korea.) The distance from camp to the firing site was two-and-a-half miles. Part of the way could be traveled by jeep, but the final five hundred yards was a steep climb to the ridgeline.

Three trucks were sent out at ten-minute intervals. The squad, led by Lieutenant Pederson and Sergeant Ralph Sherman, and weapon went out first, followed by Reckless in her trailer, and finally, the ammunition. When they reached the base of the ridge, Reckless sensed something was up. She clambered out of the trailer, and headed straight to Latham's pocket, sniffing for chocolate. But her trainer stopped her. "No pogey bait 'til this is over,"[35] he said as he strapped on six canister rounds of high-explosive shells on her and slapped her backside for encouragement. ("Pogey bait" is Marine-speak for non-issued food or drink, especially sweets.)

Coleman took Reckless's lead rope and started up the steep hill. When they passed the gun crew, Sherman told Coleman to unload Reckless and bring up more ammunition. Pedersen and Scout Sergeant Berry were already searching for targets.

Pederson and Berry were at the first firing point. Once fired, a recoilless rifle was easy to spot. So to minimize the danger, gun crews were trained that once a target was established, the gun should be fired quickly, only four or five times, before being picked up and moved to another location before counter fire came. This meant the crew would hopscotch around the ridgeline, at different firing sites, until a mission was completed. Infantrymen weren't particularly fond of recoilless rifle crews because when they started firing, so did the enemy.

The only time the recoilless crew members didn't have to play hopscotch was when they used the restricted area of Panmunjom and the corridor as a shield, as they did with the shelling of Kamon-dong.

The key to a successful mission was speed and teamwork. And now they were about to see how their newest recruit would handle

Reckless on the battlefield. *Camp Pendleton Archives and* Leatherneck *Magazine*

the pressures of battle. Reckless and Coleman had just returned to the firing line with their second load when Sherman began blasting away.

The roar of the weapon echoed through the hills and dust exploded from the back of the gun. Even though Reckless was laden with six shells totaling about 150 pounds, the force of the blast frightened the horse right off the ground. Coleman saw the whites in her eyes and moved quickly to calm her.

While Reckless became accustomed to the sounds of battle, the first few times she jumped off all four hooves! *Command Museum, Marine Corps Recruit Depot, San Diego*

The second shot roared just as loudly. Again, Reckless went airborne, although not as high this time. Coleman managed to talk her down. As she shook her head trying to stop the ringing in her ears, the third round left the tube. This time, Reckless stood closer to Coleman and shook from the concussion of the blast. That third time was the charm for the rookie recruit because she didn't jump and was breathing more easily.

She watched the gun crew fire the fourth shot and hardly jerked her head.

Sherman quickly directed his crew to move the weapon to the next firing position, with Reckless and Coleman following close behind. She delivered her second load and was heading to the truck for number three when enemy counter fire hit the old site. Reckless began to sweat more from the terrifying explosions overhead than from the weight of her loads and the stress of climbing the steep, craggy terrain. A lather of sweat formed under the packsaddle straps.

At the truck, Latham checked her over and rubbed her down. He felt her wet neck and rubbed her ringing ears as she nuzzled him. This seemed to calm Reckless a bit, and Latham loaded her up for another trip.

"They talk about her sweating profusely," said Sergeant Wadley, an avid horseman and author of a book on horse training. "They didn't realize how critical her fear was. A horse only drips sweat all over like that when they are scared half to death, or in extreme pain. How I felt for her! She adjusted on her own, and for the love of Gunny [Latham]."[36]

"The whole idea of what that horse was able to do was remarkable...," observed Sgt. Ralph Sherman, "and she did everything they expected her to do."[37]

On that first firing mission, Reckless and Coleman delivered five loads of ammunition. Afterward, she relaxed by grazing grass and a surprising side dish: an old helmet liner she found in a hole.[38]

As an adjective, "proud" didn't do justice to how the Marines felt about Reckless's first battle performance. When they returned to camp, Latham offered her a can of beer to celebrate with her comrades. She gulped it lustily and naturally wanted more.

That night, the wind and rain kicked up and Reckless sought refuge in Latham's tent, where the technical sergeant welcomed her warmly. Latham dried Reckless off and tossed a warm blanket over her. In a matter of minutes, she was asleep by the stove.

Reckless had survived enemy fire with flying colors. She had kept her head in the heat of battle. She was now one of them, a true Marine.

CHAPTER 4

RECKLESS TAKES CENTER STAGE

She could string more communication wire in a day than ten Marines, and nobody could pack as much 75 mm ammunition.
—David Dempsey, *New York Times* reviewer

I n late November 1952, the Recoilless Rifle Platoon was called into action at Outpost Bunker, about 550 yards northeast of Outpost Hedy on a ragged hill. Outpost Bunker was a hotspot, with the entrenched Communist forces striking it repeatedly "with greater alacrity and fierceness than anywhere else along the line,"[1] according to author Andrew Geer.

Pedersen had the intuition to leave Reckless behind on this mission mainly because there was more barbed wire than she was accustomed to handling. Pedersen's foresight paid off because the Chinese blanketed the area with shell fire—looking to annihilate anything in range. Mortar rounds exploded everywhere; Pedersen was wounded in the leg but refused to be evacuated. The action at Outpost Bunker led to Pedersen being awarded a Bronze Star and a third Purple Heart—not an honor he welcomed, because three Purple Hearts meant an automatic transfer out of combat duty.

The platoon worried about losing an officer they admired and respected and also feared their beloved Reckless would leave with him. Of the two, Reckless was considered to be the greater loss, if it came to that. Officers come and go, but Reckless had become so critical to the platoon that she could not easily be replaced. The sergeants called a meeting in their tent to discuss the situation and decided to take up a collection to buy Reckless from Pedersen. Within an hour, the men had raised enough money to cover Pedersen's investment.

Lieutenant Pedersen
Pleads His Case

Pedersen fought hard to stay, pleading his case to Major General Pollock, the division commander. The general was no fool, directly asking the lieutenant if Reckless had anything to do with his wanting to stay with the platoon. Pedersen came clean. "Yes, sir, in a way," he told Pollock. "If I leave and take her with me, it will be a blow to the platoon. If I leave her behind, it will be a double loss to me…losing her and the platoon."[2]

The lieutenant proved persuasive. Pollock cancelled Pedersen's transfer. As Pedersen was leaving, the general asked if Reckless really was as good under fire as he'd heard. "Yes, sir. She got used to it a lot quicker than some Marines I know. The first day she might have panicked, but she figured out we knew what we were doing. Nothing shakes her now."[3]

Maj. Gen. Pollock admired Pedersen's insight and leadership skills, especially when it came to Reckless. He would later write, "Lt. Pedersen deserves full credit for the purchase of Reckless…when he obtained this horse, he was thinking only of his men, trying to save them from the back-breaking loads over extremely rugged and difficult terrain. I am sure also, that he was thinking of saving the lives of his weary ammunition carriers. This is all a part of good leadership. Reckless no doubt was imbued with this same spirit, because she became a true Marine."[4]

That night at the camp, the men toasted Pedersen's news. Reckless was already enjoying a late snack: a half loaf of bread with strawberry jam. But because bread always made her thirsty, Reckless's latest trick came in handy: she had learned how to drink from a glass. Latham poured her a Coke, and the heroic mare joined in the toast. The ever-cautious Pedersen, however, knew his days with the platoon were limited and decided Reckless needed a backup companion in case he was transferred and something happened to Coleman. Pedersen chose another private first class, Arnold Baker, for the assignment.

The Ride of His Life

The platoon was assigned another fire mission, this one to support Captain Dick Kurth's Fox Company of the 2nd Battalion, 5th Marines. "On the line they referred to us as the 'horse Marines,'" recalled Sgt. Ralph Sherman. "It seemed to me that once we were moving around with the horse to different locations that was a phrase that I heard on a few occasions. 'Oh, it's the horse Marines...yeah, come on up!'"[5]

Reckless went along, but only for the ride because the jeeps could reach the firing sites. An enclosure was built for her in a valley, shielded from the enemy by Hill 114. Baker, who was accompanying Reckless, decided she needed more exercise and brushed aside Pedersen's directive forbidding anyone from riding her. He leapt onto

Reckless's back—and she bolted as if shot out of a recoilless rifle. What happened next was a blur to Baker. He cried out for the horse to stop, but Reckless ran like the racehorse she was out of the pasture and down the road.

"Whoa! Reckless, Whoa!" he wailed, pulling furiously on her halter rope. He considered jumping off but feared Latham's punishment for disobeying Pedersen's orders and abandoning the prized horse. All the hapless Baker could do was hold on for dear life as Reckless turned onto the road leading to the main line.

Reckless streaked through the patrol "gate" where a sentry stood by with a field telephone. Now Baker was really scared. Past the gate were fruit orchards and a countryside covered in flowers. But just north of the orchards were minefields. As Reckless ran past, the frenzied sentry yelled into the telephone, "Reckless is loose! She's through the gate an' heading for Unggok!"

Unggok was enemy territory.

Reckless raced downhill into a rice paddy. Lookouts relayed Reckless's position via field telephones. When Latham heard what was happening, he jumped in his jeep and tore after her, as did some of the men of Fox Company. To the horror of her pursuers, she turned and bounded into the minefield. The helpless Marines could only pray, which seemed to work because Reckless turned around and galloped back to camp. Reckless spotted Latham waiting for her by his jeep. She casually trotted up. Baker slid from her back, landing in a heap. Baker had lived to tell the story, but he would no longer be caring for Reckless.

The Work of Ten Marines

The 5th Marines went in reserve, which meant a temporary break from fighting and a change of duty for Reckless. When she didn't have to carry ammunition for the recoilless rifle, she became a transport

Reckless loaded with a reel of communication wire. *Nancy Latham Parkin*

animal for grenades, small arms ammunition, rations, sleeping bags, and even barbed wire. She also helped string communication wire from a pack on her back that unspooled as she walked. "She could string more [communication] wire in a day than ten Marines and nobody could pack as much 75 mm ammunition,"[6] one reviewer would note.

Even though the 5th Marines were in reserve, they could be called into action if the 1st and 7th Regiments needed them in the line. But for the most part, it was a relaxing time.

Aussie Honors

Occasionally, Latham and the men of the RR Platoon gathered with an Australian unit also in reserve. "The [Aussies] thought a lot of her," Latham recalled. "They'd let her come right in their

Reckless models the Australian bush hat with Hospital Corpsman George "Doc" Mitchell. *Nancy Latham Parkin*

club. One Sergeant Major thought there was nothing better than ol' Reckless."[7]

The Aussies were so impressed with the four-legged Marine that one offered his own bush hat to Reckless as a gift. Latham cut holes in the hat for her ears and it actually fit quite well, but it was clear Reckless didn't like it.

Pat O'Rourke agreed with Reckless. He found the hat demeaning and "something for the likes of that Army mule, Francis, to wear. He's a clown.... Reckless ain't."[8] Still, in snapshot after surviving snapshot, Reckless is seen wearing the hat.

One night Reckless couldn't take it anymore. She found the perfect solution to the headwear she hated so much: she ate it. All that was left the next morning was the sweatband and part of the brim and crown. Problem solved.

"Read 'Em and Weep"

One bitterly cold winter night, Latham, Gunnery Sergeant Norman Mull, and some of the men were tucked warmly in their tent, playing poker. All was nice and toasty until Reckless poked her nose through the tent's overlap flap and ambled inside. She reminded them how cold it was with "a chilled blast from her hoarfrost-rimmed nostrils."[9] Latham quickly closed the flap, Mull motioned Reckless over to the stove, Latham tossed a blanket over her shoulders, and the sergeants returned to their card game.

Reckless moved over behind Latham to watch the action over his shoulder. Latham placed his bet. Everyone passed but Mull, who looked to Reckless for some kind of signal. But the cagey equine showed only her best poker face. Mull called, and lost the hand. As the game went on, Reckless became bored—no one was paying attention to her. So she grabbed Latham's cigarettes and began to eat them.

By then, Latham—who hurriedly tried salvaging some of his smokes—was on a roll. He won the next three hands and his stacks

of chips began to grow. Something about the little blue discs fasci-
nated Reckless, and before Latham could say, "Read 'em and weep,"
the heroic war horse created a gambling problem uniquely her own.
She leaned in, took a big bite of Latham's substitute winnings and
started chomping the chips.

Latham tried valiantly to rescue his plastic winnings straight from
the horse's mouth. The others howled as the unamused Latham
managed to wrestle back just two whole chips and a few broken
shards; the rest went the way of all (usually organic) things.

This inspired an argument as to how many chips Reckless had
actually swallowed. But the poker-faced pony grew bored with the
bickering, strolled back to the stove and was asleep before the guys
cashed in their chips. Latham figured Reckless owed him at least
$30—possibly more. "At least she goes first class—only eating the
blue ones,"[10] O'Rourke said, climbing into his sleeping bag. Latham
moaned as he turned out the lights.

Staff Sergeant Jack Railo pays a visit to Reckless. *Jake Dearing*

At Christmas 1952, the men spoiled Reckless with a holiday bounty of rich fare including candy, apples, carrots, cake, cola, and the occasional beer. Doc Mitchell complained about the fattening diet, but Latham assured him, "Christmas comes only once a year. She'll work it off as soon as we get back on the line."[11]

She sure did—and more.

CHAPTER 5

RECKLESS
HONES
HER SKILLS

I didn't think she would make it onto the hill that last time.
She had to make two runs at it, but she wouldn't quit.
—PFC Monroe Coleman, Recoilless Rifle Platoon

In January 1953, after thirty days in reserve, the 5th Marines returned to combat, replacing the 7th Regiment on the line. They were placed to support outposts East Berlin, Berlin, Vegas, Reno, Carson, and Ava. It was here Reckless would earn her stripes.

Everywhere Reckless went, new accommodations had to be built for her. If the fighting was heavy, the Marines would willingly shed their own flak jackets and cover her head to tail to protect her. While Command frowned on this behavior, no one put a stop to it.

Sergeant Kenneth Lunt from Fort Scott, Kansas, a Browning automatic rifleman with Charlie Company, 5th Marines, remembered how much Reckless meant to those she befriended. "Her eyes were special to me—seemed to look right through you and your mind—so I tried to think of something nice," he recalled, laughing. "She was very gentle and loved to be brushed, and was very protected by the 75 [mm] recoilless team."[1] Lunt summarized his feelings to a newspaper reporter in 1989: "I'll never forget her. In a funny way, one I can't explain, her being there helped."[2]

Reckless made friends wherever she went. Until now, she had worked mainly with the 1st Battalion, 5th Marines. But here, she would fight with the men of the 2nd Battalion, 5th Marines. Lieutenant Pedersen realized Reckless was no longer "his," that she'd become a full-fledged Marine. When the time came that he was unavoidably transferred, Pedersen knew he'd have to leave her behind with the platoon.

Pedersen had divided the RR Platoon into three sections, each with several squads or gun teams. While Reckless was sent where she was most needed, she was primarily attached to the 2nd Squad of Section 1, where she worked mainly with Staff Sergeant John Lisenby's guns on Hill 120. PFC Monroe Coleman remained her main handler. Lisenby's guns could fire in support of Outposts East Berlin and Berlin and into the enemy strongholds of Detroit and Frisco. They also could fire into enemy-controlled Hills 153 and 190, which faced onto Outpost Vegas.

Platoon Sections 2 and 3 were situated farther west down the main line and reachable by jeep. Sergeant Leon Dubois led Section 2 near Carson, with Staff Sergeant Harry Bolin in charge of Section 3 farther west, toward Ava. Because vehicles could reach these two positions but not Lisenby's on Hill 120, his squad had Reckless pretty much to themselves. Because 120 was a brute of a hill, it was impossible for conventional two-legged Marines to haul the heavy ammunition up to the gun sites.

Korean winters were especially hard on the Marines, and in this sector the enemy kept them busy—even in the freezing cold. The men found and secured a pasture for Reckless near a tiny burned-out village named Panggi-dong. While the enemy couldn't see Reckless's pasture, which was blocked by a portion of Hill 120, they were frequently content to lob exploratory rounds in that direction. The Marines built a bunker to protect Reckless if incoming became heavy.

Another problem for the Marine equine was her pasture's lack of sufficient winter feed. With the Marines engaged in regular combat, there was little time for them to make trips to get hay and grain for her. Even though she was getting C-rations—the hard candy was her favorite—she was losing weight and not doing well.

Pulling Grass

A worried Latham traveled to the gun site to talk with Lisenby, the section leader, who had put some of the men on grass-pulling duty. The plan was for each to gather an armload a day until there was enough feed for their hungry horse. In addition, Latham contributed vitamins he had picked up from Doc Mitchell. But Reckless did not like the pills, and Latham had to force-feed them until he realized her tongue was swollen. Mitchell then put her on the antibiotic Terramycin, assuming her tongue had become infected, and within a week all was back to normal.

Reckless nibbling grass in pasture.
John Meyers

Colonel Lew Walt, the new commander of the 5th Marines, was visiting the troops along the line in the Fox Company sector when he caught an intriguing sight:

Marines down on all fours pulling grass on the slopes of Hill 120. When he found out why, the colonel made sure the next truck south of the Imjin would return with food for Reckless.

Walt sensed he had, "inherited something special in this little red pony," according to author and Korean War veteran Andrew Geer. "He had seen her on the trails loaded with equipment; he had been told of Marines shedding their flak jackets to cover her during heavy bombardments. This little horse was becoming as important to his men as the sight of another horse, Traveller [General Robert E. Lee's Civil War horse], had been to the fighting men of the Army of [Northern] Virginia."[3]

During her winter of deprivation, Reckless must have appreciated what PFC Booker T. Crew brought her: the breakfast of champions. Crew, a recent addition to the platoon, returned from the regimental Command Post with a crate of Wheaties and other foodstuffs. The cereal and another favorite, graham crackers, became a nice supplement to her diet of grass, C-rations, and vitamins. She started to feel better and even began to put on some weight.

Daylight Raids

Reckless's improving health was critical because she assumed a significant role in a series of daytime raids devised by Colonel Walt. The colonel wanted to stop the enemy's "creeping offensive" toward Marine positions and in the process capture prisoners who could be interrogated.

Walt thought daylight operations had several advantages over night raids. The most important was that the raids could be conducted with close air support, as well as support from artillery, mortars, recoilless rifles, flame tanks, and smoke that could be delivered by aircraft, artillery, and mortars to disguise the infantry's advance. Reckless helped ensure that the men providing covering fire for the raids were fully supplied with ammunition.

Reckless and her gun section moved into position to support the 2nd Battalion, 5th Marines, on January 24, 1953. Two days later they were on a firing mission that destroyed a machine gun bunker. Five days after that came Raid Tex.[4]

Raid Tex—January 31, 1953

Raid Tex was unlike any battle challenge Reckless had yet faced because, for the first time, she'd have to carry the heavy, awkward ammunition on her back from daybreak to sunset.

Reckless and Lisenby's gun section were in position on Hill 120 and provided the all-important smokescreen in support of the advancing troops.

The trail from Reckless's pasture to the ammunition supply point was about two-tenths of a mile south and east, an easy walk that bordered a vacant rice paddy and ended in a box canyon. Once there, the six-round, 150-pound ammunition payload would be gingerly installed atop Reckless, and Coleman would lead her up to the firing sites Lisenby had established.

Those gun sites were east and north of her pasture, up a ridge on Hill 120 that overlooked the Main Line of Resistance. And while the path to the ammunition supply point was a relatively easy walk, the route to the gun sites was difficult at best. It was a tough, sometimes treacherous hike for Coleman just to lead Reckless up to the guns and back. The most daunting challenge was the narrow, twisty trail rising at a forty-five-degree angle to the first ridge line of Hill 120. This was where Reckless showed her heroic nature—because she preferred to meet this obstacle with a running start.

Again and again, as shell canisters bounced threateningly atop the would-be racehorse, she charged the steep, craggy hill. Monroe Coleman knew better than to try to accompany her. So the PFC simply dropped the reins, allowing her the freedom to do it her way. And each time, she would make the top of the ridge on the strength of a final, urgent lunge.

Each climb left her winded and exhausted but standing triumphant atop the hill. Reckless would wait for Coleman and then make her own way, without assistance from her guide, to the guns.

"The gun crew would see her coming," Geer reported, "and would call out to her."[5]

Reckless made the perilous delivery an estimated fifteen times that day.

According to the USMC Command Diaries, eight rounds of high explosive (HE) and ninety rounds of smoke (WP) were used for the raid.[6] All told, this meant Reckless, packing six rounds a trip, delivered *more than a ton* of explosives on her back.

Lieutenant Tom Bulger from Dog Company, 1st Battalion, 5th Marines, led the raid which attacked Hill 139, just north of Outpost Berlin. Prisoners were taken, two active machine guns were destroyed, and the raid was deemed a tremendous success. Over the next month, Reckless took part in ten smaller but still dangerous firing missions along the line.

Operation Charlie—February 25, 1953

Reckless's next major raid was Operation Charlie, which was so intense and required such meticulous planning that five full rehearsals were needed. Charlie proved Reckless's most difficult assignment yet because of the sheer volume of ammo she had to deliver to Lisenby's constantly firing guns. Once again, she carried ammunition from dawn to darkness.

According to Pedersen and the USMC Command Diaries, Reckless made two dozen trips to the firing sites during Operation Charlie. The lieutenant estimated she covered more than twenty miles and hauled 3,500 pounds of explosives on her back—144 rounds of ammunition, six rounds a trip.[7]

"I didn't think she would make it onto the hill that last time," Coleman later told Latham. "She had to make two runs at it, but she wouldn't quit."[8]

Captain Dick Kurth's Fox Company, 2nd Battalion, 5th Marines, led a raid on Outpost Detroit, which had been lost to the enemy in October 1952. The Marines didn't want to keep the hill. They just wanted to, "get there, kill a few people, capture some if possible, 'kick over a stove or two,' and leave."[9] The operation was successful in that it destroyed eight enemy bunkers, burned out three caves, destroyed five enemy machine guns, and captured one gun.[10]

Sergeant Ken Latham remembered seeing Reckless from a distance during the raid, and not knowing what to make of her. "It looked like a trench she was in," he recalled. "You could just see part of her body, half of a horse and I had no idea what I was looking at because I had no idea there was a horse out there.

"And I didn't even think about a horse! And I said, 'What the hell am I looking at?' It was really spooky."

He got on the radio to find out what was happening. "I didn't know if it was a trap of some kind; I was afraid the horse might be the enemy's horse because of all of those explosives on her back...like a suicidal animal. That's what I was afraid of. You can imagine my relief when they said, 'Yeah, that's *our* Marine.' I didn't know what the hell they were talking about, 'our Marine.' But I sure was glad to know she was on our side."[11]

When Reckless came off the hill the last time that night, her head hung low on the walk to her bunker. Coleman knew she was utterly exhausted when she didn't even nuzzle for pogey bait. Pedersen brought Reckless one of her favorite dinners that night—warm bran mash. When she caught scent of the warm food, Reckless perked up. Still, she ate unusually slowly that night. Pedersen, Latham, and Coleman gave Reckless a thorough rubdown and then covered her with a blanket. She had performed like a great Marine—a true testament to the Corps. And yet, her finest hour was still to come.

Spring 1953

The men knew spring finally had arrived when the hillsides and paddies began filling with fresh green grass and colorful flowers. Reckless loved the fresh greens added to her diet.

When she wasn't carrying ammunition or supplies, Reckless burned off extra energy by chasing her own shadow. If there was any kind of audience watching, she'd break into her special prance to show off.

Yet as nice as the fresh, warming weather felt, spring also brought the sadness of a replacement draft from the states. This meant Reckless had to say goodbye to a lot of friends. Gunny Sergeant Mull and Sergeant Harry Bolin were two of the many who came to bid her farewell. New friends arrived, including Sergeant Elmer Lively, who joined the squad in Lisenby's section and formed with Reckless a partnership and friendship that would last a long time.

Around this time, Lieutenant William Riley Jr. volunteered to join the Anti-Tank Company. In a March 14, 1953, letter to his sweetheart back home, Riley wrote, "I got my assignment, which was to the 5th Marine Regiment.... The officers were interviewed and we were told they wanted a man for the 75 recoil rifle platoon, so I volunteered. I now find I'm executive officer of the Anti-Tank Company for this week (you have to wait 5 days until you can go up on the MLR). I'm learning the trade—on the job training. Next week, I go up and work with the present platoon leader and take over in three weeks. We are part of Regiment, which means I'll do a lot of traveling. We lend support to any platoon on the MLR that is having trouble. The colonel is a hot shot so here at Regiment (even though we're up front) you have to look sharp all the time. My captain is named Shain [actual spelling is Schoen] and is from Milwaukee and Marquette U."[12]

When Riley met Pedersen, he was quite surprised to learn about Reckless.

"I was flabbergasted," Riley said. "Nobody had briefed me on her ahead of time. I came down from regiment thinking everything was just the normal platoon thing, and all of a sudden Pete [Pedersen] introduces me to this horse. And I said, 'Is the horse going with you?' And he said, 'No, it's yours.'"[13]

Later, Riley wrote home about her. "I went out with the recoilless platoon (where I am assigned) and met my men and oriented myself with the terrain. I guess I told you we have the only horse in the 1st Marine Division (the platoon leader I am relieving bought it to haul ammo). It's name, her name...is 'Reckless,' which is the nickname the regiment has given to the 75 mm platoon. Quite a nag. (So I have sixty men and one horse.) I really have a good bunch in the platoon—plenty of spirit."[14]

As March roared on, the shelling increased in the sector. One afternoon, three mortar shells exploded near Reckless as she stood in her pasture. She didn't need anybody to tell her what to do; Reckless headed to her bunker for protection. Latham saw it happen and ran to make sure she was okay. Later, he told Pedersen, "She knows what incoming is and she knows what the bunker's for. When those mortars exploded she didn't exactly run for cover, but she didn't let any grass grow under her feet either."[15] Such excitement didn't happen very often. On the other hand, Reckless had a tendency to get bored if she wasn't working or being attended to.

Reckless Ventures Out on Her Own

One night, Reckless ventured out of her pasture. But instead of going into camp to visit friends, she headed the opposite way—out of camp, toward the Main Line of Resistance, where fierce fighting continued. The Marines of Captain "Big Dog" Young's C Company were stunned when Reckless walked into the line. They heartily welcomed the local heroine and tried to make her comfortable.

Word spread fast via field telephone that Reckless was in the line. And what was she doing there? Eating C-rations, of course.

The men of C Company decided not to tell the RR Platoon they had their secret weapon. Why not make them sweat a bit? Yet when the enemy opened up with the heaviest bombardment to that date, the men were sorry they hadn't notified Pedersen—God forbid something would happen to Reckless. The men became more concerned about protecting her than fighting back.

Reckless was rushed into the deepest part of the trench, since there was no bunker big enough for her. She surprised the men when she knelt down in the trench. The men covered her with their flak jackets, yet she shook off the one that covered her head. Several shells came close enough to pelt her with dirt and debris. Suddenly it wasn't so funny to have her in camp.

When the shelling stopped near daybreak, Pedersen was finally notified. Reckless was never that adventurous again. But she had plenty of work to do. The Command Diaries for March 1953 showed Reckless and her squad participated in eighteen firing missions conducted over thirteen days. It was the Battle for Outpost Vegas, near the end of March, that would make her a legend.

CHAPTER 6

THE "BATTLE OF THE NEVADA CITIES"— THE NEVADA COMPLEX

THE BATTLE OF OUTPOST VEGAS, MARCH 26–30, 1953

The spirit of her loneliness and her loyalty, in spite of the danger, was something else to behold. Hurting. Determined. And alone. That's the image I will always remember … that's the image I have imprinted in my head and heart forever.
—**Sergeant Harold E. Wadley, USMC**

The Battle of the Nevada Complex was among the fiercest clashes ever fought by the United States Marine Corps. "The savagery of the battle for the so-called Nevada Complex," Lieutenant Colonel Andrew Geer wrote later, "has never been equaled in Marine Corps history."[1]

At stake in the pivotal confrontation: an eccentrically shaped, strategically critical patch of wartime turf called the "Iron Triangle." The three-sided area, with angles anchored by outposts Vegas, Reno, and Carson, was targeted by the Chinese Communists who wanted a major victory to weaken the hand of the United Nations at the continuing peace talks. A victory here would not only be an embarrassment for the United Nations forces, it would put the Communists in a position to threaten to attack the South Korean capital of Seoul.

The Nevada Cities were surrounded by higher ground held by the enemy and each outpost depended on the others for flank defense. Reno was situated atop the off-kilter triangle—it appeared to be listing to the left—almost a mile north of the Main Line of Resistance. Carson, southwest of Reno, was itself a half-mile north of the Line. Vegas was southeast of Reno, three-quarters of a mile in front of the main battle line.

Battalion commander Lieutenant Colonel Tony Caputo said the hills were named after Nevada gaming towns because "It's a gamble if we can hold them."[2]

Between Carson and Vegas was a comparatively small area called Reno Block, manned by a handful of Marines charged with keeping the enemy outside of the triangle. If one of the Nevada outposts fell, the odds were high that the others would too, and with that kind of victory, the Communists might be inclined to withdraw from, or stall yet further, the Panmunjom truce talks.

Battle of the Nevada Cities
Outpost Vegas
Thursday, March 26, 1953

The day started out normally enough for Reckless and her platoon mates. No fire missions were scheduled for her that day. For a

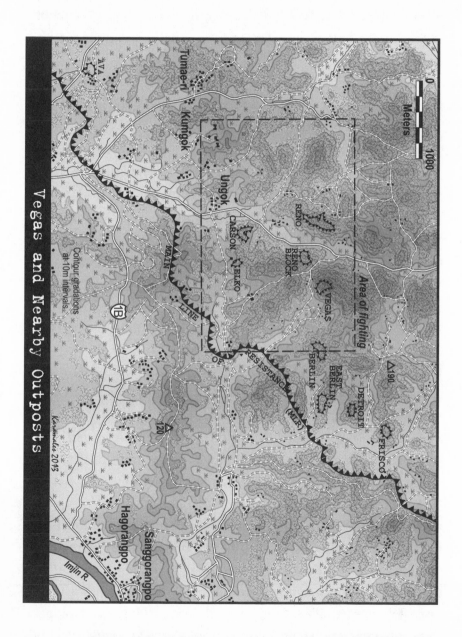

Vegas and Nearby Outposts

month, she'd been working the line around the Nevada Cities. The bitter winter cold was gone, replaced by mild, cool spring conditions in the Korean hills. Except for the occasional shower, the seasonal change was a pleasant one.

Reckless loved this weather. Grass was finally starting to grow in her pasture, so there was plenty to eat. All was good in her world. That would soon change. Before she knew it, Reckless would be smack in the middle of a defining battle of the Korean War.

The day began, "like all the other days while on the line, with a pre-dawn 100-percent alert," wrote Sergeant William H. Janzen, a platoon guide in Charlie Company, 1st Battalion, 5th Marines, who was stationed at Outpost Reno. "It was a routine and uneventful day...cold weather gear had all been turned in and it felt good to only need a sweater or field jacket.

"There was something ominous in the air, though." How else, the sergeant wrote, to interpret three straight days of Chinese artillery and mortar fire, "across the front of our outposts, the known trails through the mine fields to the outposts, the Main Line of Resistance and beyond to our main supply routes and known or suspected battalion and company command posts.

"Yet, beyond maintaining our normal state of readiness, there was nothing that would alert us to what was about to befall [us] during the coming night and the next five days."[3]

Sergeant George Johannes from Willingboro, New Jersey, was a forward observer (who directs artillery fire) attached to How Company. Johannes and two buddies were about to make the trek up to Outpost Vegas to relieve the forward observer there when they spotted Reckless. "I'm standing there petting her before heading up the line," Johannes recalled, "and one of the guys with me said jokingly, 'Hey, Johannes, that's quite a cow you got there!' and laughed. I said,

'Ollie, you're a farm boy—you should know better.' We got a good laugh out of it, and the three of us headed on up the line."[4]

Marine demolitionist Sergeant Harold Wadley, working with Corporal Allen Kelley and Lieutenant Milton Drummond, set off explosive charges that blew holes in the hillsides of Reno and Vegas. The blasts helped the Marines carve out caves that would be turned into shelters for the wounded. All hell was about to break loose at Outpost Vegas.

Sixty years later, Wadley's memories of the day remained vivid. "I left to get supplies. Actually, when the (reinforcement squad) came up to the outpost, they forgot half the mail and the best part of our C-rations—these candy bars of pressed jellies of red and black licorice.

"I said, 'Dad gummit, you guys left all the good stuff.' Since I wasn't designated to a specific position, I asked Lieutenant Ken Taft, our [officer in charge] if I could go get them. He agreed and called the [Command Post] on the Main Line of Resistance [saying] that one Marine would be coming in. That's how I missed it. I told Lieutenant Taft that I would be back as soon as I got loaded." Wadley had made the run many times, but that night it seemed different. "As I made my way down the trail into the dry creek bed, I could hear low, muffled coughing *on both sides of the trail*." Taft had told him no Marine patrols were out that night, which was meant to reassure him that he would not be mistaken for the enemy. But who, then, was coughing?

"When I left the dry wash below the gun gate, I began yelling, 'Marine coming in!' The Marines on the A4 [Able Gate] were expecting me. I ran to the [Command Post] to report what I had heard along the trail. There was an air of excited apprehension in the bunker. They already knew—the listening post had reported the same thing. I looked back at Vegas to see it suddenly light up like a Christmas tree! Vegas was covered with smoke from Willie Peter [white phos-phorus] rounds and a mosaic of red and white hot shrapnel, mixed with Chinese white and green tracers crisscrossing and striking our red tracers."[5]

Sergeant Johannes was helping carry a wounded Marine down from the outpost when things really got hairy. "I had to shoot my way down," said Johannes. "Halfway down the hill, a gook with a burp gun appeared in the trench about twenty feet in front of me. Five or six rounds of my carbine dropped him very quickly." Yet sniper fire continued as they made their way down. When he looked back at Vegas, his description echoed that of Wadley. Vegas looked "lit up like a Christmas tree."[6]

At 7:00 p.m., simultaneous, surprise attacks began on Vegas, Carson, and Reno. The enemy's barrage was crashing into the Marines' lines at an astonishing rate—180 rounds of artillery and mortar shells a minute. The Marines intercepted an enemy radio message: "We are standing by for the signal."[7] Ten minutes later, masses of Communist Chinese soldiers came swarming down from Unggok, Arrowhead, and Hills 25A and 190, hitting all three Marine outposts at once. As one historian described the opening of the battle, "Choreographed with artillery, mortars and machine guns, two full battalions of Chinese troops [3,500 men] attacked a handful of Marines defending three outposts."[8]

There were only forty to fifty Marines on each outpost at any given time. The overwhelming numbers confronting them meant that each outpost had to focus on defending itself as opposed to support-ing the others. The enemy conducted diversionary attacks against seven other outposts along the five-and-a-half mile front covered by the 1st Division, including Old Baldy, Bunker, Dagmar, Hedy, and

Esther just west of the Nevada Cities, and Berlin and East Berlin to the east.

Geer wrote later that "for a period of seventy-two hours," the battle "reached a bloody crescendo seldom matched in warfare."[9]

The Battle of Outpost Vegas

A barrage of fourteen thousand artillery shells assaulted the crest of Vegas. When the shelling began, Latham ran to check on Reckless in her pasture. He found she had taken refuge in her bunker, where she was nervous and sweating. But she was glad to see Latham and rubbed up against him when he checked her over. When darkness fell, flares lit up the sky. Latham had left Reckless grain and water—which she ignored, given the heat of the battle—before he went to get his orders.

Forty minutes into the attack, the Marines at Vegas thought their only hope to hold the position was to use an artillery round fused with "variable time" (VT). When an outpost was overrun, the Marines rushed for cover in caves and trenches and called for VT, which meant artillery shells with proximity fuzes that would explode over the position—a step just short of suicide, but usually effective. The Marines moved into a large cave on the reverse slope of the outpost and waited.

All Communication Lost on Vegas

By this time, ground-based communication with Vegas had been lost because enemy artillery fire destroyed ground telephone wires connecting the outpost to the battalion Command Post. Command

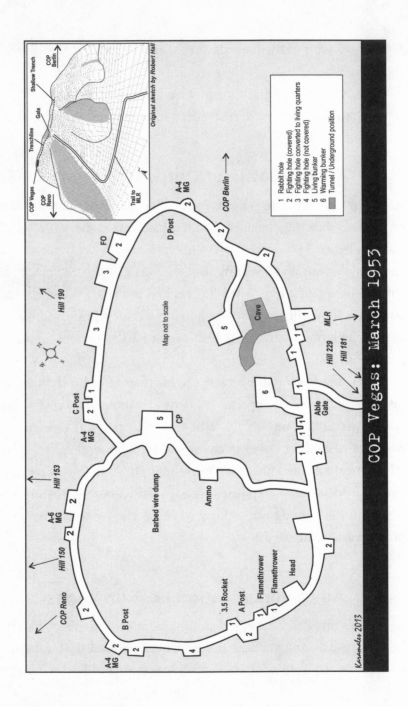

COP Vegas: March 1953

tried switching to radio—but had no luck reaching anyone on Vegas. Because of the communications breakdown, it wasn't clear if the outpost had fallen into enemy hands.

At 10:05 p.m., Dog Company, 2nd Battalion, 5th Marines, sent a platoon of forty-two men to find out what was happening on the outpost. But as they approached Reno Block, the troops were hit with mortar fire and looked up to see the enemy atop Vegas.

Even with an extra platoon from Easy Company, the Americans could not advance and had to retreat to the Main Line of Resistance—not knowing the fate of those back on the outpost.

But by midnight, the horrible truth seemed clear enough: all the Marines at Outpost Vegas were likely dead or captured. The first round of the battle had gone to the enemy.

Friday, March 27, 1953

At 2:00 a.m. Colonel Walt regrouped his men, summoning all his battalion commanders, as well as many staff officers, and Lieutenant Pedersen representing his Recoilless Rifle Platoon. He planned a coordinated attack to retake both Reno and Vegas in daylight. The rest of the night was spent evacuating the wounded and dead and supporting the stubborn defense at Outpost Carson.

Through the night, Sergeant Latham and the rest of the RR platoon listened to the radio for updates. Occasionally, Latham and Coleman broke away to look in on Reckless, who seemed on edge but otherwise all right.

Returning from Command in the early morning hours, Pedersen briefed his men on plans for the counterattack. It was set for 0930 that morning.

Captain John B. Melvin of Dog Company, 2nd Battalion, 5th Marines, led his men into the attack. "We had been just pulled back (in reserve) not more than two or three days when the Chinese struck and I had to turn around and come back up," Melvin recalled, "and when I saw Vegas, I didn't even recognize her."[10] Reinforcements from the 2nd Battalion, 7th Marines, were brought in to help with the counterattack on Reno and Vegas.

Reckless's Work Begins before Dawn

Before daylight, Coleman made his way to Reckless's pasture. Enemy shelling had ceased temporarily—the Chinese were saving ammunition for the pushback they knew was coming—and Reckless had calmed down a bit.

Coleman tried to persuade Reckless to have some barley, but she only nibbled at it. She then tried to return to her bunker but didn't get the chance. Coleman tied a sack of grain to her pack, along with C-rations for himself, and headed away; Reckless hung back for a moment, but understood it was time to work, and slowly followed Coleman into the darkness.

The trail to the ammunition supply point was not an easy one. Coleman could feel himself sweating under his flak jacket. They had to cross a steep hill, and at the top of the ridge, before they made the descent down the other side, they stopped for a moment, giving Coleman the chance to better secure the lead rope to Reckless's pack. But it was Coleman who had trouble going downhill. As he started, the PFC slipped and skidded his way down, tearing his pants and cutting his knee on a rock. Getting up, he could hear Reckless sliding down the hill in front of him, braking on all four legs until she safely reached the bottom. They found Sergeant Latham waiting for them.

Latham laced the eight canisters to Reckless's pack to see how she would handle the load. "She packed three each side, and two on top," recalled Wadley. "That's 192 pounds she would have to carry up and down the steep terrain."[11]

Latham gave Reckless a slap on her backside for encouragement, then sent her out. Reckless charged the hill, Latham and Coleman following close behind. The load was heavy, but she didn't falter.

"I took her up near the guns," Latham said, "checked the pack-straps to make sure the ammo would ride securely and pointed her in the direction of the gun. From then on she worked like a charm."[12]

Able to make better time on her four legs, she did not wait for Latham and Coleman, but walked ahead on her own, bound for Lisenby's firing sites on Hill 120. But that hill was a steep, challenging climb, especially for a horse laden with such a heavy payload.

Reckless instantly knew what she had to do. She took off in a trot, then broke into a gallop. As she tackled the hill, the canisters bounced perilously; with all that extra weight strapped to her pack, Latham feared the bindings would give way. Reckless clambered up the abrupt forty-five-degree incline, struggling to maintain her balance and fight gravity, but she made it to the top of the ridge and then navigated her way along 250 feet of twisting trail to get to the gun sites. Nothing was going to stop her.

"To know she ran up the steep slope fully loaded, with the load and saddle bouncing on her back," Wadley said, his air of wonder undimmed by the six intervening decades, "that's the biggest no-no there is in packing. It's a wonder that horse didn't have a galled back or worse. Reckless had to be one of the smartest, most trusting horses on the planet."[13] (A horse's "galled back" is soreness from rubbing or severe chafing.)

The Main Line of Resistance was located directly below Lisenby's guns atop Hill 120. On the far side of the line: 1,200 feet of deadly mine fields in the rice paddies leading to the enemy hills. The line was extremely curvy, and Vegas and Reno were southeast of the guns. Lisenby's guns could fire into enemy positions on Hills 190, 150 (25A), and 153.

The Firing Begins

Daylight approached, still without signs of enemy activity atop Vegas as Pedersen squinted through binoculars, searching for targets. The tanks moved into position behind the ridgeline and began firing. Pedersen waited for orders to cover the advancing Marines with smoke. He received them in the form of friendly fire—144 rockets sailing overhead, bound for enemy-controlled Hill 190. "At the sound of them, Marines all along the line looked northward. On the forward slopes of Hill 190, there was the clustered twinkle of dozens of orange lights—and then the lights were lost in the Bikini blossom of yellow smoke and dust. Long seconds later came the roar of thunder."[14]

At long last, the battle had begun.

Just as the guns began firing, Reckless delivered her load of ammunition. At first, the gunners had a small stash of ammunition to get the attack started. Five rounds were fired from one site, with the gun quickly picked up and moved to another position before enemy incoming could target them.

Reckless's travels varied that day. The farthest hike to a firing site was 700 yards; the nearest run was 550 yards from the ammunition supply point. She was covering a round-trip to the farthest site in twenty minutes; the closer location was a twelve-minute trip. Some of the men were also hauling rounds—three shells each—and the terrain quickly took its toll on them. Reckless, meantime, was making two trips for every one of theirs, carrying eight rounds at a time.

At 11:00 a.m. the decision was made to abort the retaking of Reno, at least for the time being, so all efforts could be focused on Vegas. Within twenty minutes, Vegas and the surrounding areas were blanketed with smoke as Captain Melvin's Dog Company, 2nd Battalion, 5th Marines, launched an attack on Vegas. Within an hour, the first platoon of forty-two had been reduced to just nine Marines. Yet they worked their way valiantly toward Vegas.

Pedersen kept looking for enemy gun and mortar positions where he could direct his guns. (Recoilless rifles and tanks were the only weapons whose gunners could actually see their targets without relying on forward observers to direct them, unlike the artillery and heavy mortars. Pedersen could line up his guns and fire directly in front of the troops.) The targets were plentiful and when the backlog of RR rounds dwindled, the gun crew simply began loading the shells right off Reckless's pack. Pedersen moved the gun sites forward to help the advancing Marines, which meant a longer haul for Reckless. These positions also exposed Reckless and the two-legged shell carriers to the enemy, who could fire on them from outposts Detroit and Frisco.

At one point, Pedersen faced a massive Chinese charge that didn't give him time to fire and move. He had to keep the gun at the site even though they were now easily targeted by the enemy. But by holding his ground and his unit's quick and precise firing, he helped prevent enemy reinforcements from reaching Vegas.

Reckless maintained her charging starts up the hill, pausing only briefly at the ridgeline to catch her breath before moving on again.

She was kept in near constant motion to keep the men supplied with shells. "It's difficult to describe the elation and the boost in morale that little white-faced mare gave Marines as she outfoxed the enemy bringing vitally needed ammunition up the mountain," said Sergeant Major James E. Bobbitt.[15]

On Reckless's twenty-first ammo delivery, the team was unloading her pack in a shallow bunker when three enemy mortars blasted around them. The mortars' burning white phosphorous engulfed Reckless and the men as they all dived for cover. Latham yanked off his flak jacket and threw it over her eyes, then stroked her neck to help settle her and make sure she didn't bolt away. Soon Reckless was fine, and when he gave her a slap on the backside, she ran out of the shallow trench.[16]

During the battle, "as we were catching all kinds of hell," Sergeant Chuck Batherson periodically tracked Reckless through his binoculars. "She was getting hailed all over the place and she was jumping all around," he remembered.[17] She never flagged in keeping up her deliveries.

"Incoming fire," described Lieutenant J. C. McCamic, "was like a tremendous rain storm with each drop of rain being a shell."[18]

"The battle was indescribable," Harold Wadley noted. "It was horrific. I still don't know how that mare lived through it."[19]

"The Image of That Small Struggling Horse Was Unbelievable"

At one point, on the way back to the ASP, Latham found a protected area, pulled off Reckless's packsaddle, and gave her food and water. As she ate, Latham gave her a thorough rubdown, paying special attention to her legs and hooves. After a thirty-minute rest, he strapped the packsaddle on her back, and she returned to the fight without a fuss.

Reckless continued the heroic eight-round ammo deliveries all day, seemingly undaunted by the deafening noise and blinding smoke of battle. "The roar and crack of the 90 mm tank rounds hammering Reno and Vegas was numbing," recalled Wadley. "The rush of air that our 4.5-inch rocket ripples made passing overhead sounded like wild birds of vengeance.... I looked through the flickering light at the hillside beyond and could hardly believe my eyes. In all that intense fire, in the middle of that chaos, the image of that small, struggling horse—putting everything she had into it, struggling up that ridge loaded with 75 mm rounds ... —it was unbelievable."[20]

Sometimes Reckless made the trip with Coleman, sometimes with other Marines, but she was so intuitive that most of the time she went solo; they would just load her up and send her on her way, knowing she'd make it on her own. "How in the world she managed to climb that slope," Wadley continued, "with all the incoming turning the earth to powder all around her, is beyond me.

"I was raised on horseback, working cattle and horses in Oklahoma, and know that the best of our horses could not, or would not, attempt to do what this little mare was doing. And by *herself!* I thought surely there was a Marine leading her, but in the flare light all I could see was her alone. She struggled along with her head and neck stretched out to help balance her load of 75 mm rounds like she knew where she was going. Indeed she knew."[21]

Wadley also recalled seeing Reckless carry wounded soldiers off the battlefield. "They would tie a wounded Marine across her pack-saddle and she would carry them out of there with all of this artillery and mortars coming in. The guys down at the bottom would unload the wounded off of her and tie gun ammo on her and she would turn around right on her own and head right back up to the guns. She was always moving and unforgettable on that skyline in the flare light."[22]

On one trip, Reckless shielded four Marines heading for the front line. They returned the favor, throwing their flak jackets over her for protection, thus risking their own lives. Reckless sometimes looked like a, "prehistoric hump-backed monster covered with large scales,"[23] wearing flak jackets head to tail, but the Marines valued her that much.

Sgt. Reckless. *Reprinted by permission of Boots Reynolds.* ©2003 *Boots Reynolds*

An Incomprehensible Sense of Duty

On one trip to the guns, Reckless suffered a shrapnel cut just above her left eye. Blood oozed down into her white blaze, but she kept going. Arriving at the guns, Pedersen checked her out, cleaned the wound with iodine, and sent Reckless on her way.

Later that day, she was wounded a second time when another shard of hot, sharp shrapnel struck her left flank, behind the ribcage and in front of her hind legs. Again, the wound was dressed and she returned to work.

Neither gash slowed the horse even one step.

Reckless was resolute. "Fatigue had taken its toll and drained her free of nerves," Andrew Geer wrote, "but as long as they would load and unload her, she kept to her task. No longer did she run at the hill rising sharply from the paddy...rather she crept up the twisting trail and paused to take two or three rest periods en route."[24] But she never stopped for long. No matter how tired she was, the mare with an almost incomprehensible sense of duty just kept going.

Latham took great care of her. Short on water, he nonetheless poured what little he had into his helmet, to replenish some of what she lost from raw exertion. Finally, later in the day, he cut her some slack, reducing her load to six canisters and providing another twenty-minute rest. Latham even dug into his own C-rations for one of Reckless's favorite treats—chocolate—to give her an energy boost.

The Sound, the Fury...and the Red Rain

Little was gained in the initial efforts to retake Vegas, despite the valiant work of the Dog and Easy companies of the 2nd Battalion, 5th Marines. Captain Melvin reported that incoming from the enemy "literally rained on the troops...(it) was so intense at times that you couldn't move forward or backward...the noise was deafening. They would start walking the mortars toward us from every direction possible. You could only hope that the next round wouldn't be on target."[25] Incoming artillery and mortar shells slashed through the air at a rate of five hundred rounds a minute, averaging eight rounds a second.

"You talk of the Fourth of July," Wadley remembered. "The tonnage of incoming mixed with the outgoing was unbelievable. The concussion waves from the explosives hit every fiber in our bodies. The rounds were coming in and going out so fast, a lot of them would collide mid-air over us. The rounds were hitting each other up there and causing aerial bursts.

"The counter mortar radar (team) that tracks the incoming rounds so they can return the fire—they said there were so many rounds, it just blurred their screen device and they couldn't tell anything except it was all coming in their direction.

"The concussions from the incoming…we were so sore, it was as if somebody had beat us with a hammer, just from that pounding of the concussions. The concussion against that mare…I couldn't believe she was still doing what she was doing."

Reckless remained steadfast. "I can still remember the flare light and seeing that little Mongolian mare heading up that slope without anybody leading her and going up to that gun pit," Wadley said. "She was packing three canisters of 75s on each side and two on top to balance the load. From that distance it was difficult to see what shape she was in, but just from her stride I could tell she was very tired.

"I had ridden lots of tired horses. She was tired. She wasn't crying in the dirt about her uncomfortable pack rigging, or the stark terror of the screaming 76 mm rounds coming from the enemy. She knew exactly what her job was."

Every time they sent her out, they didn't expect her to come back. And when she did, they couldn't believe it. She kept her Marines fighting just on her own willingness to keep at it. And that she survived is just astonishing.

"There's not another horse in war history that could even touch that mare," Wadley continued. "Even Alexander the Great's horse,

Bucephalus, who was a warhorse and personal protector of him, I bet he wouldn't have gone up that ridge with all that incoming. She was just something else. I truly felt for her.

"The spirit of her loneliness and her loyalty, in spite of the danger, was something else to behold. Hurting. Determined. And alone. That's the image I will always remember. That's the image I have imprinted in my head and heart forever."[26]

One particular image still haunted Sergeant George Johannes sixty years later. "The 2/5 was getting ready to retake the hill," he recalled in 2013, "and the guys started making their way up Vegas amidst a heavy barrage of incoming. My job was to set up a Forward Observer post to tell where to send the outgoing artillery. I had two Marines with me. We needed to get up to the top of Vegas so we could see. As I recall, it was misting at the time—a very fine rain. We were twenty to thirty yards from the top when I look up and I see these four Marines leaping—all four of them together— and you see their weapons in each of their hands and all of their legs flying in mid-air as a 120 mm mortar round landed right in between them and *vaporized* them—there was nothing left of them.

"I'm looking at these other two guys with me, and they're looking at me, and our helmets, our clothes, our faces were all red from the blood and the rain. We were dazed and dripping in their blood. I could taste it. I could taste it, and I said to myself, '*red rain*.' To this day I can still remember the salty taste of that blood."[27]

Later in the day, Fox Company of the 2nd Battalion, 7th Marines, added some reinforcements to Dog 2/5 and Easy 2/5. In doing so, they were able to gain control of the lower trenches at the bottom of Little Vegas.

In the Heat of the Night

Reckless and her gun crew were so effective, and she kept them so well stocked, that as night fell, the intense heat of non-stop firing had melted Lively's gun barrel; the gun was inoperable, and his crew had to head back to camp.

Coming off the hill, Reckless stumbled a bit, betraying her utter exhaustion. Walking home, the men showered their war horse with praise, telling her what a great Marine she was. Overhead, the battle raged on, but for Reckless and her squad, the day was done. Her head hung so low it almost dragged on the ground, but her pace quickened as she neared her pasture. Reckless sighed loudly when Latham retired her packsaddle for the day.

The battle-tested mare savored every morsel of a large helping of grain and greedily gulped fresh water. As she ate, Latham and Coleman rubbed her down; Reckless began nodding off before they could finish.

Latham spread fresh straw in her bunker and, after more water, coaxed her to lie down. Reckless's overseer gently draped a blanket over his charge, who was asleep by the time he crept out of the pasture.

Lieutenant Pedersen's Fears Realized

Thanks in part to Reckless and the RR platoon's efforts, the Marines now held Vegas's reverse slope and the Chinese held the forward slope. No one controlled the summit. Fox Company, 2nd Battalion, 7th Marines, stayed the night to hold what they'd gained, while the other companies evacuated, returning to the Main Line of Resistance to regroup.

Communist gunners had fired almost 41,000 shells into Allied positions during the twenty-four-hour period ending at 6:00 p.m.,

March 27. Approximately 36,000 of these shells were concentrated on Marine defenses.[28]

After Latham had finished caring for Reckless, he reported to Pedersen and received his orders for the next day. The lieutenant had some news of his own. His earlier fears had been realized: he had been transferred, to Command as it turns out, where he would take control of the entire Anti-Tank Company.

But he was being relieved of the RR platoon. Lieutenant Bill Riley would take his place.

Pedersen still would be close by, but Reckless was staying with the platoon because that's where she was needed most. Latham had mixed feelings. He was upset Pedersen was leaving but relieved Reckless was staying. Pedersen also told Latham a new rifle was coming for Lively and that everyone would need to be in position to fight at first light.

A Battle Far from Over
Saturday, March 28, 1953

In the early morning hours, Pedersen turned over command of the platoon to Lieutenant Bill Riley. But before reporting to the Anti-Tank Company Command Post, he took Riley to see Reckless and to make his goodbyes to the horse. Technically he still owned her, but he knew Reckless would no longer belong to him.

It was still dark when Coleman arrived at Reckless's pasture. She was thin and hungry and had obviously lost a lot of weight in a single day. Coleman gave Reckless extra barley, rubbed her down, and checked her two wounds. When she had finished eating, he strapped on her pack, which she accepted without fuss. But as they set out, Coleman saw she was walking stiffly. Returning to battle after only a few hours rest, Reckless clearly was bothered by the wound in her flank, her muscles were still tired, and she appeared to show effects of the disorienting concussion waves that had pounded all day.

They met up with Latham at the ammunitions supply point. He examined her hooves and legs and declared that while Reckless was gimpy from overwork, she would be fine once she warmed up. This proved correct, and by the end of her first trip, she was walking true and straight.[29]

Bombing "Seldom Experienced in Warfare"

Reckless was now accustomed to the sounds of battle—even a battle as fierce as this. When she broke into a sweat, it was from exertion, not fear. Andrew Geer noted, the "second day of the battle for Vegas was to bring a cannonading and bombing seldom experienced in warfare"[30]—and Reckless withstood it.

Within a twenty-three-minute period later in the morning, the First Marine Aircraft Wing dropped twenty-eight tons of bombs on Vegas, completely obliterating its crest. The bombs fell at the rate of more than a ton every minute. Yet miraculously, not a single Marine was wounded, even though the bombs landed a perilously close 450 feet in front of them. Reckless "shivered under the shock of the concussion, but it was a muscular reaction, rather than from nerves."[31]

Up until then, the Marines hadn't used air bombardment on Vegas, hoping it could be retaken with its defenses intact. But when it became clear the Chinese wouldn't let that happen, Command decided to target Vegas with heavy bombardment.

By 1:13 p.m., Easy Company reported it had finally gained control of the hill, although fighting remained heavy. By 2:55 p.m., Outpost Vegas was securely in the hands of the Marines.

Reckless and her squad had played critical roles in the final surge to reclaim the hill. The squad did so by firing directly into the trenches ahead of the advancing infantry; Reckless did so by keeping the squad fully supplied with ammunition. Now, the Marines had to hold onto the turf they had recaptured.

Garlic and Grenades

As Marine casualties mounted, a converted mess tent had become the only aid station on Vegas's reverse slope. Bayoneted M-1 rifles became poles to hang plasma bags for the wounded. By 11:00 p.m., there were more than two hundred wounded soldiers crammed into the makeshift hospital. Outside the tent, the dead were laid out in rows.

At times, the roar of battle was so loud that the Marines couldn't talk to each other. Even screaming was useless. They resorted to hand signals and passing notes.

"All individual sounds," recalled Dr. William E. Beaven, "were absorbed by one continuous, thunderous roar." Beaven, a battalion medical officer in the 1st Marine Division, was tending to the wounded when, at 2:00 a.m., Melvin came by the aid station with a battle update, but the noise of the explosions was too great for anyone to hear him. "Captain Melvin appeared through the far end of the tent flap, arms in the air, a gesture of utter futility" at making himself heard over the incessant roar.

Finally, he found a blank card and large black crayon and, according to Beaven, "scratched out a message: 'Gooks by-passing Vegas; coming around your side...close to battalion strength...laying down smoke screen first. Can't bug out! Load walking wounded with grenades...send them down far path...pitch them into smoke screen!'"[32]

The card was passed by hand among the nearly one hundred walking wounded.

This was it. Whoever could walk out of the tent prepared for the worst.

"There was a moment's pause," Dr. Beaven recalled, "then, spontaneously, the entire complement arose and, without a word, loosened the remaining hand grenades carried on their ammo belts. Deliberately, they filed out, crept along the fifty-yard path to the end of the hill, stepped a few yards into a thick smoke screen and lobbed the grenades at the unmistakable garlic smell[33] seeming to emanate from the advancing Chinese troops.

"For more than an hour, there was a continuous procession of men jettisoning explosives down the far end of the path. The dead were stripped of all remaining grenades and [and the grenades were] loaded onto returning Marines who then returned to the edge of the smoke screen, and in a last act of defiance, hurled some 500 more grenades into the area. That was it. There was no more; and we waited for the end to come."[34]

But it never did. For two days the Chinese had led counterattack after counterattack. But finally, having gone through two regiments—at least four thousand men—they couldn't afford more casualties. The barrage of artillery began to quiet, the smoke screen disappeared, and the garlic smell of the Chinese infantry faded away. "Simultaneously, every man dropped to his knees and wept unashamedly. The Chinese had been stopped."[35]

At 2:30 in the morning on March 30, 1953, the tide had turned. While the Marines continued firing on the enemy throughout the night, by eleven o'clock that morning, the Battle for the Nevada Cities was over. The last confrontation was when five Chinese approached on foot, appearing to surrender. Instead, they tossed grenades and fired their weapons. Three of the Chinese soldiers were killed instantly by the Americans; the other two were taken prisoner, one of whom later died.

The Red Mongolian Mare with Two Purple Hearts

"Outpost Vegas broke the back of the enemy," Lieutenant Riley recalled, "and we give a lot of credit to Reckless. As far as we were concerned, she was kind of the hero in that battle."[36]

The brass agreed and made sure that, despite being an animal in a man's Army, her sacrifices didn't go unrecognized. Reckless was awarded two Purple Hearts, one each for the wounds she shrugged off in the heat of battle.

Reckless did more than just keep the guns so well supplied that at least one melted. She helped carry the wounded and dead from the battlefield and was a shield for troops who walked beside her against shell fire.

Harold Wadley recalled being asked about Reckless transporting a wounded Marine to How 3/5 Med bunker the day after the outpost was overrun. "LtCol Oddy asked me to get KSC's [Korean Service Corps—aka "chiggy bearers"] from their camp and go with the reaction force to Reno Block. Heavy casualties were taken and we could not get up to Outpost Reno. We were called back to the line. It was the next day while bringing dead and wounded back to the How Company Command Post that I was asked if the horse that carried a wounded Marine back was with me. My reply was that the mare was with the Reckless Rifle team. I only had Chiggy Bearers."[37]

It's impossible to say how many lives her devotion to duty saved over those final, harrowing days of March 1953.

Wadley put it best: "I never thought she would survive. I figured she'd end up dead. But there was an angel riding that little mare's back every time she went up and down Vegas—no doubt about it."[38]

Reckless's Finest Hour

In a single day, Reckless had made *fifty-one round-trips* to the various gun sites, moving solo through the combat zone ninety-five percent of the time. She *carried 386 rounds* of ammunition—nearly five tons of explosives—on her back, up and down treacherous terrain as the hellish battle raged all around her.

Overall, Pedersen estimated she *covered more than thirty-five miles* that day, through open rice paddies and up steep mountain terrain, where the final climb was always a forty-five-degree angle. She safely delivered all fifty-one loads of the powerful shells amid "an inferno of explosives,"[39] with the buzzing and screaming of enemy fire coming in at a rate of *five hundred rounds per minute*. No horse—before or since—has come close to such selfless acts of bravery. She was a horse truly worthy of the United States Marines.

The Human Cost of the Nevada Cities

The Turkish Brigade came in to relieve the Marines on April 4, 1953, and the 1st Marine Division went in reserve. According to the Division Command Diaries, casualties for the month of March were heavy: 1,488 killed, wounded, or missing.[40] Of that, the Battle of the Nevada Cities alone accounted for 1,015 casualties—nearly 70 percent—including 156 killed in action, 801 wounded (441 wounded and evacuated; 360 wounded and not evacuated) and 98 missing, which included 19 captured.[41]

R&R for the RR Platoon

Reckless and her regiment moved to the relative safety of Camp Casey, south of the Imjin River, for R&R. Only at night could they hear the vague murmur of distant gunfire. Reckless was elated to be in a new pasture, one teeming with fresh grass and colorful flowers.

Riley wrote home, describing both the battle and his taking command of the platoon. "The 'panic button' was pushed sometime last week, and since then I've put in some long hours; right now, however, the 5th Regiment is in reserve and off the line," he wrote on April 5, 1953. "The Chinks attacked the entire 5th Marine front a week or so ago and captured one of our outposts (a hill about 1,400 yards in front of the MLR called Vegas). It took a few days and quite a few casualties to get it back and set the Chinaman on his heels. An unbelievable amount of ammo was expended against [them] and [they] withdrew. In my platoon the 75s fired more ammo in four days than all last summer. Also, only a handful of my men were wounded."

Riley added the platoon had gone into reserve on April 4 and, "are supposed to remain here for twenty days and then move up and relieve the other regiment. The only trouble we had moving was when 'Reckless,' the horse, decided he didn't want to get into the trailer. We finally coaxed him in after a forty-five-minute delay. During the time of attack she hauled quite a bit of ammo up the hills and earned her feed."

Riley ended with, "Tomorrow I get ten new men from the incoming draft—now I'm up to sixty-four men, one truck, two jeeps, six 75s and one horse."[42]

(He later wrote home to correct himself on a personnel matter: "As far as Reckless is concerned, it was my error if I called her a he—as she is not a he, but a her."[43])

The Battle for the Nevada Complex was a turning point of the war. Skirmishes continued, but for the RR platoon, fierce battles like Outpost Vegas were over. In fact, peace was just four months away; the ceasefire would be signed July 27, 1953.

CHAPTER 7

THE WAR
WINDS DOWN

*I asked Lieutenant Quinn, our platoon leader, "What about Reno
and Vegas?" He just shook his head and said, "They get to keep
them." I just sat down in the mud and cried hot, bitter tears.*
—Sergeant Harold E. Wadley, USMC

While the down time at Camp Casey was a welcomed
respite, it coincided with bittersweet news for the RR
platoon: Eric Pedersen was giving up command of the
Anti-Tank Company. Bill Riley wrote home on April 12, 1953, that
Pederson had managed to get "extended for three months so he can
be an air observer—fly around in a Piper Cub"[1]—but Pedersen
would no longer be close by. His place would be taken by Captain
James Schoen, soon to win a Bronze Star for his leadership in battle.

Joe Latham again offered to take up a collection to buy Reckless
from Pedersen and keep the horse with the platoon. But Pedersen
wanted to maintain a financial stake in the heroic horse and would

only accept partial payment, so Reckless was sort of kept on loan to the platoon.

For Pedersen, it wasn't about money, or investments, or the refracted glory of being associated with such an unusual war hero. Actually, he'd worried for a long time that after the war Reckless might be abandoned. In the back of his mind, he'd always hoped that when the time was right, he could arrange for her to be brought stateside so she could be properly cared for.

Bill Riley drove Pedersen to the pasture so he could say goodbye to his four-legged, battle-tested Marine conscript. When Reckless saw Pedersen, she stopped eating and joined him at the fence. Pedersen gently stroked her neck and back, and Reckless seemed to know something was up. She nuzzled the lieutenant. Pedersen turned to Riley. "He told me to take good care of her," Riley said. "I told him, 'Don't worry, Pete. She's in good hands.'"[2] When Riley drove him away in his jeep, Pedersen did not look back.

With her heroics a few weeks earlier, Reckless was basking in her new status as the local hero of Camp Casey. Reporters eagerly snapped her picture and quizzed the men about their famous pal. Reckless's visitors included a steady stream of officers from the Corps' highest ranks, who dropped by to make sure she was doing okay, among them Major General Edwin Pollock, commander of the 1st Marine Division.

Rest and a regular diet seemed to restore Reckless's playful spirit. She began putting on shows for her new fans—running, jumping, eventually finishing with that good-natured prance from the long-ago days at Sinseol-dong racetrack. She even took delight in teasing Latham by pretending she was going to run him down. After a few near-misses, Riley dryly offered Reckless's target a warning: "I told him that one of these days she's going to make a mistake and we'll be looking for a new gunnery sergeant."[3]

Reckless loved the attention, but there still was work to do. And for all that they loved and respected her, Reckless presented issues different from the usual Marine. Not only did she eat more, but, as Riley noted in a letter home, "Every time we move, the same old question pops up—how to move the horse. Right now, the men are trying to get her into a jeep trailer and the mud and rain aren't helping out any."[4]

Recklessly Assaulting the "Cleanest Vessel in the Fleet"

The regiment was scheduled for a ten-day amphibious exercise starting May 8, 1953.[5] Riley organized his unit for the exercise, known in Corps jargon as MAR RCT LEX I (LEX I, for short). "I put down on the manifest, 'One horse, so many inches high, and a trailer,' and I thought it was a joke. But it turned out that everybody thought that was cool, so we took the horse with us."[6]

Just before leaving, on May 7, 1953, Riley wrote home about the amphibious landing. "We leave here by train around 1 a.m.—arrive at a seaport around 10 a.m., board ship and go on a landing exercise somewhere in South Korea. We'll be away about ten days. I don't know if I told you or not, but we are taking the horse along and she sure causes a lot of problems. The landing exercise is a practice one, on a friendly shore, just to get us in shape in case a real one is needed if the talks in Panmunjom fail."

The loading lists were forwarded to the Navy. According to the Battalion Operation Plan, Reckless would ride on the USS LST-1084[7], the vessel that carried the tanks. The ungainly ferry craft, formally called a "Landing Ship, Tank" (LST), could be described as a sea-going flatbed truck. The platoon rode on the USS *Talladega* APA-208. The mission called for the men to "land on MARLEX beaches, advance inland, seize force beach headline, protect landing of supporting elements and additional enemy forces in the area."[8]

Captain Schoen and PFCs Monroe Coleman and Eagle Trader[9] transported Reckless to Inchon, fifty-five miles away, by trailer. The rest of the unit traveled to Inchon by train—everyone but Joe Latham, who stayed behind to find a blacksmith for Reckless.

In a letter home, Riley wrote that before embarking for Inchon, "We took the horse into a village blacksmith to get her 'shoe'd,' but she had other ideas and tore apart the blacksmith shop and knocked over the 'village blacksmith.' Conclusion—she makes the trip with her 'tender hoofs.' I have a few pictures of myself on the horse—I'll send them on when they are developed. I'll mark the horse...just in case you've forgotten what I look like."[10]

When the Navy's LST loading officer saw the shipping list of equipment and men, one item stood out: "One horse with gear and two day's rations. Weight: 850 pounds." It's not known if he laughed, but it's clear the officer thought the Marines were trying to pull a fast one. He considered the possibility they might actually be trying to sneak beer or other non-issued food or drink onto the ship. Everything else on the list looked legit; only the horse entry seemed, well...*fishy*.

If there truly was a horse, he knew they would have a problem because for the second year in a row, the ship had just been honored as the cleanest vessel in the 7th Fleet. A horse on board could easily jeopardize that distinction.

Surely, he thought, this must be a Marine gag.

As Coleman unloaded Reckless from her trailer, arriving Army replacement troops stood by and watched. Unaware of Reckless's identity or exploits, they shouted out:

"Hiya, Man o' War."

"Naw, that's Seabiscuit."

"Looks like a walking can of dog meat. Where'd you get that nag, Marines?"[11]

Reckless parades in front of the Army replacement troops as she readies to board the ship for the amphibious landing exercise. *J. R. Willcut*

Reckless and her Marine handlers ignored the misguided taunts.

Still, as Monroe Coleman led Reckless up the LST's boarding ramp, her presence caused a stir, especially with the Navy skipper.

"I recall that as Reckless and her party approached the LST, they were halted by a loud hail from the bow," said Lieutenant Colonel Ed Wheeler, the regiment's executive officer (and 1st Battalion commander after Pedersen was wounded for the third time). "The hailer proved to be the Navy skipper. He was considerably exercised over the proposition of transporting livestock in his clean tank deck. It was obvious his embarrassment was profound when the Marines pulled out a loading plan approved by him, which included in its myriad columns and figures, '1 horse, w/appurtenances.' From that point on, I imagine that this officer is a firm believer in reading 'the small print' in any loading list he signs."[12]

At last on board, Coleman set up Reckless with two days of rations and a stall between the tanks. The rest of her food would be brought by a truck (boarded on another ship) after they landed.

The amphibious exercise called for the regiment to land at Yong-jong-Ni Beach ("Red Beach"), thirty-three and a half miles southwest of the U.S. Air Force's Kunsan Ai- Base on the Yellow Sea. The landing would be followed by a mock battle, an advance of several thousand yards, and then withdrawal from the "battle" and re-boarding the ship.

Shortly after setting sail, the ship hit bad weather. The rank smell of gasoline from the tanks and the unsettling roll of the ship nauseated Reckless. Coleman sought out the ship's doctor for nausea pills. But the doc thought Coleman was crazy and denied the request. Worse, the weather also forced a change in plans: only the infantry would be landing—Reckless and the tanks would stay on board.

Command Diaries for the 2nd Battalion, 5th Marines, May 1953, noted that in the morning hours of the thirteenth, "personnel of the Battalion participating on LEX-1 made the planned landing, took the objective and dug-in and spent the night there." (Coincidentally, at 2:07 p.m. that same day, Lieutenant Colonel Andrew Geer, Reckless's future biographer, took over command of the 2nd Battalion, 5th Marines.)[13]

Because Reckless was left aboard ship during the landing, and so there was no rendezvous on the beach with the truck carrying her food, a serious new problem arose: she had finished the few rations brought aboard for her, and there still were four days before they would be back at Inchon.

First Lieutenant William Cross, a Marine tank commander, asked for shredded wheat, cornflakes, or even bacon and eggs for Reckless. The request was refused. Instead, all they could get for the heroine of Outpost Vegas was oatmeal and cabbage.

What happened next served the Navy right for being so uncooperative. The cabbage gave Reckless another stomach ache. "My ship has won the 'CE' for being the cleanest vessel in the fleet two years and running," moaned Navy Captain John Kaufman, commodore of the LST squadron, "but I can assure you Reckless is going to end that tenure."[14]

Not only was Reckless depositing onto the tank deck proof of her illness, she was also losing weight. Kaufman finally sent a mordant dispatch to a Marine commander: "Reckless out of rations. We may have to eat her before she eats us."[15]

The "cavalry" finally arrived in the form of Corporal Howard Richie, who docked a small boat piled high with barley and hay for the famished filly.

The rest of the trip went smoothly. Yet, strangely, the Navy never invited Reckless back for another cruise.

Back at camp, Riley wrote home about the trip. "I just returned from a ten-day cruise on the Yellow Sea," he told his sweetheart. "It was a good change for the troops, plenty of good food and sleep. (Except the three days used in making a landing and running around the hills and through Korean villages.) The tide was too rough to land heavy vehicles, so our horse 'Reckless' didn't get ashore. She

Jimmy Lee

Joe Latham and Jimmy Lee

Latham, Jimmy, and unidentified Marine

Jimmy and Capt. Ted Mildner in front of Commanding Officer's Tent

Jimmy and Capt. Mildner with Reckless

Jimmy on the back of Reckless

Jimmy on Reckless with unidentified Marine

Various pictures of the Korean orphan, Jimmy Lee, that Latham took under his wing, riding Reckless with Latham and Capt. Ted Mildner. *Nancy Latham Parkin*

spent her ten days aboard an LST. She wasn't too happy about the whole deal, either."[16]

When she returned to Camp Casey, Reckless met a new caretaker, a young Korean orphan taken under the wing of Sergeant Latham. This was Jimmy Lee, who struck up an immediate rapport with the horse and was her constant companion through the spring.

Challenging the Champion: Native Dancer, Reckless, and the Paddy Derby

Reckless's roots in racing were not forgotten by the men of the RR platoon.

"We challenged Native Dancer," Riley recalled. "She was the big horse of the day."[17]

In letters home, Riley wrote giddily of the platoon's publicity stunt. "By the time you receive this, our horse Reckless will be hitting the U.S. papers and a few TV programs. The division public info officer was here yesterday taking shots of the horse, the 75 and a few of the men from the platoon. Today, an NBC telecaster showed up and took television pictures of the horse, the 75 and two squads of men. How is this for a publicity angle? The division is challenging Reckless against the horse that won the Kentucky Derby, providing the race is in Korea and the K. Derby horse carries 75 ammo. They took a picture of the horse and a sign, 'The Paddy Derby.' The TV publicity will be on either *The Dave Garroway Show* or the John Cameron Swayze TV show about the time you receive this letter."[18]

It's not clear why the Marines changed horses from the Kentucky Derby winner, Dark Star, to the Preakness winner, Native Dancer, but on June 9, 1953, the Tokyo edition of *Stars & Stripes* ran a story—headlined, "'Night-Mare' In Shape: Marine Mare Dares

Throwing down the gauntlet: U.S. Marines challenge a champion at a makeshift war zone racetrack with a punny name. The dare went unacknowledged. Top: Lt. William Riley, Reckless, Platoon Sgt. Joseph Latham, Corpsman "Doc" Mitchell, Sgt. John Lisenby. Bottom (L-R): Edward A Kujawa, PFC Joe Gordon, PFC Billy R. Jones, Sgt. Elmer Lively, PFC Monroe Coleman, Cpl. Kenneth H. Schumacher, PFC Jose B. Cordova, and PFC Booker T. Crew. *USMC History Division, Quantico, VA*

Dancer"[19]—about the Marines' offer to race Reckless again the great thoroughbred racehorse Native Dancer in a "Paddy Derby." Back home, a Florida newspaper picked up the story: "'Mare of the Mad Marines' Challenges Native Dancer."[20]

Latham and Riley drafted a letter to Native Dancer's owner, Alfred Vanderbilt. The note laid out race terms and conditions: "There are two stipulations we must make. Because Reckless is a very busy horse, Native Dancer must come to Korea and agree to a handicap."[21]

The contest was to be held at "Upsan Downs," a makeshift mile-and-a-half course of hills and rice paddies. The handicap: each rider-less horse would carry four rounds of 75 mm ammunition weighing 96 pounds.[22] The first to reach the Recoilless Rifle team waiting at the finish line would be anointed the winner. "I guess," Latham speculated, "that you'd call Reckless a dark horse, maybe even a 'night-mare.' She makes most of her races after dark."[23] The purse: a whopping $25,000, equivalent to about $215,000 today. It was proposed that each man in the 1st Marine Division would put up a dollar, but the Marines had so much confidence in their little mare that they easily could have raised three or four times the proposed purse.

They never needed to because their daring challenge went unanswered. They never heard from Mr. Vanderbilt. While Native Dancer endured his only loss in twenty-two career races in the Kentucky Derby on May 2 to 25 to 1 longshot Dark Star, Native Dancer rebounded by winning the Preakness at Pimlico and would soon compete in the Triple Crown's final race, the Belmont Stakes.

The disappointed Marines remained cocksure of Reckless's superior speed, even after Native Dancer took the Belmont plus the historic Travers Stakes at Saratoga. (At year's end, the Thoroughbred Racing Associations named Native Dancer the 1953 American Champion for three-year-old male horses.)

A Change in Command

When Major General Edwin Pollock rotated back home from his tour of duty in Korea, he was replaced by Major General Randolph McCall Pate, future twenty-first Commandant of the Marine Corps and one of the horse's greatest admirers.

Pate would later write about his first meeting with Reckless. "I was surprised at her beauty and intelligence, and believe it or not, her *esprit de corps*. Like any other Marine, she was enjoying a bottle

Latham in a photo shoot with Reckless. Top right image was used on the cover of Lt. Col. Andrew Geer's book, *Reckless: Pride of the Marines*. *Command Museum, Marine Corps Recruit Depot, San Diego*

Bottom right: Joe Latham and Reckless. *Mary Alice Gehrdes*

of beer with her comrades. She was constantly the center of attraction and was fully aware of her importance. If she failed to receive the attention she felt her due, she would deliberately walk into a group of Marines and, in effect, enter the conversation. It was obvious the Marines loved her."[24]

But before Pollock left, he gave Reckless one last inspection. He was appalled at the poor condition of her shoes. Lieutenant Riley assured him that Sergeant Latham was on top of the problem. Reckless had a bad track record with farriers, he said, but he assured the general, Latham was taking her to a racetrack in Seoul the very next day where they thought a qualified farrier with a good horse-side manner might be found.

It proved to be an eventful trip.

Latham and Jimmy Lee loaded Reckless into her trailer and drove to the Sinseol-Dong racecourse. Pulling up, Latham sensed the horse's excitement. And while Latham knew nothing of Reckless's previous owner, everyone at the track remembered Kim Huk Moon's spirited mare.

When Kim's one-armed friend Choi Chang Ju stepped from the crowd to greet them, Reckless perked up. She was thrilled to see Choi and walked over to greet her old friend warmly.

Latham explained why they had come. Choi slipped an arm over Reckless's neck, turned, and shouted something to a Korean boy, who scurried out of view behind the stables.

Choi turned back to Latham. "I know Ah-Chim-Hai long time," Choi said. Latham had never heard Reckless's Korean name before.[25]

Choi led Reckless to her old stall, and another young Korean man raced over to see her. It was Kim Huk Moon, reunited with his beloved horse, the one he called Flame. Reckless nuzzled Kim's chest, as her former owner draped his arms joyfully around her neck.

Latham had no idea who Kim was—and actually assumed he was the farrier—but saw she was in good hands and so left with Jimmy to get something to eat and look at the planes while waiting for Reckless to get new shoes.

One can only imagine Kim's emotions at getting to see his dear friend again. He took loving care of Reckless, fixing her shoes, then brushing and massaging her as he used to do nightly. He stayed as long as he could but slipped away before Latham and Jimmy returned to the stables.

Latham studied Reckless's shoes and found they were perfect. He looked around for Kim to thank, but the young man was gone. Latham paid Choi, led Reckless into the trailer, and headed back to camp.

It was the last time Kim Huk Moon ever saw his beautiful Flame.

War's End

Summer was upon them when the Marines were ordered back into action. This time, Reckless found herself in almost the same spot as where she had begun her military career, near Changdan, where her unit was charged with supporting Outpost Hedy from Molar Hill with recoilless rifle fire to keep the Communist Chinese from extending their trenches. Reckless was kept busy, roving the line, supporting fire missions, until one day in July it was over.

At 10:01 a.m. on Monday, July 27, 1953, Lieutenant General William K. Harrison, representing the United Nations forces, and North Korean General Nam Il signed the first of eighteen armistice documents. It was an anti-climactic end to a savage war—what the United Nations insisted on calling a "police action"—which had taken almost thirty-seven thousand American lives, wounded more than twice that number, and possibly killed more than five million people in total. The armistice was a "cease-fire," which remains in effect today. There has never been an official peace treaty ending the Korean War. At 10:00 p.m., Marines on the Main Line of Resistance fired off a star cluster—a sort of wartime fireworks display—to acknowledge the Marines would observe the cease-fire, and also for a practical reason.

"I was on Outpost Dagmar when it ended at 2200 hours, 27th of July," recalled Harold Wadley. "And when they shot up in the air—dad gum, our artillery was really banging and so was theirs. And those of us that were hunkered down in holes didn't have the privilege of knowing what was happening.

"We thought they were still fighting. But we learned later why they were doing it—they were firing up to get rid of all their extra ammo so they didn't have to pack it. And there we were, sitting under the middle of it all on Outpost Dagmar, and gosh Almighty it was something.

"And we were told to clear our weapons and leave. And Lieutenant Quinn and I said, 'Dad gum, we weren't going back through this crap, that's seven, 800 yards back to the line.' And so he just acted like he couldn't hear the radio and we stayed because we thought it was a trick of some kind.

"And then the next day we were ordered to come back…and there again, we said, 'We're not going to cross there in daylight.' There were Chinese all over; you couldn't count them, they were so thick around us. And we said, 'We aren't going back.'

"And so then, Lieutenant Quinn radioed back and said he'd had radio difficulty, but he understood we were to proceed to the MLR immediately, but he said it will be after dark. And we were told not to have a round in our chamber.

"Well, *we had a round in our chamber.*

"It was terrible. Looking out there at Vegas, Carson, and Reno—dad gum. I asked Lieutenant Quinn, our platoon leader, 'What about Reno and Vegas?' He just shook his head and said, 'They get to keep them.' I just sat down in the mud and cried hot, bitter tears. A big hand grasped my shoulder and I looked up. It was Lieutenant Quinn. And tears were running through the grime on his face also. All that blood-soaked earth and we gave it back to them! Every 27th I go out and fire one round to the [northwest]."[26]

For what everyone hoped would be the last time, the dark Korean hills rocked with flame and noise. Then the hills lay quiet. At sea, ships backed away from the cold gray waters off North Korea. On land, aircraft stood silent on the fields.

When the reality of the cease-fire sank in, the American troops celebrated. That night, Reckless partied alongside the boys—and not just her pals from the RR platoon.

"It was like a family reunion when we all got together, because we were all stretched out across the front lines, with different platoons and different companies," recalled PFC Don Menzies, a gunner with the Anti-Tank Company of the 5th Marines.

"On Armistice Day, she got drunk on beer with the rest of the guys," Menzies said, "and she staggered about the camp. It was a sight to see and one I will never forget."[27]

Camp Semper Fidelis

Because the Armistice called for a demilitarized zone (DMZ) a military demarcation line (MDL) was drawn up. Each side retreated 2,000 yards, thus establishing a 4,000-yard DMZ between them. A new "No fly zone" was created, its corridor extending to the town

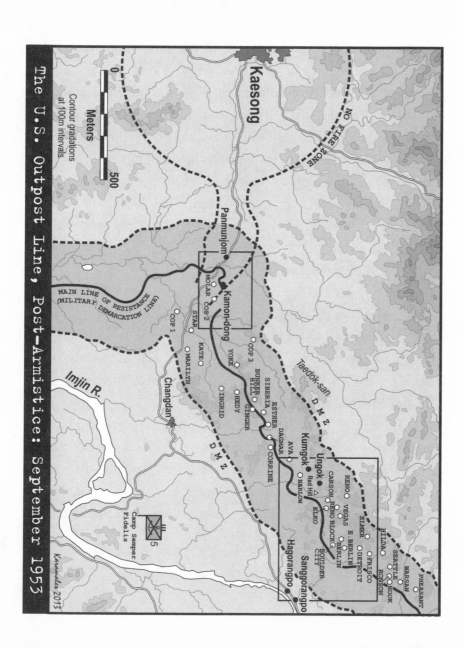

of Kaesong, west of Panmunjom. Within seventy-two hours of the ceasefire, "combatants were to remove 'all military forces, supplies and equipment'"[28] from the DMZ. Old defenses were torn down, and new ones were built within a forty-five day deadline ending September 13, 1953. Some old outposts like Bunker Hill, Esther, and Ava lay north of the MDL. The agreement also called for each side to maintain a force of a thousand "civil police" to provide a buffer across the 155-mile front. To meet this mission, the 1st Provisional Demilitarized Zone Police Company was formed on September 4, drawing its personnel from the 1st Marine Division's infantry regiments. Each regiment furnished twenty-five enlisted men and one officer. On September 21, the DMZ Police Company was attached to the 5th Marine Regiment.

Camp Semper Fidelis, built specifically to house the 1st Provisional DMZ Police Company, was situated just north of the Imjin River, southeast of Changdan. Constructed in four days, the new police unit occupied the camp for about eighteen months, until March 17, 1955, when they were replaced by the 24th Infantry Division and returned to the States.

At the camp entrance stood a Torii, the traditional Japanese gateway to a sacred place said to bring good luck. It also made a beautiful backdrop for taking pictures. No records survive to indicate precisely when Reckless visited the camp, but by the stripes on her blanket in Marines' snapshots, she was a corporal at the time.

Navy Hospital Corpsman Sam Saba, the Marine 1st Provisional Demilitarized Zone Police Company corpsman, poses with then-Corporal Reckless. Leatherneck *Magazine*

Reckless poses with Rene Morin at the entrance of Camp Semper Fidelis. *Rene Morin*

CHAPTER 8

OLD FRIENDS LEAVE, NEW FRIENDS ARRIVE

She just stood still. They read off everything and it was
almost like she was just a part of it. She knew what
was happening. She was a proud Marine.
—Navy Corpsman Bob "Doc" Rogers

With the cease-fire, the 2nd Battalion took a new position, moving from the Panmunjom Corridor to the Imjin River. Reckless spent her days stringing communications wire. Life was good, though some of Reckless's friends began heading home.

The first to go was Colonel Andrew Geer, commander of the 2nd Battalion, 5th Marines, who thought she "displayed attributes and intelligence never before seen in an animal."[1] He knew what a great story Reckless was, steered journalists her way, interviewed everyone connected with her, and took copious notes. "From the day I joined the 5th Marines to command the 2nd Battalion, I knew I would one day write about this little red horse."[2] He also tracked down Kim Huk Moon for his side of the story.

Latham told Geer he was worried about what would happen to Reckless when everyone went home. Because her name was not on any rotation list, presumably she would be left behind in Korea. Latham was haunted by thoughts of her becoming a broken down carthorse. Geer promised Latham and Lieutenant Riley he'd do everything possible to get Reckless to American soil.

The night before Geer left, Latham, Riley (who was being transferred to Fox Company), and Reckless took him to say goodbye to the various units. Reckless acted as one of the guys, drinking beer and posing for pictures. "She'd put out her left lip," Latham recalled, "and the colonel would mix her a drink. He'd pour it in her and she'd never drop a drop. We sure got a kick out of her."[3]

"You know, Colonel," Riley said, "Reckless has forgotten she's a horse."[4]

By the time they returned to camp it was late, but they raided the mess tent anyway for old times' sake. Reckless drank a cup of coffee and scarfed down peanut butter sandwiches; the others settled for Spam sandwiches.

Col. Andrew Geer pours Reckless a beer as he says good-bye to the men in his unit. *Camp Pendleton Archives*

Reckless provoked wild laughter as she struggled vainly with her tongue to scrape peanut butter off the roof of her mouth. The more she scrunched up her face trying to sweep her palate clean, the more the men roared. A second cup of coffee helped a little, but not much.[5]

The next day, both Geer and Reckless paid the price for too much celebration; both visited the unit surgeon for help with hangovers.

A General in Her Corner

Next to say goodbye were Latham and Coleman, in October. Latham had been hoping to take the young orphan Jimmy Lee back to the states with him. Circumstances prevented that, so he arranged for Jimmy to live with a family near the base, which meant the platoon could help look after him and Jimmy could help look after Reckless. Many of Latham's worries about Reckless had been alleviated because Major General Randolph Pate made her well-being a priority. Lieutenant William McManus, who relieved Riley, put it best: "The surest way I know of getting locked up is to have the general find her bunker dirty and Reckless unhappy."[6]

New People Toss Out the Old Rules

Reckless quickly and easily made new friends. Yet with the arrival of newcomers, many of the "rules" regarding Reckless gradually gave way. Marines began riding her at will, even guarding her at night instead of allowing her free rein around camp.

"Reckless had her quarters, a small shed with a small fence around it," Private John Newsom of the Anti-Tank Platoon recalled, "and at night, it was cold as all get out (felt like 20 or 30 below!) and people had guard duty. Word was out that she might be kidnapped for food.

We didn't know who would kidnap her; only that it might happen—and after all she'd done, we couldn't let that happen on our watch. Every night we had to stand guard on her, four hours per man. It didn't matter that she wasn't more than a hundred feet from our tents; we still had to do our watch duty. We would put her blankets around her and [she] would be all bundled up. She'd have full run of the place during the day, but at night we'd have to guard her."[7]

Corporals Paul Hammersley and Quentin Seidel more or less adopted Reckless when they joined the platoon. Both had been raised on farms and ranches and knew a lot about horses. Reckless took a particular shine to Hammersley.

"It was lonesome sometimes walking guard duty," he recalled. "We had to walk guard over our Command Post and it could be dangerous, too, because the Koreans were just over on their outpost a few thousand feet from us and you couldn't have good enough ears—and we knew Reckless had good ears. So I'd coax her sometimes with a little pogey bait and she was just happy to walk along with me, to walk guard duty in the middle of the night. And it was very comforting to have a companion like that with you. She was also a very neat little lady. She would just walk in and out of your tent and never make a mess. She was just so sweet. She loved to be petted—just like a dog or cat—and she never resisted. But the fun thing about Reckless was you could jump on her and ride her at will."[8]

It became Corporal Quentin Seidel's job to "doctor up" Reckless after she cut her head and ear on barbed wire fencing.

"I can't say how she cut it or where she cut it," he recalled, "but she needed stitches and I had to take care of her. When she cut herself, I was the only farm boy in the crew that had any idea what to do. So I went down to First Aid because back on the farm we would use sulfa powder when we treated cuts on livestock on the farm. And

The old rules give way: one corporal astride another as Paul Hammersley rides Reckless, something unthinkable only months earlier. *Paul Hammersley*

I asked the doctor for some sulfa powder and he wondered…why was I looking for that? And I told him that Reckless had been cut and needed doctoring."

Seidel said the doctor became irate. "And he said, 'I'm a *person* doctor, not a *horse* doctor.' When I told him *I* was going to do it," Seidel remembered, "he gave me a whole big bottle of sulfa tablets and I took them along with needles and thread and whatnot that they used in operations and stuff. He gave me all that I needed to stitch her up.

"I took the sulfa tablets back to my tent and mashed them up so I could get the powder out of them and then we just took her and tied her down so she would hold still and I started sewing her ear up. I sewed it all the way up and tied it off and we wrapped bandages around it as you see in the pictures.

"So she was running around there for the longest time with bandages all wrapped around her ear and her head. And she would go from one person to another and get sympathy here and sympathy there. Just like a spoiled kid.

"They were the kind of stitches that dissolved normally, so we just took the wrapping off after it healed together. And then she had a little notch on the top of the ear that I should've taken one more stitch and then her ear would've been complete, but she ended up with one ear with the notch on the top of it."[9]

Paul Hammersley (back facing out) lets Reckless out of the back of the truck to get stitches. *Quentin Seidel*

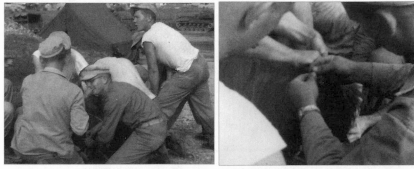

Reckless is held down while Quentin Seidel stitches up her cut ear. *Paul Hammersley*

Cpl. Quentin Seidel's lack of a medical (or even veterinary) degree didn't stop him from successfully stitching up Sgt. Reckless's badly cut head and ear following an encounter with barbed wire fencing. *Quentin Seidel*

Baby Needs New Shoes—Again

Only a few months had passed since Latham and Jimmy had taken Reckless shoe shopping, and already she needed a new set and her hooves trimmed. After getting the okay from their sergeant, Corporals Seidel and Hammersley did the honors this time.

"We loaded Reckless in a trailer," Hammersley said, "which wasn't very high and didn't have sides on it and we took her to Seoul to try to find someone to shoe her. We found a Korean person, but she did *not* like him. Not one bit. And she just flattened her ears back and showed her teeth and she was ready to bite him or kick him, either one. And she would not let him even touch her.

"So we talked to him a little bit, and he didn't understand English, and we didn't understand Korean, but we all understood that she needed to go someplace else. And he was sure happy that she was going someplace else."

But when they found a second blacksmith, Reckless "didn't like him much either. But we held her head and petted her and he trimmed her and put shoes on her," Hammersley said. Maybe Reckless changed her mind about the second blacksmith. Or maybe she was just happy when he finished because as the corporals walked her to her trailer, Reckless flashed her old showboating self:

"She just jumped on and rode like a dog would, with her mane just flowing in the wind and her head up high. And when we got back she just jumped off. I don't even know if we put a halter on her to tell you the truth. She was quite some little horse."[10]

Just One of the Guys

In the early spring of 1954, Navy Corpsman Robert "Doc" Rogers of "Baker" Co, 1st Bn, 5th Marines, had temporary duty as a corpsman with the Anti-Tank Platoon. He learned quickly how special Reckless was and how much fun the platoon had with her: "I heard stories about the guys. Marines would come in drunk off of liberty and they'd go down and say, 'Let's go down and let Reckless out.' And they'd do it—just to see what trouble she'd get into."

But what Doc Rogers remembered most fondly was how she fit in as one of the guys—and the lengths to which they'd go to protect her.

"Sometimes the guys would be standing around talking and she'd walk right up to us and just stand there. And somebody would be talking and she would look at him. And the other guy would start talking and she'd look at *him*. And another guy would talk and she'd look at *him*.

Paul Hammersley shows the special bond he had with Reckless. *Paul Hammersley*

Leroy Struble also steals a little nuzzle. *Paul Hammersley*

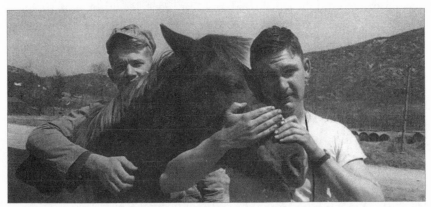

Paul Hammersley and an unidentified Marine show Reckless some affection. *Paul Hammersley*

"It was like, 'Hey, I'm a Marine. I'm one of you.' She had the right-of-way in that compound and she knew it, too.

"One night a bunch of us were all standing around in a circle, talking. There was a Marine lieutenant there. Lieutenant Louie was his name and he was of Chinese ancestry. And while we were talking, Reckless came up behind this one soldier and muzzled the back of this guy's neck. Nipped him on the back of his neck. It scared him half to death and he screamed, 'What the *f---!*' and jumped and turned around. And he's right face to face with Reckless, and shouted, 'Get that motherf——— nag out of here!'

"And Lieutenant Louie exploded on the guy and said, 'That horse has done more for the United States Marine Corps than you have, or ever will do. And besides that, she outranks you. And if I ever hear you talking to that horse like that again, I'm going to have you written up and court-martialed.'"[11]

Recklessly in Pursuit of Anything Edible

Reckless's new friends soon learned the hard way that beyond her playful personality and battlefield bravery, Reckless had another distinctive trait: an insatiable appetite and unstoppable drive to satisfy it. "Everybody had to chip in and pay for Reckless's feed," recalled Private Newsom. "Each payday, we all divvied up. With me being a private, I didn't make a lot of money and to have to give up part of it to feed a horse wasn't a priority for me. So some of the men weren't too pleased with having to do that."[12]

Doc Rogers in particular fell victim to the consequences of Reckless's incredible sense of smell, discovering that when she detected food, Reckless might as well have been named Relentless.

"We all lived in tents, had thirteen-men squad tents, and she could smell from outside the tent what was inside. So I made the mistake of going to the PX one time and I got a package of cookies and I had them stashed away in the tent. We went out for the day and when I got back, it looked like a bomb had hit the place.

"The blankets were off of my bunk and everything was just all torn up in there. Reckless went in the tent, tore the place apart and found those cookies. She ate every last bit of them—wrapper and all."[13]

Pancakes, Pudding, and
the Spray of Satisfaction

When Sergeant John Meyers joined the Anti-Tank Company, 5th Marines, he was assigned to the staff mess tent for about six weeks, more than enough time to see firsthand how spoiled Reckless had become with food—especially when pancakes and chocolate pudding were involved.

"I would feed her an apple a day, so every time she'd see me, she'd trot over to me.

"I worked closely with the head cook at the time...Manny, from Brooklyn, New York, developed the practice of giving Reckless some of our rations for breakfast, which often included pancakes. I would often make sure that Reckless would have a serving and as a result the horse got to know me.

"She knew exactly where I slept. So when Manny was late in getting things started some mornings, Reckless would walk into my tent and wake me up by licking my face, reminding me that it was time for her to eat. It would be the funniest thing. On one occasion, Manny attempted to make chocolate pudding to boost morale for the troops. However, Manny did not have enough sugar to sweeten the dark chocolate treat. It turned out to be too strong and no one really ate it and the 55-gallon drum trashcan became full of the discarded pudding.

"Well, Reckless found the barrel of 'bad' pudding and had a feast. Unfortunately, several hours later, that horse was spraying chocolate diarrhea all over the camp. After a day, there wasn't a safe spot to step."[14]

Sergeant Michael J. Mason slept in the same tent as Meyers. "I first made contact with Reckless in the reserve area, where she had a free roam of the compound. She appeared to be a gentle horse, or should I say Marine. You would never know just when or where she might appear.

"On a number of occasions she would roam into our tent and where John [Meyers] would be laying and tug at his blanket or clothes to get his attention…John always had a few goodies for her.

"On other occasions the cooks would make sheet pies in pans that were 2 foot by 3 foot and about an inch deep. They would put the pies out on a ledge to cool. They soon learned they had to know where Reckless was, as she would suddenly appear and eat the center out of the pies. Her favorite was cherry pie; however, she was just as fond of apple and peach pies as well."[15]

Just a Few Beers with the Boys

Just as before, the new Marines shared whatever food or drink they had with Reckless. Especially their beer.

"She *loved* beer and it didn't matter what brand it may have been," Sergeant Mason recalled. "To her, beer was beer and she loved it. If we had a ration of beer and were sitting around drinking a few, Reckless would trot on over, nudge you in the back until you tipped your can up for her to lick up the beer. She'd drink from the can and I'm sure a lot dropped to the ground, but she wouldn't stop until she had enough. Then she would stagger back to her stable to rest. Or, should I say, to *sleep it off*."[16]

"There was no way to ignore her if she wanted your attention or something to eat or drink," Corporal Hammersley remembered. "She would just give you a nip if you ignored her and she would always come into the tents when she wanted attention."

One night, Hammersley was asleep in his bunk after doing guard duty, "and suddenly I felt a bite on my arm. I awoke and there she was—and she wanted some pogey bait." The corporal got up and looked around, but found little more than, "a case of warm beer under my cot.... So I shared my beer with her. I opened it up and I had a little wash basin that we shaved out of, and I poured the beer in there and she drank it. And she nipped me again. So I said, 'Hey, does anybody else got something for this horse?' And by golly the beers started popping open, and she probably drank a half a dozen beers right there."

One Marine fetched some bread from the cook and, according to Hammersley, "they made a peanut butter and jelly sandwich because she wasn't going to leave that tent until she was satisfied. So we gave her a half of a peanut butter and jelly sandwich—but she ate the whole thing.

"You know, I had lived on a farm as a boy and I'd never seen any animal eat bread and peanut butter before. She was something else."[17]

"Kidnapped" in a Good Cause

In the fall of 1953, the Marine Corps War Memorial—also called the Iwo Jima War Memorial—remained unfinished. More money was needed to complete the huge, cast bronze statue and deliver it to Arlington National Cemetery in Virginia.

Based on the iconic World War II photograph of five Marines and a sailor raising the second flag on Iwo Jima, the memorial was being paid for with private donations. But support had slowed, and a fundraising effort began in Korea. "Many ideas were initiated," Major General Pate told Colonel Andy Geer, "to promote competition among units to see which could raise the most money."[18]

One scheme inspired disbelief and horror among the men of the RR Platoon. Marines from the 4.2-inch mortar unit (Four Deuces) "abducted" Reckless from her bunker and held her for "ransom" in a nearby camp. "We had her for three days," Navy Corpsman Robert Pontius recalled. "Our unit kidnaped her and I remember us guys all talking about how long we could keep her before they found her."[19] The unit had printed ransom tickets that sold for a dollar apiece.

The men of the RR Platoon were not amused. While assured Reckless was safe, they remained deeply concerned about her care; the Four Deuces had no idea of Reckless's unusual feeding and drinking habits or how she preferred to sleep near a stove on cold nights.

Paul Hammersley shares a beer with Reckless. *Paul Hammersley*

The division scrambled to get her back, with Sergeant Elmer Lively raising $400 from the platoon for the "Ransom Reckless Fund."

"Her ransom was quickly forthcoming and the fund oversubscribed,"[20] Major General Pate wrote later. When receipts were tallied and Reckless returned, the kidnap stunt had generated more

Reckless with her handler feeding her a snack of bread. *Command Museum, Marine Corps Recruit Depot, San Diego*

Reckless with her handler feeding her a snack of bread. *USMC History Division, Quantico, VA*

Dollar raffle tickets raised both money for the Iwo Jima War Memorial—and the ire of the RR Platoon

than $28,000 from the division, equivalent to around $237,000 today.

Recognizing Reckless:
The Marine Corps Makes It Official

In February 1954, Master Sergeant John Strange, the senior NCO in the Anti-Tank Company, along with the company commander, Captain Andrew W. Kovach, decided it was time Reckless was formally recognized and rewarded for her incredible service to country. She would be promoted to sergeant, with details of her courageous acts read aloud at a company formation.

The men felt Reckless deserved an official uniform for the occasion—and it seemed unlikely the Corps had any uniforms to fit her properly. So Kovach turned fashion designer, creating a beautiful red silk parade blanket trimmed in gold, with the Corps' emblem—the Eagle, Globe, and Anchor—on each side and her unit identification. They found a tailor in Seoul, and the platoon took up a collection for the $51 cost.

A week later, Reckless modeled her uniform for the first time. Unlike the Australian Army hat she had hated, Reckless was proud of this obviously special blanket. Yet after awhile, she couldn't help herself and began to nibble at the front edge. Lively put a stop to that, instructing his men to "never leave her alone with that blanket. She'll eat it like she did that hat and we can't be putting out fifty bucks every few weeks."[21]

A small reviewing stand was built, a citation written, and the national and Marine Corps colors displayed as the unit readied itself for the big day.

Biting Off More Than She Can Chew

On March 31, 1954, just a few days before the promotion ceremony, a newspaper ran the headline, "New Ammo Diet Gives 'Reckless' Loose Denture." According to the story, Reckless had "attempted to vary her usual diet of such delicacies as laundered undershirts, talcum powder (seasoned with metal can) and a tasty brand of shaving cream with tube. She tried sinking her molars into a clip of 30-caliber ammunition."[22]

Regimental surgeon Nathaniel E. Adamson Jr. and Navy corpsman Robert Pontius were called in to treat the problem. "She bit down on a clip of ammo and it fouled up her mouth," Pontius recalled. "Several times a day, we washed her mouth out with saline using a large syringe we got from the motor pool."[23] The instrument, a hydrometer, normally used to determine the alcohol content in radiators, was the only thing available that could help Reckless with her teeth. "She just stood there—she didn't mind," Pontius said. "She was really something. And she really loved the guys and was part of the unit."[24]

"This horse has the strangest appetite I've ever seen," Captain Kovach remarked as Reckless snatched from his outstretched hand an apple, then a slice of bread with jelly.

Another officer agreed. "The troops sure spoil this nag," he replied while delivering her breakfast, which included donuts.

"'And then there was the undershirt incident,' chuckled the company first sergeant. 'Reckless found it drying on a clothesline and decided to digest it. She was caught in the act by the owner,' he added, 'and galloped around the parade ground in high gear, the shirt flapping from her mouth with the sergeant right on her hooves.'"[25]

Major General Pate Promotes Reckless

On April 10, 1954, Reckless was officially promoted to sergeant—an honor never bestowed, before or since, on an animal.

There have been animals, especially dogs, which surpassed their roles as military mascots and were recognized with awards and even medals. For example, in World War II, an Army German Shepherd named Chips attacked an enemy pillbox in Sicily and took four startled prisoners. Chips was awarded a Silver Star and Purple Heart for valor. (The medals later were revoked following complaints that presenting service medals to a dog diminished their prestige.)

In World War I, a pit bull mix named Sergeant Stubby served with the 102nd Infantry, 26th (Yankee) Division, in France. Stubby was on solo patrol in the Argonne when he heard something in the bushes and found a German spy mapping American positions.

Stubby charged, the spy ran, Stubby gave chase, tackled his prey, and bit him in the leg.

When the patrol followed Stubby's barking and a man's cries, they found the German on the ground, Stubby's steely jaws clamped emphatically onto his rear end.

The commanding officer of the 102nd reportedly was so impressed that he "promoted" Stubby to sergeant. But it was an honorary promotion, not an official one.

(Returning to the states, Stubby's celebrity grew so great that he commanded an audience with three presidents—Woodrow Wilson, Calvin Coolidge, and Warren Harding.)

But honorary Sergeant Stubby wasn't actual Sergeant Reckless, who was held in the same high esteem as any human Marine of the same rank. No other animal has ever held any legal, officially sanctioned U.S. military rank and been genuinely respected for that rank, except for Reckless.

So April 10 was a big day for Reckless and her platoon. Not just because of the promotion, but especially because Major General Randolph McCall Pate made a special trip to do the honors of presenting Reckless with her sergeant's stripes.

The company paraded and General Pate "trooped the line." Sergeant Elmer Lively and Technical Sergeant Dave Woods escorted Reckless into position. Master Sergeant John Strange read the citation:

> For meritorious achievement in connection with operations against the enemy while serving with a Marine infantry regiment in Korea from October 26, 1952 to July 27, 1953. Corporal Reckless performed the duties of ammunition carrier in a superb manner. Reckless' attention and

Navy Corpsman George Pontius examines Reckless's teeth. *George Pontius*

devotion to duty make her well qualified for promotion
to the rank of sergeant. Her absolute dependability while
on missions under fire contributed materially to the success of many battles....[26]

Reckless stood at attention as Pate pinned the stripes onto her beautiful, though slightly chewed blanket.

The native Korean, born Ah-Chim-Hai, and raised to race at a
Seoul thoroughbred track, was now officially a sergeant in the United
States Marine Corps.

Navy Corpsman Doc Rogers was there that day. "They broke us
all out in formation," Rogers remembered, describing the formal
gathering, at attention and by rank, "and they had Reckless there.
And they had her corporal blanket on—had corporal stripes on the
side of it, had all of her ribbons on there—and they promoted her to
sergeant.

"They took the old blanket off and put the new blanket on her
that had the sergeant stripes on there. And, of course, the same ribbons. It was the most beautiful horse blanket I ever saw.

"But, you know, I think back on that and I think she just acted like she knew everything that was going on. She just stood still. They read off everything and it was almost like she was just a part of it. She knew what was happening. She was a proud Marine."[27]

Reckless's Military Decorations

Reckless's war heroics earned her no fewer than ten military decorations, all worn proudly on her red and gold blanket including the prestigious French fourragère,[28] awarded to the 5th Marines after World War I. The other decorations included:

- Two Purple Hearts
- Marine Corps Good Conduct Medal
- Presidential Unit Citation with Star
- Navy Unit Citation
- National Defense Service Medal
- United Nations Service Medal
- Korean Service Medal with three Stars
- Republic of Korea Presidential Unit Citation

Had she been able to speak up, Reckless probably would have said none of the medals was as meaningful to her as those hard-won sergeant stripes.[29]

Reckless is promoted to sergeant. On the platform, (L to R) Gen. Pate, Capt. Andrew Kovac, Col. Elby D. Martin Jr. listen as MSgt. John Strange reads the citation. Standing beside Reckless are Sgt. Lively (L) and TSgt. Dave Woods (R). *Camp Pendleton Archives*

Capt. Kovac watches Gen. Pate pin sergeant stripes to Reckless's blanket, as Col. Martin and Sgt. Strange watch from the platform. *Camp Pendleton Archives*

Reckless troops the line at her promotion ceremony. *Command Museum, Marine Corps Recruit Depot, San Diego*

Reckless shows off her beautiful blanket. *USMC History Division, Quantico, VA*

CHAPTER 9

"OPERATION BRING RECKLESS HOME" BEGINS

It doesn't matter who owns her. I'll transfer any claim I have to her for a dollar, but let's get her home.

—**Lieutenant Eric Pedersen**

Within a week of Reckless's promotion to sergeant, her name was a household word, thanks to the *Saturday Evening Post*. The April 17, 1954, issue ran Lieutenant Colonel Andrew Geer's four-page spread, "Reckless, the Pride of the Marines," which included a photo of the newly promoted NCO, four rounds of ammunition strapped to her back, posing with Sgt. Joe Latham.

Lieutenant Bill Riley received a copy of the *Saturday Evening Post* story while stationed in Japan. He wrote to his sweetheart Patty O'Leary that he and Latham had "spent an hour a night for a week

"Reckless at Chang-dan, Korea, with TSgt. Joseph Latham, the Marine who put
her through 'hoof camp.' A Seoul race pony, she thrived on bacon and eggs."
Caption courtesy the Saturday Evening Post. *Photo: Nancy Latham Parkin*

last September giving the author Andy Geer the scoop.... He certainly did a good job in writing about 'Reckless.'"[1]

Letters poured in to the *Post* from across the country. Americans
inspired by her story wanted to know when Reckless would be
brought to the states. Picking up on the developing story, the *San
Diego Union* reported on April 22, "Plans now call for Reckless to
be rotated, after long service, to the green hills of Camp Pendleton
... [Lieutenant] Pedersen thinks she rates rotation."

The rotation question took months to answer. The Navy was
willing to transport Reckless to the States—a minor surprise, con-
sidering how messy her previous seagoing adventure had been—but
first, the Navy demanded from the Marine Corps "an official request
for passage for one horse with feed and handler."[2] In short, the Navy
wouldn't budge without properly authorized paperwork.

Thanks to the popular interest generated by the *Post* article, Operation Bring Reckless Home was underway. Geer got things started with a letter to Colonel Victor "Brute" Krulak, staff secretary to the Commandant of the Marine Corps, proposing Reckless be assigned permanent duty at Camp Pendleton in Oceanside, California, just north of San Diego.

Colonel Krulak was happy to intervene on her behalf. Yet even his best efforts failed to prevent bureaucratic stumbling blocks and assorted delays. Despite her valor on the battlefield, which saved untold American lives, some military bureaucrats evidently had a problem with providing a mere horse with "free" transportation—even if she was an acknowledged heroine and decorated noncommissioned officer of the United States Marine Corps.

One such objector was Colonel Raymond Crist of the Marine Division of Public Information. Crist was one of several Marines asked to gauge the likely public reaction should Reckless be rotated to the United States. Crist's hair-splitting written analysis to Colonel Krulak included the following:

> Marines who now have custody of Reckless are actually her legal owners, and they would have to be consulted before any action was taken to bring her to this country. Moreover, government transportation could only be furnished if this horse were owned by the Marine Corps. I realize that we possibly could buy the animal for one dollar, but I cannot see how we could justify the expense of transporting her to the United States for no other purpose than the attendant publicity. Even if we did overcome official objections and bring Reckless to this country, I am

afraid that the publicity might be construed by some as Marine Corps assistance in the promotion of a commercial venture.[3]

In hindsight, it seems unlikely that the public would have regarded the Navy's transporting of Reckless to America as a squandering of taxpayer dollars, or as a shameless publicity stunt, or as a cynical, money-making scheme by the Marines who technically owned her. Yet at that time it was widely believed by those involved that, "the Corps would be laying itself open to censure if some junketing congressman learned of Reckless hitchhiking a free ride with the Navy."[4]

Precious Cargo

When it became clear government transportation was not an option, the disappointed Geer telephoned Ernest Gibson, a family friend who worked for Pacific Transport Lines, a cargo operator. Geer explained the situation to Gibson, who asked, "Is that the Marine horse I read about in the *Post*? The one who carried ammunition?" Assured that she was, Gibson picked up the phone and, within moments, had Stan Coppel, executive vice president of the shipping company, on the line.

"My kids and I loved that story about Reckless and we'd like to help get her home," Coppel told Geer. "I'll tell you what we'll do: we'll bring her home free of charge, if you'll furnish the stall and pay for the feed."[5]

The irony in this flurry of activity was that while the Korean-born-and-bred horse had never set hoof on U.S. soil, she nevertheless was regarded as much an American as any of the Marines with whom she served.

And so at last, this (sort of) naturalized citizen had snagged a ride to her adoptive homeland.

Three Weeks That Shook Her World

The Marines had three weeks to deliver Reckless to Yokohama, Japan, before the SS *Pacific Transport* shoved off for the states on October 22, 1954. Geer devoted himself to arranging Reckless's transportation to Japan and securing other necessities, which included construction of a stall and enough hay and oats for feeding and bedding.

When Major General Pate heard the news, his response was immediate: "I can't tell you how delighted I am that Reckless is soon to be on her way home."[6]

But Major General Robert E. Hogaboom, commander of the 1st Marine Division in Korea, then passed along details of the plan to the Recoilless Rifle Platoon in Korea, which still had custody of Reckless. In a minor surprise, Hogaboom actually left it to those men to decide Reckless's fate. The platoon voted to allow Reckless to be shipped stateside, but only under certain conditions:

First, majority ownership of Reckless would remain with the RR Platoon, not Lieutenant Pedersen, who still owned a piece of her;

Second, Reckless would be kept at Camp Pendleton;

Third, any money she generated from public appearances or promotional events would go to families of deceased platoon members;

Finally, her latest handler, PFC William Moore, would escort Reckless on the trip.

Colonel Geer contacted Lieutenant Pedersen, then on duty at Pendleton, to discuss the horse's disputed ownership. Geer found that Pedersen, "shared the feeling that the present members of the RR Platoon were being high-handed in the matter. As had been pointed out in earlier correspondence, none of the present membership had been in Korea at the time Reckless was purchased."[7]

Pedersen recognized it was not a good time to nit-pick, but to strike while the iron was hot. He promised to do everything he could to ensure Reckless was aboard the *Pacific Transport*. "It doesn't matter who owns her," Pedersen said. "I'll transfer any claim I have to her for a dollar, but let's get her home."[8]

But the bureaucratic snags and cross-currents continued. A mail subsidy contract between the shipping company and the government forbade Reckless's handler, PFC Moore, from traveling free aboard the *Pacific Transport* while accompanying her. Andy Geer would not let that technicality stop Reckless from getting aboard the ship. He personally paid Moore's way. There was still the logistical challenge, however, of getting Reckless from Korea to Japan.

A Whole Lotta "Horse Shift"

On October 12, 1954, General Hogaboom's chief of staff asked the 1st Marine Aircraft Wing if they could fly Reckless from Korea to Yokohama, Japan. Up until then, they had moved jeeps, 105 mm howitzers, and every other conceivable load of war equipment. But horses? In fact, delivering any kind of livestock would be new for them.

Luckily for Reckless, they considered the request a welcome challenge for their training program and for the R4Q aircraft—"the

Flying Boxcar"—which had been the Marines' heavy hauler through-out the Korean War since its introduction in 1950.

Four days later, Hogaboom's top aide heard back from the Marine Aircraft Wing. The response tucked a little wry humor within its arsenal of otherwise dry military jargon and bureaucratic gobble-dygook:

HEADQUARTERS
1st Marine Aircraft Wing, FMF
c/o Fleet Post Office, San Francisco
16 October, 1954

MEMORANDUM
From: Chief of Staff, 1st Marine Aircraft Wing
To: Chief of Staff, 1st Marine Division
Subj: Operation HORSE SHIFT
Ref: (a) CG, 1st MarDiv Memo of 12Oct54
    (b) CG, 1st MAW disp 130745Z Oct54
    (c) MarCorps GO No. 111

1. Your request contained in reference (a) has been approved as indicated by reference (b). Certain personnel, logistical and medical details related to subject operation may have been overlooked by members of your staff and are cited for your action:

a. Reference (a) failed to specify the sex of the passenger. It should be remembered that regulations require that *female passengers in Naval aircraft must be suitably clothed in a trouser type uniform.* Male passengers must be in the uniform of the day (ribbons optional). *All passengers must wear dog tags and must be sober.*

b. In-flight box lunches are not furnished for passengers by this command. Present rations (Army common) do not include food fit for a horse. Recommend advice be obtained from the Army's First Cavalry Division.

c. Although the responsibility for loading has been assumed by your headquarters, certain in-flight unloading problems must be anticipated. Responsibility for solution of these problems must naturally be assumed by you. A **HORSE SHIFT** Liaison Officer (hereafter referred to as *DUNG-HO*) is recommended.

d. Close coordination between the pilot and **DUNG-HO** is required in this matter. Provisions must also be made for inspection by the Neutral Nations Inspection Team on return to Korea.

e. Medical regulations require that passengers returning to CONUS must be dewormed and de-malariaized prior to departure. Compliance is requested in subject case.

f. Passengers riding in the R4Q aircraft are *required to don parachute harnesses prior to flight. This promises to be a difficult task, but the ingenuity of your staff is being counted on to find a solution.*

2. It is noted that paragraph 2 of reference (a) makes mention of precautions to insure safety of the animal in flight. While the sympathies of this command are solidly with

Reckless, it must be remembered that the pilot will also be interested in maintaining the structural integrity of his aircraft. *Therefore a horse adrift will be viewed with disfavor, and in case of unforeseen events he (or she) must be warned to stand clear of the pilots' compartment.*

(Signed)

E. A. MONTGOMERY
Chief of Staff[9]

Operation Horse Shift had begun. It looked like Reckless finally would be joining her friends back in the States. Now, the hard part: saying goodbye.

Halftime Ceremony, Fulltime Heroine

On October 17, 1954, Reckless's rotation ceremony took place during halftime of a football game between the 7th Army Division and the 1st Marine Division. Accompanied by a drum and bugle corps, she was paraded before the troops in a moving ceremony that acknowledged her unique contributions and allowed Reckless a chance to say farewell to the men.

The division adjutant read the farewell citation:

General Hogaboom, officers and men of the 1st Marine
Division, guests and Sergeant Reckless, Pride of the
Marines.

Reckless began her career in the Marine Corps in
October, 1952, when she was purchased in Seoul by the
75 mm Recoilless Rifle Platoon of the Anti-Tank Company, 5th Marines. Her boot camp was different from that
of the ordinary Marine; she was trained to carry seventy-
five Recoilless Rifle ammunition during actual combat.
For outstanding conduct during this period, she was promoted to the rank of corporal.

It was in the battle for the Outpost Vegas that Reckless
proved her merit as a Marine. With enemy artillery and
mortar rounds coming in at the rate of 500 a minute, she
carried 75 mm shells into the front lines. Each yard was a
passage under fire. Reckless made a total of fifty-one trips
to the outpost during the Battle for Vegas to keep the guns
supplied with ammunition.

Disregard for her own safety and conduct under fire
were an inspiration to the troops and in keeping with the
highest traditions of the Naval Service.

Corporal Reckless received her Meritorious Promotion
to sergeant on April 10, 1954. The citation reads in part,
"Corporal Reckless performed the duties of ammunition
carrier from October, 1952, to July 27, 1953, in a superb
manner. Reckless' attention and devotion to duty make
her well qualified for promotion to the rank of sergeant.
Her absolute dependability while on missions under fire
contributed materially to the success of many battles."

Reckless stands proudly beside PFC William Moore at her rotation ceremony.
Camp Pendleton Archives

Rotation to the United States is her due and in a few
days she will be on her way to Camp Pendleton…home
of the 1ˢᵗ Marine Division. Good luck, Sergeant Reckless
and *bon voyage*.[10]

The men standing at attention had to wonder what was going
through Reckless's mind at that moment. How much did she intui-
tively grasp of what was happening? After all, this particular horse
had always seemed supernaturally attuned to the people and circumstances around her. Did she understand the surrounding pomp
reflected more than just respect and affection? That it also meant she
soon would be leaving behind her comrades-in-arms for a long voyage to a new homeland, one she had served with pluck, skill, and
almost unimaginable valor? She probably had at least a vague idea

that she was being honored. She was quick to recognize human appreciation. The Marines dedicated the game to her—and won, 23 to 7.

Reckless's life in her native Korea was over. Soon she would join her friends in the "land of the free and the home of the brave" which also happened to be the "land of plenty," which for Reckless meant plenty of ice cream, candy, cokes, beer, and good times. She was about to embark on a new adventure, but first, she had to get to the embarkation point, an adventure in itself.

PART II

A HERO'S JOURNEY

Californians are proud to join with our United States Marines in welcoming Sergeant Reckless home from Korea.

—California governor Goodwin J. Knight State Proclamation

CHAPTER 10

AMERICA-BOUND

Sergeant Reckless, the fabulous horse of the Marine Corps
with a fantastic war record, is coming home ...
—Newspaper columnist Louella Parsons
Louella Parsons on Hollywood

Almost two years to the day from Reckless's forced conscription, Operation Horse Shift began in earnest. On Friday, October 22, 1954, Reckless undertook the long voyage to her new homeland. While she didn't take kindly to the first leg—the flight from Korea to Japan—she was happy to board the SS *Pacific Transport* V/36E with her "date," PFC William Moore.

The Marines furnished a four-by-ten foot portable stall with a sloping roof seven-and-a-half feet high in the front, slightly shorter in the back, with room enough for oats, hay, and her bed. The stall was placed up on deck to provide plenty of fresh air. The hope was the fresh, salty sea air would help her to avoid another bout of seasickness.

Colonel Geer spread the word quickly to (recently promoted) Lieutenant General Pate, Lieutenant Eric Pedersen, Gunny Sergeant Joe Latham, Sergeant Elmer Lively, and PFC Monroe Coleman that Reckless was on her way. Pedersen and Lively, already stationed at Camp Pendleton, arranged to meet Reckless in San Francisco with a trailer for the nearly five-hundred-mile drive south to her new home.

Joe Latham excitedly called Pedersen from Camp Lejeune, North Carolina, where he was stationed, to say he would do everything possible to be there for her arrival. Monroe Coleman, back in civilian life and living in Utah, said he could drive in for the event.

But the welcome would be much bigger than that. Major General Evans Ames, managing director of the Marines Memorial Club, named Reckless the guest of honor at the Marine Corps 179th Birthday Banquet in San Francisco the evening of November 10, 1954.

There was much to do to get ready for the celebration.

Clearing Customs

First and perhaps most important, Geer had to figure out how to get Reckless into the country. Reckless did not have a passport (most Marines didn't, let alone horse Marines, because it wasn't necessary for military travel). Ernest Gibson, his friend at Pacific Transport, suggested Geer call Clarence Ogden, his contact at the U.S. Customs Service.

Like Gibson and millions of others, Ogden had read the *Post* article and was moved by Reckless's story. He told Geer he could bring her in on the same orders that brought him home from Korea.

All Geer needed to do was list her as special baggage. Or he could simply declare her value as being under $50 and pay a duty of $3.75.[1]

Geer chose the latter option, adding with a smile, "But don't let Reckless or any of her Marine friends know I put that valuation on her."[2]

Ogden also suggested Geer contact the U.S. Agriculture Department. As easy as Customs made things for Geer, Agriculture was just the opposite. For starters, they insisted on an on-board hoof inspection by a bureau veterinarian. The department also required a blood draw to be sent to Washington, D.C., for analysis, testing for two serious horse disorders—the dangerous bacterial disease glanders, and dourine, an often chronic venereal disease found mostly in Asia, Africa, and the Americas.

Reckless was required to remain aboard ship or at the dock until test results cleared her— which typically took a week or more. Geer realized if Reckless couldn't leave the dock, she would miss the banquet where she was guest of honor.

Geer again sprang into action, contacting the Department of Agriculture in Washington to plead his case to Dr. C. L. Gooding, chief of the Animal Inspection Quarantine Branch in the department's Agricultural Research Service. In a telegram, Geer asked if they could take a blood sample in Japan before she left port and airmail it to the lab.

The answer: Request Denied.

Geer was undeterred. After overcoming every other hurdle, he was not about to let paper-pushing bureaucrats prevent Reckless from getting off the docks and taking her place at the big party.

Eventually, Geer won concessions for Reckless to attend the banquet in San Francisco. He also gained permission for Reckless to be transported south to Camp Pendleton, provided tests were negative.

If either test came back positive, she would have to return immediately to Japan—or be destroyed.

Star Treatment

The news media jumped on the story of her impending arrival and attendance at the coming banquet. Among the first to report on Reckless was Bob Considine, a popular radio show host and syndicated newspaperman, who launched a welcome home campaign on the October 24 broadcast of his Sunday night radio show, *On the Line*. The next day, he followed up in his syndicated column, suggesting there would be overwhelming emotions at dockside when Reckless and her Marine friends were reunited: "There are sure to be tears, shared in by Reckless herself."[3]

When wire services got involved, papers around the country excitedly jumped on the story. On October 28, 1954, the Hearst newspapers' syndicated Hollywood gossip columnist Louella Parsons—her once-commanding influence in decline but still potent—reported on a letter she received from Colonel Geer: "Sergeant Reckless, the fabulous horse of the Marine Corps, with a fantastic war record, is coming home." She told readers Reckless would be pastured at Camp Pendleton and that "Andy" was writing a book for Dutton which he hoped to finish in five weeks. She added, "The story of Reckless would certainly make a good motion picture. There was never a braver Marine."[4]

Ed Sullivan had already been a television variety host for six years, but he still wrote the syndicated show business gossip column that had brought him to prominence two decades earlier. Sullivan wrote appreciatively about Reckless in the New York *Daily News*, then sent a telegram inviting the decorated war horse to appear on *Toast of the Town*, his weekly revue series that a year later would be renamed *The Ed Sullivan Show*:

> I have written my Sunday November Seventh column about Reckless as part of my annual observance of the Marine Corps Anniversary. I'd like very much to have Reckless appear on our stage November Seventh as General Devereaux will be in our audience that night. How much would it cost to send her east? In addition to transportation I will earmark an extra one thousand dollars for your fund for Marine families. Wire me.
>
> Sincerely Ed Sullivan[5]

As details were being worked out for her appearance on *Toast of the Town*, Captain Shannon, master of the SS *Pacific Transport*, radioed the ship was caught in a typhoon. He determined the storm would delay their arrival until the evening of November 9, two days after the Sullivan broadcast, so she would not be making her television debut after all.

Feeling Low on the High Seas

For Reckless, the voyage across the Pacific must have brought back memories of the failed amphibious landing. Despite traveling topside for the fresh air, the high seas made her seasick and unable to eat; and she was nearly swept overboard. One of the huge waves washing across the bow knocked Reckless completely down, out of her stall, and almost into the raging ocean. By the time the crew scrambled to reach her, Reckless was sprawled across the deck, her front legs braced against the edge of the ship. The mates managed to steady the thoroughly drenched, frightened horse upright and back into her stall. Bales of hay were stacked around her to prevent any further near-disasters.

San Francisco, Open Your Golden Gate

In California, excitement mounted as preparations were made for the grand arrival. California's interim governor, Goodwin J. Knight, issued a ceremonial proclamation welcoming her to the state. (The proclamation came on the same day Knight won a full term as California's chief executive; he had been appointed to the office a year earlier after Governor Earl Warren resigned to become chief justice of the United States Supreme Court.)

> Executive Department State of California
> November 2, 1954
>
> Californians are proud to join with our United States Marines in welcoming Sergeant Reckless home from Korea.
>
> Fighting with our men of the First Division this great-hearted little mare became the symbol of their spirit. During the bitter days, while carrying ammunition to the Reckless Rifles of the First, she was twice wounded. Yet, despite her bloodied flanks, she continued to plod the Korean hills. Such courage understandably won the respect of the men who know courage best. Therefore, I

am proud California has been chosen as home for this heroic animal.

I know the years ahead will hold affection for her by those who fought beside her. But more important, as time goes on, this little mare with the blaze will mingle with Marines-yet-to-be and, in her inimitable way, instill in them the spirit of *Semper Fidelis;* life's breath to the Eternal Corps.

Goodwin J. Knight   Governor of California[6]

Old Friends Gather and Reminisce

Eric Pedersen and Elmer Lively pulled into San Francisco with a trailer full of alfalfa, grain, and blankets; Kay Pedersen would fly in the following morning to join her husband and finally meet the "other woman" in his life. Monroe Coleman already had arrived from Utah with his bride. Joe Latham tried every trick in the Marine book in increasingly desperate attempts to get there—and failed. Latham was heartbroken, as were many others who knew how close he and Reckless had become.

On the night of November 8, 1954, the eve of her arrival, the wartime comrades and their families gathered at Colonel Geer's home in San Francisco for drinks, to reminisce, and to arrange final touches for the reception. Out at sea, Reckless was inadvertently making extra last-minute work for them.

The Geer cocktail party was cut short by a call from Captain Shannon. The good news: Reckless's appetite was back after her days of seasickness and almost being washed overboard. The bad news: Sergeant Reckless had devoured not only her beautiful parade blanket, but also all her chevrons and ribbons; only a few scraps remained.

Otherwise, she was just fine, thank you very much.

The men couldn't believe it.

Again, Geer took charge. Reckless's ship was set to arrive the following night, with a dockside press conference the next morning at 0900. He knew how important her appearance would be, especially with all those photographers on the dock, cameras poised. Geer and the gang needed a blanket, lettering, sergeant chevrons, and ribbons for her. And they needed them fast.

Before Pedersen could pick up Kay at the airport, Geer assigned him to swing by Olsen Nolte, a landmark saddlery in San Francisco, for a new, replacement blanket.

Coleman's orders: find someone to sew on the lettering.

Lively would track down a pair of sergeant's chevrons. And Geer would handle the ribbons.[7]

November 9, 1954—the Frantic Rush to Get Things Right

Creed Haberlin of Olsen Nolte Saddle Shop produced a blanket correct in both color and size and donated a fine leather halter, hoof pick, currycomb, and brush. When Pedersen took out his wallet, Haberlin refused to take the lieutenant's money. "It's a present," he told the former platoon leader. "If I went home tonight and told my kids I'd charged you for anything for Reckless, they'd chase me out of the house."[8]

Something similar happened at Emerson Manufacturing Company, where the manager, Arthur McLorg, stopped cold all routine production of flags and banners and immediately put all hands to work on cutting and blocking the letters for Reckless's blanket. It read: "Sgt. Reckless: 1st MAR. DIV."

B. Pasquale & Company, the historic military outfitters founded in San Francisco in 1854, created two bars of ribbons in record time—each measuring eighteen inches long by an inch-and-a-half wide.

With all the elements—blanket, lettering, ribbons, and chevrons—collected, Kay Pedersen managed to finish sewing the chevrons and ribbons onto the blanket just as the call came in that the ship was about to dock.

The twelve-day voyage home was over. Reckless had arrived.

That night, Pedersen, Coleman, and Lively met Reckless aboard the ship. Eighteen months had passed since Reckless and Eric Pedersen had said their goodbyes half a world away. But when she spotted him, on the hatch and at night, and he returned the gaze, it was evident neither time nor distance had loosened their special bond.

Reckless strained against the stall cross bar, trying to reach out to him as Pedersen, along with Coleman and Lively, excitedly welcomed her. When the trio reached her, the little war horse buried her face in Pedersen's hands. She was safe. She had to spend one last night on board, but maybe on some level she understood she had arrived at a new home with her old friends.

November 10, 1954—Off to Meet Her Public

At dawn, Reckless's friends were back aboard, readying her for the media. With a thorough brushing and rubdown, her coat gleamed. Reckless's hooves were cleaned and polished, and that trademark blaze and three white stockings brightened by a refreshing shampoo. Naturally, Reckless loved the attention, and when they were done, she looked absolutely beautiful.

Lieutenant Arthur Newell, a veterinarian with the 6th Army stationed at the Presidio, arrived early with the bottles and needles necessary for her blood tests. But he had to wait for Inspector Eddy of the Department of Agriculture before he could go to work.

When Eddy and a second inspector showed up, Newell expressed concern that Reckless could hurt herself if she reared when he stuck her with the needle. "Go ahead," Pedersen deadpanned, "she won't even nod."[9]

So Newell took off his barracks cap, placed it on a fender, and gave Reckless several sharp taps on the neck to numb it. Reckless didn't flinch; she was too busy finishing off a carrot.

He inserted the needle, and blood filled the vial. Reckless noticed the barracks cap, reached over, and snatched it between her teeth. But thanks to Lively's quick hands, it was only slightly mangled.

Ready for My Close-Up, Mr. DeMille

The time had come for Reckless to meet the press. The ship was so jammed with reporters and photographers that one veteran newsman observed wryly, "She has more cameras and reporters to meet her than Vice President Nixon had a week ago when he came to town."[10]

The *San Francisco Examiner* reported, "Not since the days when troopships were coming back from the Korean War had the waterfront seen such a welcome as that given the fighting veteran at Pier 7 yesterday."[11]

Reckless was in her glory. For more than an hour, she "posed with various Marines, she ate carrots, she walked into and out of her stall a dozen times while flash bulbs popped and cameramen shouted for different poses.

Reckless's very first press conference. Leatherneck *Magazine*

Left: Pedersen secures Reckless into her stall for the trip ashore. *Command Museum, Marine Corps Recruit Depot, San Diego*

Right: Reckless and Pedersen are lowered down to the San Francisco dock. *Camp Pendleton Archives*

Pedersen leads Reckless out onto American soil. *Command Museum, Marine Corps Recruit Depot, San Diego*

"Then she became bored and let Pedersen know it."[12]

It was time to go.

The lieutenant led Reckless into an unloading stall, and the two were winched over the ship's side and lowered to the dock.

Pedersen opened the stall gate and led her onto American soil— and into a whole new life. Sergeant Reckless had arrived in a style and fanfare befitting a great heroine.

Newspaper headlines across the country reflected the triumphant atmosphere at the docks that day. "Heroine's Welcome Given as Mare Marine Arrives" trumpeted Southern California's *Long Beach Press Telegram.*

In Massachusetts, the *Springfield Union* proclaimed, "Horse Marine Has Landed: Sgt Reckless, Little Sorrel Mare, Reaches West Coast; Real Heroine of Korean War."

The local *Oakland Tribune* seemed to get the story slightly backward: "Heroic 'Sgt Reckless' is Greeted in Korean Return."

Splashed across the nationwide newspaper coverage were pictures of Reckless being petted by a "beaming" Andy Geer, Eric Pedersen, Monroe Coleman, and Elmer Lively.

Pedersen was widely quoted on how he came to acquire her and about the last-minute scramble to replace the blanket and ribbons she'd munched on during the ocean voyage. The governor's welcoming proclamation was read for the press, followed by an electric morning of interviews, photos, and celebration.

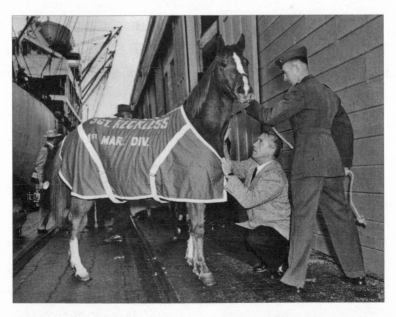

Pedersen and Geer dress Reckless in her replacement blanket. *Nancy Latham Parkin*

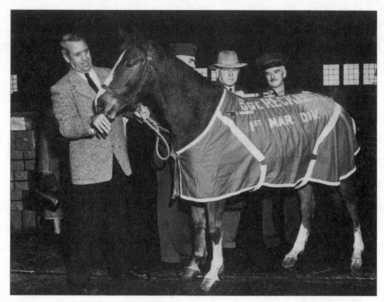

On dock, Maj. Gen. Evans O. Ames presents Reckless with a new set of ribbons. *Nancy Latham Parkin*

In a bit of serendipity, Reckless touched "hoof" in the United States the same day President Dwight Eisenhower was dedicating the Iwo Jima Memorial—for which Reckless helped raise donations—in Washington, D.C. The *San Diego Union* ran a photo from the ceremony of Vice President Richard Nixon standing with the mothers of two of the Marines who had lost their lives after hoisting the flag on Iwo Jima. It appeared right next to the coverage of Sergeant Reckless's arrival.

An Immaculate Reception

From the docks, Reckless and her entourage headed straight to an afternoon reception in her honor at the Marines' Memorial Club arranged by Major General Evans O. Ames.

The Marines' Memorial Club and Hotel, a landmark in San Francisco's Union Square since 1946, was created as the nation's first "Living Memorial." The entire building pays tribute to "those who have gone before; and to provide a service to those who carry on." Each floor has a different theme, and walls are adorned with historical and heart-tugging memorabilia, "to honor the memory and commemorate the valor of the members of our armed forces who were killed, lost or died in military service for their country."[13]

The November 1954 Anniversary Issue of *Crossroads of the Corps*, the Marines' Memorial Association magazine, devoted its cover to Technical Sergeant Joe Latham and Reckless, "the winsome equine lass that had her coming out party on the rugged terrain of Korea and who makes her formal stateside debut at the Marines' Club." The feature story previewed how Reckless "will make an unprecedented appearance as the honored guest...and be given due recognition"[14] at her stateside "coming out" party—the annual Marine Corps Birthday Dinner and Dance, celebrating both the Corps' 179th anniversary and the eighth birthday of the Marines' Club. Reservations for the event reportedly were "in extremely heavy demand," as it promised to include a memorable salute to America's most unlikely war heroine.

The press went wild when Reckless, clip-clopping onto the club's historic theater stage, was greeted by at least fifty cheering Marines. (It is not clear whether Reckless took the freight elevator to the second floor or waltzed through the lobby and up the stairs to the auditorium.) When calm returned, she was toasted again and again—with Coca-Cola.

Poor Reckless. She was a decorated war heroine and belle of the ball, yet she had to consider her pristine public image. So when a photographer suggested that, in print, the caramel-colored soft drink could be mistaken for alcohol, Reckless obliged and also drank a glass of milk.

When the reception was over, the stage lights were dimmed and Reckless had time to rest, since there was still a big night ahead. So as she had done often in her friends' tents, Reckless quietly lay down and went to sleep.

You *Can* Have Your Cake and Eat It Too

After the brief respite, it was time to get the party started. Some skeptics in the crowd doubted a horse would ever willingly board an elevator. But they didn't know Reckless, who strode into the freight elevator, adjusted her stance to fit more comfortably, then rode confidently to the tenth floor's banquet dinner in the main dining room.

Who needs cake when there are carnations? Reckless eats the centerpieces.
USMC History Division, Quantico, VA

Escorted off the elevator by Pedersen and Lively, the little mare strode into the banquet hall of four hundred Marines and their dates to thunderous applause as, "flash bulbs popped like mortar shells along the Main Line of Resistance."[15] Keynote speaker Andy Geer regaled his audience with "the story of Reckless' transition from a racing pony to a traditional Marine Corps hero."[16]

While being introduced to the crowd, Reckless "spied a two-foot-high anniversary cake and before Pedersen or Lively could restrain her, she was up to her nostrils in it. She sighed gustily. This was the best food she had since the peanut butter sandwiches in Korea. When the cake was gone, Mrs. Veda Ames, wife of Major General Evans O. Ames, USMC, leaned far over the table and served Reckless ice cream from her hand."[17]

But for the famished filly, these were mere appetizers. During the speeches, Reckless started in on the rose and carnation centerpieces. By the time the last speaker was finished, so were the flowers.

When the General Deferred to the Sergeant

Around 10:00 p.m., Reckless made her second appearance of the evening. Again she ambled onto the elevator and was whisked to the eleventh floor's Crystal Ballroom for the birthday dance and official cake-cutting ceremony. (Someone had had the foresight to order more than one cake.)

The traditional cake-cutting ceremony symbolizes the annual renewal by every Marine of commitment to the Corps and its pledge to seek peace and freedom worldwide. The Mameluke sword used in the ceremony, according to the Corps' official website, "gets its name from the cross hilt and ivory grip design, similar to swords used for centuries by Ottoman warriors." The Marine Corps' ceremonial use of the Mameluke sword can be traced back to 1805

Kay Pedersen feeds Reckless the first piece of birthday cake as guest of honor. *Top: Camp Pendleton Archives; Bottom: Corbis*

and Marine Lieutenant Presley O'Bannon's leadership in success-fully retaking Derna, Tripoli. Marine lore claims Tripoli prince Hamet Karamanli showed his gratitude by presenting his own Mameluke sword to O'Bannon.[18] The historic battle is celebrated in "The Marines' Hymn" with the line "to the shores of Tripoli."

A version of the Mameluke sword remains part of the Marine dress uniform.

Traditionally, the first slice of cake is presented to the guest of honor; the second goes to the oldest Marine in the room, signifying "the honor and respect accorded to experience and seniority."[19] This Marine then passes that second slice to the youngest Marine present, a gesture representing the hand-off of Corps' history and traditions from one generation to the next.

Major General Henry D. Linscott did the honors of cutting the first piece. But it was Reckless who received the symbolic slice, heartily slurping it up from the outstretched hand of Kay Pedersen.

The moment was captured for posterity in the December 1954 *Crossroads of the Corps* beneath the headline, "'Reckless' Hit of Birthday Celebration."[20]

November 11, 1954—Last Hurrahs

The next day, Reckless took her victory tour to the San Francisco Cow Palace. "She put on one of her greatest performances...the rocking horse strut, the whirling run, the charge at Pedersen as though to run him down, the stiff-legged bucking action."[21]

Later that day, Colonel Geer took her to the exclusive, men-only Bohemian Club, where the sergeant had the distinction of being the first female ever to enter the Cartoon Room. "That sort of thing wasn't done," noted Geer's nephew, James Taggart, "but Andy Geer was such a rollicking huge guy, he could do whatever he wanted."[22]

Mingling freely through the crowded room of all-male members, Reckless shared drinks and hammed it up for photographers. When the bartender presented Reckless her first drink, Kay Pedersen noted the barkeep's wry observation: "That's the first time I've ever served a drink to a four-legged lady."[23]

It was her last hurrah—the moment had come for final goodbyes to friends, old and new. Pedersen loaded her into the trailer and, with Lively in the passenger seat, started the long drive to Camp Pendleton.

It was time to go home.

Reckless enters the Bohemian Club's Cartoon Room in style. *James Taggert*

PART III

LIFE AT CAMP PENDLETON

*We had Reckless make her mark in the guest book—and if it hadn't
been for Lieutenant Pedersen, she would have eaten the pen.*
—Major General John T. Selden, USMC
Commanding General, Camp Pendleton

CHAPTER 11

HOME, SWEET HOME

*It is suggested her "court" be in the vicinity of
the commanding general's quarters and properly marked
with appropriate signs, so that all will know this is to be
the home of Sergeant Reckless, Pride of the Marines.*
—**Andrew Geer**

After her San Francisco triumphs, fanfare followed Reckless all the way to Camp Pendleton, five hundred miles south. On arrival, Reckless was greeted by no less than the base boss, Major General John T. Selden, who wrote:

I was at the main entrance to meet Sergeant Reckless. She is every bit as beautiful and well trained as I had been told. Although she joined the Division after I had turned over command to Al Pollock, I have heard from many Marines about her valiant service in Korea. It was with pride I welcomed her to Camp Pendleton.

After she met the guard, we drove to the Ranch House where she met Mrs. Selden. It was a case of love at first sight for both. We had Reckless make her mark in the guest book—and if it hadn't been for Lieutenant Pedersen, she would have eaten the pen.

As for her future, I can assure that there are 25,000 Marines on this base who are determined she will want for nothing—ever. When the 1st Marine Division returns from Korea, that number will be doubled. Need I say more?[1]

Top left: Reckless arrives at her new home, Camp Pendleton. *Command Museum, Marine Corps Recruit Depot, San Diego*

Top right: "Marine sentries pay honor to the heroic Sgt. Reckless, held by owner 1stLt Eric T Pedersen, as she returns to her home base, Camp Pendleton." *Original photo caption. USMC History Division, Quantico, VA*

Left: Maj. Gen. John T. Selden greets Lt. Eric Pedersen and Reckless. *Command Museum, Marine Corps Recruit Depot, San Diego*

"Sgt Reckless signs guest log on her visit to the historic Ranch House, quarters of Base Commanding General, MajGen John T Selden, accompanied by her owner, 1st Lt Eric T Pedersen." *Original photo caption. USMC History Division, Quantico, VA*

Hangin' with the Pedersens

While the Marine Corps waited for the results of the USDA blood tests performed on Reckless, she was "quarantined" at Pedersen's five-acre ranch in Vista, California, a short drive from the base. The Pedersen children had apparently never heard about the no-riding-Reckless rule, because while she was there, according to Pedersen's son Eric Jr., the children rode her as they did the other horses on their ranch.

Reckless was with the Pedersens for just over a year before she was officially sold to the 1st Marine Division, then transferred to the base stables. The family loved her as one of their own—so parting with their heroic houseguest was not easy.

How to Handle a Heroine

Reckless was never just another horse put out to pasture when she took up permanent residence at Pendleton. In a letter to Lieutenant

General Pate on November 19, 1954, Colonel Geer emphatically declared that because Reckless was no ordinary horse, she deserved special care and consideration at the base:

"She should have a large and luxurious box stall constructed for living quarters. Her pasture should be commodious and watered to provide the best grass. It is suggested her 'court' be in the vicinity of the commanding general's quarters and properly marked with appropriate sign [sic], so that all will know this is to be the home of Sergeant Reckless, Pride of the Marines.

"Never should she be ridden by oversized, leaden-seated, heavy-handed cowboy types, nor should she ever be considered one of the post stable horses."[2]

The colonel also noted Reckless's weakened left hip, the result of being hit by a jeep in Korea, adding that "overwork will bring on lameness." Geer, who sounded like an overanxious father delivering his teenaged daughter for her freshman year of college, wasn't finished:

"She should never be ridden by anyone weighing in excess of 130 pounds, and then only enough for exercise and light training. Every six months, she should have a thorough physical examination. She likes children and is gentle in their presence. Because of her having been savaged by wild Korean dogs, she is committed to the destruction of the canine race and dogs should be kept clear."[3]

(In time, the orders were changed to a directive—that nothing was to be put on her back heavier than her blanket.)

Instructions for grooming and hoof care also were specific, including a caution about selecting the right blacksmith:

"Her shoes should be removed and she should be allowed to go barefoot for a period of six weeks. At that time, her feet should be trimmed and new shoes fitted. Only the most knowing and patient horseshoer should be employed. Sergeant Reckless is extremely proud of her feet and will not stand for inexpert attention. Several Korean horseshoers will painfully attest to this statement. She should be groomed each day and her mane and tail, which have become ragged by inexpert clipping and, perhaps, dietary deficiency, should be encouraged by daily brushing. The headquarters duty officer should be directed to inspect her and her quarters in each twenty-four hour period."[4]

And Geer made clear Reckless had earned the right to expect her own preferred delicacies.

"Reckless came to know and like certain liquids other than water. She is fond of Coca-Cola and milk, even the powdered variety. Under the stress of battle she has been known to drink beer. However, all liquids should be served in a common variety water glass. When drinking from [a] bottle, she has been known to bite off the top and this could prove injurious.

"Cola in limited amounts (no more than two or three glasses a week) could be provided. Of milk she should have all she and the budget will stand. As a change from her usual ration of grain and alfalfa, she can be served an occasional plate of scrambled eggs, lightly salted and without pepper. She also relishes carrots, apples, sugar and kimchi, although it is unlikely this latter food will be found in Southern California....

"Reckless will not take salt from a lick. It must be placed in her grain or on her eggs and never too much at one time."[5]

Reckless was quite the celebrity when she finally settled in at the Marine base. In fact, her fame had been building since her grand arrival in San Francisco a year earlier. Reckless might have captured an even bigger slice of the public's imagination. But she never did make it onto Ed Sullivan's variety show, even though he pursued her tenaciously in 1954 and the next year for his Marine Corps anniversary shows.

In a letter to Marine Corps Commandant Lemuel C. Shepherd Jr., Geer laid out suggestions for handling Reckless's celebrity.

To begin, Geer reported, there was no shortage of offers attempting to capitalize on Reckless's good name. Among them: a "Wild West show," which wanted to feature her; some television producers envisioned building a series around her; and "a stock-feed company asked for an endorsement."

(Evidently when offered a taste of the feed, Reckless nibbled at it for a moment, then turned away. As Sergeant Lively put it, "She'll never go for that kind of chow unless they mix a lot of cake or peanut butter with it."[6])

Colonel Geer then laid out strict requirements for Reckless's personal appearances. Never should she appear on a program that was not dignified, nor one that might appear to compromise her integrity as a war heroine. Endorsing alcoholic beverages was out of the question, although she could back other products (feed, milk, etc.), assuming she actually liked the product and that it had a good reputation.

Reckless would appear without charge to certain charities, such as Navy Relief, the March of Dimes, and the American-Korean Foundation.

Geer was especially concerned about movie and TV offers. "One Hollywood producer," he explained, "was ecstatic over the idea of having Reckless do a talking-mule type of routine, à la Francis. Such antics may be all right for the Army, but there is as much difference between Sergeant Reckless and Francis as there is between a horse and a mule. After all, one is a Hollywood clown and the other a gallant Marine who won honors in one of the bloodiest battles fought by American troops."[7]

A television producer also had approached Geer, hoping to star Reckless in a twenty-six-episode series in which the producer's company stood to make a considerable profit.

When Geer asked how much the producer would donate to the Marine Fund, he was told, "Nothing." Geer curtly informed the producer, "This was the exact amount of footage he would be allowed to shoot."[8]

Because Reckless was such a hot commodity, Geer proposed a $1,000 fee for personal appearances or product endorsements, in part to weed out hucksters and others whose offers were less than serious.

In a letter to General Pate, Geer mentioned that his new book about Reckless would bring television and movie offers and that he saw no reason why she should not play herself in any production.

"Life in Hollywood, over an extended period," Geer summed up, "is not recommended, but it is possible she would find a few weeks interesting and profitable."[9]

Regulations over her public appearances were drawn up and approved by General Pate. They included Geer's suggestion that if Reckless assisted recognized charities like the Red Cross or Navy Relief, or any effort to benefit the Korean people, she would do it free of charge. Appearances for commercial ventures would be

"Sergeant Reckless of Korean fame, stands at attention for the inspection of the public, during the Carlsbad, California Spring Holiday celebration. Handling Reckless is Private Walter R. Wilson, of Peoria, Illinois who is going thro[u]gh training…His parents are Mr. and Mrs. W. R. Wilson of RR #1 of Bellflower, Illinois." *Original photo caption. USMC History Division, Quantico, VA*

carefully screened and any monies earned would go to the 1st Marine Division Association Fund, "devoted to the care and education of children of Marines killed in Korea."[10]

Star of Parades

In May 1955, Reckless was featured in two local parades. On May 7, there was a large Spring Holiday Parade in Carlsbad, California, and two weeks later an Armed Services Parade in nearby Vista. Thousands turned out at each event to catch a glimpse of their heroine, Sergeant Reckless.

October 1955—a Big Month for the Little Lady

In early October 1955, Andy Geer's book, *Reckless: Pride of the Marines*, was published by E. P. Dutton & Company. *New York Times* book critic David Dempsey was "disappointed" that Geer abandoned Kim Huk Moon halfway through the story—after Kim sold Reckless to the Marines. Especially since Geer had "skillfully constructed a moving story of Korean life." Overall, however, Dempsey praised the book, acknowledging Reckless as the "great morale builder she was, with her ample girth and gregarious manners" and noting that in retirement at the Marine base, "far from fading away, she is just coming into her glory. Camp Pendleton is not far from Hollywood."[11]

On October 23, 1955, the Associated Press named Geer their "Author of the Week." Many reviewers echoed the sentiments of a critic with the *Pasadena Independent*, who called the book "a touching and inspiring story" that would "likely move adults as well as children."[12] Geer donated all of his book royalties to the First Marine Division Association Scholarship Fund.[13]

The Duke Takes Notice

In late October 1955, a second feature article in the *Saturday Evening Post* revealed interest from a Hollywood legend in Reckless's story. According to the *Post*, John Wayne and his Batjac Productions were in talks with Geer and work was underway on a screenplay for a semi-documentary picture called *The Outpost*.

It would focus on the titanic outpost battles in Korea and feature Reckless playing herself during the dramatic climax of the Marine counterattack on Outpost Vegas. "She'll probably steal every scene she's in," Wayne was quoted as saying.[14] The film, however, was never produced.

The final paragraph of the *Post* story promoted Geer's book, cheerfully predicting great things for the book's subject, the newly retired Marine sergeant Reckless: "Never again will she be asked to carry 75 mm ammunition into the caldron of enemy fire unless it is in a Hollywood battle scene, where, of course, she will have star billing and salary."[15]

Art Linkletter's in the House

On October 25, 1955, Reckless and now-Captain Eric Pedersen appeared on CBS television's *Art Linkletter's House Party* to boost interest in the story that appeared in the October 22 issue of *The Saturday Evening Post*, according to a letter from John Thackaberry, supervisor of west coast publicity for Curtis Circulation Company, the magazine's publisher.

Sadly it appears this episode has not survived.

Emancipation Proclamation Doesn't Apply

On November 23, 1955, the long-discussed sale of the Marines' most decorated four-legged ammunitions transport expert was finalized.

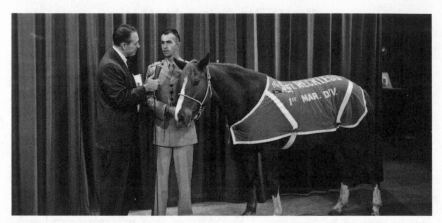

Reckless didn't have a bit of stage fright when she appeared on the Art Linkletter show in season four, episode thirty-seven. *Command Museum, Marine Corps Recruit Depot, San Diego*

Reckless officially became the property of the First Marine Division Association when Captain Eric Pedersen accepted one dollar for her.

"As the property of the Association ... the blaze-faced mare will make public appearances for which the Association will receive donations for its scholarship fund. The fund provides for children of deceased Division Marines."[16]

While now the Association's property, it was actually the 5th Marines who cared for her—and their commander quickly laid down some Reckless rules:

"Other than participation in an event which would not 'reflect unquestioned credit on the Marine Corps,'" declared Colonel James S. Blais, "the principal taboo is permitting a dog to approach the combat veteran ... the little mare is understandably dedicated to the elimination of all canines, the sooner the better."[17]

At the time, there were rumors of an "'heir of expectancy' surrounding the Korean-born mare."[18] The talk was that Reckless was with foal, and per the bill of sale, the first foal was to be the property of Captain Eric Pedersen. The rumors, however, were unfounded; Reckless was not pregnant.

"HORSE TRADERS—Col James S Blais (center), 5th Regiment commander, hands Capt E. T. Pedersen a $1 check as a token sale price for Sgt Reckless. Capt Pedersen bought the mare in Korea, later used her to transport artillery shells over bitterly-contested terrain. Reckless is now the property of the 1st Marine Division Association. At left is Col J. T. Wilbur, holding a painting donated by a Reckless fan for presentation to Col Blais." *Original photo caption. USMC History Division, Quantico, VA*

After the transfer, Reckless made one last trip from the Pedersen Ranch to stables at Santa Margarita, home of the 5th Marines at Camp Pendleton. These stables were just to the west of the Santa Margarita Ranch House (now on the National Register of Historical Sites) between the house and Basilone Road where the base commander and his wife lived. A few years later she was moved to the base stables, where she lived out her days and is now buried.

How to Handle a Hero

PFC Art Sickler from Dickinson, North Dakota, was her handler from the fall of 1956 to 1958.

"I drove jeep for Colonel Schmuck," Sickler recalled, "and that's where my story leads to about how I got the job taking care of Reckless."

Sickler remembered being called into the colonel's office. "I was shaking in my boots because he was a tough guy. I thought he was going to chew me out for a fence I just put up. And instead, he wanted to know what I knew about horses." Relieved, Sickler told him he had been around horses his whole life—that he had been plopped atop a horse before he could walk and had trained many horses on the family farm.

The colonel was convinced he had the right guy. "I got a job for you, Sickler," Colonel Schmuck told him. "I got this special horse that we brought back from Korea and you're totally responsible for her."

"I didn't know anything about Reckless at that time," Sickler recalled, "but the next day I went out to the stables to see the horse I was supposed to take care of. And I see a very fatigued horse; she was very sad looking, she was tired looking. She was combat fatigued.... So I got a veterinarian to check her over, because Colonel Schmuck made it very clear to me that, 'You better do what you think you've got to do for that horse,' and added, 'If you need a vet, we'll furnish you a vet.'"

So Sickler got a vet to look her over. "We checked her teeth and got her teeth filed down, because horses develop such points on their teeth....

"So I had her teeth done, and I know she hadn't been dewormed—and that probably was the biggest problem, or one of the problems, for looking the way she did because horses need to be dewormed at the minimum two times a year and I know she needed it.

"As I started working with her, we became really attached to each other. She was looking for a friend. And, you know, I had that horse looking happy within a month; you couldn't recognize that horse—her coat started shining and she was just a whole different 'horsenality'—after about a month."

Colonel Schmuck kept close tabs on Reckless, for whom he was genuinely worried. "I don't know what his connection was with

Reckless in Korea," Sickler said, "but he was really concerned about the horse and her condition—and we fixed that up. He couldn't believe that within a month, five weeks, how we changed her. Her coat was shiny, her feet were good; I just trimmed her up and so she looked very healthy."

As they started using Reckless as a mascot, orders were issued that she was never to pack more than forty pounds at any one time. "I took that responsibility really seriously," Sickler said, "she drew so much attention."

But what Sickler really noticed was how Reckless began to more than trust him—she began to rely on the PFC for her safety. "Some of the troops there would tease her a little and right away, she'd be looking for me for protection. And she didn't like to be harassed, and you'd get these guys kind of pestering her and she'd pin her ears and show her teeth a little bit and look around to see where I was. And when I'd go out there she'd just quiet down right away.

"And I did things like, I'd go up to her and tap her on the leg and say, 'Down Reckless,' and she would just lay down flat. And then I'd say 'Quiet!' … and I only did that once or twice, just to show them. But when I said, 'Quiet Reckless,' her eyes would just show fear.…

"It was just so sad, that combat fatigue she had in her. And so I never did that again."

Sickler also arranged special sleeping arrangements. "I made this bed for her with these leaves and pine needles and she knew what I was doing and she'd be watching me make this. And then I'd say, 'Okay Reckless…down.' And she'd come in and paw it a little bit and then she'd lay down and then she'd just go, 'Ahhhh,' and just gave a sigh of relief."

Reckless seemed to suffer nightmares, given that she'd kick and grunt in her sleep. "I felt so bad for her…but she just enjoyed sleeping in that tent. And I would sleep behind her and we were really attached."

Sickler also made sure to get just the right feed and grooming products for her. "To get her back into condition, what I did was, I got some special feed for her and I got a molasses mix, which really shines up your hair.... Just looking at the horse I could tell her condition and what she probably needed to get back in condition. And she loved it."

The private first class made sure Reckless's coat shined and soon had her looking like a spit-and-polished Marine. "I'd brush her and I'd spray her with a spray I still use today called Laser Sheen, and it gives that coat such a shine and it feels like silk after she has a couple of layers on. And she would just shine with that. She *sparkled*. And she looked very healthy after about two months and her whole 'horsenality' changed because that horse went through a lot and *no one understood* how much she went through. I think it was taken for granted that this was normal for a horse.

"But this was so not normal. And she was under a lot of stress. And I get the feeling that she tried to please so much. They'd put her [under] such stress. She showed the stress when I got her. It was bad and sad." But Sickler knew his job was to get her looking and feeling better—and he happily did everything possible to help this exceptional Marine.

"I had a special relationship with her. I loved the horse because she adapted to me. She needed a friend—desperately needed a friend when she came here—and I could sense that. And even having a friend made her look better. She was looking forward to seeing me after a week of taking care of her. And all you had to do was to go up and scratch her behind the ear—that was where her wound was—and maybe it comforted her a little bit. She looked forward to just being talked to a little bit."

Reckless even sensed when Sickler was coming to visit. "If I hadn't seen her for a couple of days she would whinny—horses can set patterns and they can tell how you drive up, where you park your vehicle and they could figure out who it is. So she would whinny when I drove up.... She got the routine and looked very forward to seeing me and I'd give her a little treat every night—and maybe that's why she looked forward to seeing me."

Sickler went back to school to learn natural horsemanship, using the Pat Parelli method, which focuses on recognizing and classifying horse behavior. "There's right-brain horses, extroverts and introverts in that class. And there's left-brain extroverts and introverts. A right-brain horse is a flighty horse, extrovert, and [is] kind of nervous. And if he hurts you, it's unintentionally. Reckless was a left-brain introvert. She was very smart, but she was smart enough to know what she could do and [what] not to do....

"A left-brain is probably much easier to train than a right-brain. But then, you get the introverts and extroverts within each classification."

Sickler prepared Reckless for the various ceremonies she attended. "I was told what the ceremony was about and to have her there at a certain time. So I went down the night before to the stable and got my Laser Sheen on her, my special spray, and got her all shined up and her mane and tail fluffed out. And I'd get her there.

"My favorite memory of her, if I had to pick out one, is when some of these guys would start pestering her and she'd look for me to protect her. And if I wasn't around close, then she would pin her ears and they thought that was funny. I didn't think it was very funny. So I guess my one memory would be, and I could see it today, is how she would look for me at these times—just like a little kid looking for its mom.

"So she was such a good horse that way. She needed comforting and I could see her in battle, the way she would stand up to pressure. She wanted to please so bad. She did all this to please you....

"It was her job, but she wanted to *please* these troops. And that's the way a left-brain horse operates. And she was more left-brain than any horse I ever had. But she did all this stuff in combat because she wanted to please. And I hope they at least gave her a little pet or something when she made these trips up and down the mountain. That's all she was looking for was just a little comforting...and she'd give her all for that. She's just a good-hearted leatherneck troop, that's what she was...that wanted to please.

"I felt very sad when I said goodbye to Reckless. I know there were a few tears. I walked up to her, put my arm around her neck and said 'Goodbye Reckless, I'm leaving,' and the tears started to come and I walked away.

"I was so attached to her and she watched me walk away...and it chokes me up today.... I guess I felt that way because I felt, 'Who's going to protect her here now?' You know? 'Are these guys going to pester her?'

"And Reckless knew I was leaving. She knew I was leaving because she watched me sadly as I walked away and said goodbye. And if I told someone who didn't love horses this, they'd think I'm a crackpot thinking that a horse knew this. But they *do!*"[19]

Old Friends Reconnect

Reckless in retirement was a magnet for old friends from the war who came to visit her at Pendleton. Bill Riley, who relieved Pedersen during the battle for Outpost Vegas, was stationed about forty miles away, in El Toro, California. More than a half-century later, he gleefully recalled trips to Pendleton to visit her. "We'd take the kids down there, and I'd go down to see Reckless.... It was funny because they would have some platoon leader lead her in all the parades and he would get all excited [angry] when he would have to clean up after her," Riley said with a mischievous grin. "I remember taking a lot of guff when there was a parade—they always seemed to want to blame me for having to clean up after the horse."[20]

Riley's children grew up hearing tales of Reckless, as did most children of the Marines who served with her. "I told my kids all about her—what she did in the war, what a hero she was," Riley said.[21] His daughter, Mary Alice, even wrote a school book report about Reckless.

As Marines returning from Korea reported to Camp Pendleton, many joyfully reconnected with Reckless. "We had just gotten off the ship that brought us from Korea and we were headed to the new barracks," PFC John Newsom recalled. "We were in a 6/6 truck as we headed down the main road coming from the main gate at Pendleton. Suddenly, somebody yelled, 'Hey look, there's Reckless!' Sure enough, there she was in the pasture in front of the general's house, just off the main road. It was sure good to see the ol' gal again, and it's an image that has stayed with me ever since."[22]

The "Mare-ternity Ward," or Foaling Around

For weeks in the early spring of 1957, a large sign placed on a hill overlooking Camp Pendleton tantalized Marines with a simple phrase: "It's a..." On April 5, the mystery ended when someone at the base completed the sentence with a simple word: boy.

Reckless had foaled her first colt, Fearless, much to the delight of the Marines and her admirers across America.

It was the kind of feel-good story the news media gobbled up—and when reporters swarmed Pendleton, they found five more words added to the makeshift birth announcement: "Mother and Son Doing Fine." The hand-painted declaration was so prominent on the hill that drivers on the nearby Pacific Coast Highway could see it.

Newsreels carried footage of the sign that announced the birth of Fearless. *USMC History Division, Quantico, VA*

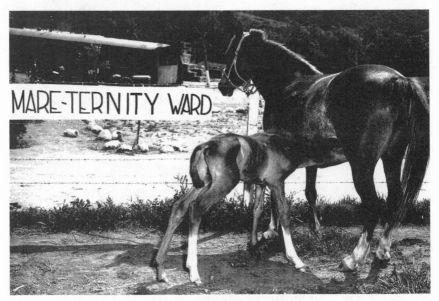

Reckless and Fearless in the "Mare-ternity Ward." Fearless was immediately enlisted in the Marine Corps. *USMC History Division, Quantico, VA*

Reckless Promoted to Staff Sergeant (E5)

On June 15, 1957, just a few months after she became a mother, Sergeant Reckless became Staff Sergeant Reckless. Her second promotion, by the 5th Marines, was acknowledgment "for attention to duty, devotion and loyalty to the Marine Corps."[23]

As before, Randolph Pate, now a full general and Commandant of the Marine Corps, was behind the order. He felt Reckless's devotion and loyalty to the Corps made her "particularly worthy of reward."[24] The honor was made doubly meaningful because it came from the Corps' highest echelon; since approving Reckless's first promotion in Korea, Pate himself had risen to his branch's top job,

"DEVOTION AND LOYALTY—For 'attention to duty, devotion and loyalty to the Marine Corps,' Sgt Reckless was promoted to staff sergeant June 12 by Col Richard Rothwell, CO 5th Marines. The CMC ordered the promotion for Reckless, a Korean racing filly pressed into serviced as an ammunition carrier during the bitter fighting for Outpost Vegas late in the Korean War. During the Camp Pendleton promotion ceremony, Reckless' two-month-old colt, Pvt Fearless, was elevated to private first class." Original photo caption, the Pendleton Scout, June 20, 1957, p.5. *Photo courtesy USMC History Division, Quantico, VA, and National Archives*

twenty-first Commandant of the U.S. Marine Corps. The Corps' magnanimity extended to Fearless, who was upgraded to private first class at the same ceremony.

Pate left the formalities to the commanding officer of the 5th Marines, Colonel Richard Rothwell. "We gave her a regimental parade and she was presented her promotion at the parade," Rothwell recalled. "I stood up and had to read the proclamation of her promotion, as if she were a human being," he chuckled. "The whole regiment was in the background, with a regular regimental parade, the same type of parade that we would give anyone else who we were so honoring for a promotion."[25]

"I was there," Art Sickler remembered more than a half-century later. "I was in dress blues and it was so dang hot.... I got her ready once the guys from the stables hauled her over in her trailer and dropped her off....

"I'd get her harness on, brush her, get her in her blanket, and I was in charge of her at the ceremony. I'd get her to where she belonged and stand there while the ceremony went on.

"We had the whole ceremony, just like she was a human being. And she got the commission and she loved it. She loved that kind of attention. I think she understood exactly what was going on and she was proud of it."[26]

Rothwell "pinned new chevrons on mother and son, and the equine-type Marines stood at attention as the unit passed in review."[27]

Losing a Friend

On December 22, 1957, Andrew Geer died peacefully, at fifty-two, after a brief struggle with melanoma. "By the time they discovered it, it was over—it just took over like crazy," Geer's nephew,

Andy Geer rides in the front seat of Governor Warren's car as the military attaché in President Eisenhower's inaugural parade. *James Taggert*

James Taggart, explained. "He was larger than life—just an unbelievable guy," Taggart said, "and he was a descendant of Daniel
Boone."[28]

John Wayne and Andy Geer on the set of *The Sea Chase*.
James Taggert

Geer was a Marine to the end, directing the Toys for Tots Christmas drive for the Corps until just before the cancer took him.[29]

According to an obituary the next day in the *Independent Journal*, Geer packed a lot of living into fifty-two years. First were the athletic achievements. In the late 1920s, he played football at the University of Minnesota, where teammates included future pro football hall of famer Bronko Nagurski. Geer also boxed at Minnesota, where he was Big Ten Conference heavyweight boxing champion two years running. He even picked up extra cash as a sparring partner for world champion fighters Jack Dempsey, Tommy Loughran, and Mickey Walker.

Andy Geer also played college baseball, turning semi-pro after graduation. And in the late 1940s, he scouted for two teams in the old All-America Football Conference, the Brooklyn Dodgers and Cleveland Browns.

Geer served with the British Army before joining the Marines as a captain in 1943. He saw action in Saipan, Guam, commanded an amphibious tractor battalion at the landing at Iwo Jima, and commanded the 2nd Battalion of the 5th Marine Regiment during the Korean War—one of only two Marine Reserve officers to command an infantry battalion in Korea.

"He was a military attaché in Eisenhower's inaugural parade," Taggart noted. "Each state governor had one military attaché to ride in his car, so Andy rode with California Governor [and future United States chief justice] Earl Warren when Eisenhower was elected."[30]

In a writing career that spanned a quarter-century, Andy Geer wrote mostly about what he knew: war. His short stories and articles appeared in magazines including *Redbook*, *Collier's*, *Detective Tales*, and, of course, the *Saturday Evening Post*. Besides the book about Reckless, Geer's other published works included the non-fiction bestseller *The New Breed*, about the Marines in Korea; *Mercy in Hell* recounted his service as a volunteer ambulance driver for the American Field Service during World War II; the front cover blurb of Geer's historical novel *The Canton Barrier* describes it as "a crackling adventure novel of a Yank pilot who would risk anything for money—and a girl." Thanks to Hollywood, his best remembered book is probably the bestselling fictionalized true story *The Sea Chase*, which followed a German freighter dodging danger on the high seas at the outbreak of World War II. *The Sea Chase* was adapted for the screen in 1955 as a vehicle for John Wayne and Lana Turner, although Geer did not write the screenplay.

However, Andy Geer did work a bit in Hollywood, receiving a story co-credit (with Charles Grayson) for 1951's *The Wild Blue Yonder*, starring Wendell Corey, Forrest Tucker, Walter Brennan, and Phil Harris.[31] And he was technical advisor on one of John Wayne's best-known war pictures, *Sands of Iwo Jima*, in 1949; Geer had actually fought at Iwo.

Andy Geer's name is also associated with a cultural contribution that had nothing to do with movies, novels, or athletics. This achievement was purely alcohol-related. According to one account, in 1954 Geer helped bring an obscure Tahitian mixed drink to prominence when he helped popularize the mai tai. Geer's collaborator in recreational mixology was bandleader and prolific composer Harry Owens of the Royal Hawaiians, the house orchestra at the iconic, famously pink Royal Hawaiian Hotel on Waikiki Beach in Honolulu.

Competing accounts maintain it was either restaurateur Vic Bergeron (a.k.a. "Trader Vic") in 1944, or his rival, Ernest "Don the Beachcomber" Gantt, in 1933, who concocted the cocktail. But in his 1970 autobiography *Sweet Leilani: The Story Behind the Song*,

Owens told his own mai tai tale. According to Owens, one evening
at the hotel's Surf Bar, Geer casually mentioned "a terrific rum drink
called a Mai Tai" he had tried during a recent trip to Tahiti. Since
the exotic drink had not yet reached the mainland, the two friends
resolved to duplicate it. After a dozen tries, and a curious crowd
growing to fifty—including Pulitzer Prize–winning author James
Michener, who suggested adding orange curacao to the mix—the
drink was perfected and the recipe printed in the next day's menu,
with the following warning: "When you're having trouble singing
the first four bars of 'Sweet Leilani,' you've had enough Mai Tais."[32]

Geer was the son of a thoroughbred trainer and breeder, so it's
not surprising that he was so devoted to the sweet-natured, impish
little Mongolian mare he met in Korea. He was her greatest advocate and ambassador, the one who stepped up to ensure she was
rotated stateside; found her passage; personally paid the fare of her
handler, PFC Moore; fought with U.S. Customs and the Agriculture
Department to clear her entry to the United States; and untangled
all the last-minute hitches so she could be so joyously honored at
the Marine Corps anniversary celebration in San Francisco, including replacing Reckless's blanket and ribbons so she would look her
best when introduced to her clamoring American fans. Geer's sister,
Marion Erickson, said her brother put his money where his heart
was. In a July 31, 1966, letter to the *San Diego Union*, she claimed
Geer ultimately paid $1,200 out of his own pocket—equivalent to
more than $8,500 today—to get Reckless stateside.[33]

But of everything Andrew Geer did on Reckless's behalf, it was
his writing that helped the most to spread her inspiring story. In his
last-ever article about Reckless, for the *Saturday Evening Post*, Geer
proposed a plaque for Reckless's quarters at Pendleton:

Home is the Warrior. Let Marines who pass this way take notice of honors won and the esteem in which she is held by those who were with her when the battle was in doubt. Remember, Marine, here is an unusual Marine. May we have a half a million as true.[34]

Fortitude in Peacetime

In March 1958, the "unusual Marine" participated in a 110-mile roundtrip hike to Camp Elliot with nearly 2,400 fellow Marines—to prove they were still good "foot soldiers." (Interestingly, "Shanks' mare" was a nickname for a foot soldier, "the common, garden-variety of gravel cruncher who picks 'em up and puts 'em down. The phrase 'shanks' mare' has all but disappeared from [our] vocabulary."[35])

The column of marchers stretched for about seven miles and evidently Reckless ran into trouble along the way. The *San Diego Union* reported that she marched just a few paces behind the 5th Marines' commanding officer Colonel Donald Schmuck, who led the hike to camp.

Reckless's problems began when she couldn't get past a road rail. According to one of her handlers, Colonel B. C. Evans, "She got her front feet over the rail, but her lame hind leg bothered her and she wouldn't go on." In short, she was stuck halfway across the rail. Several Marines, including Evans, "lifted her front legs back over the rail and walked her to a break in the fence."

This caused about a fifteen-minute delay, but Reckless needn't have felt badly; eight other Marines dropped out of the march due to, variously, blisters, an abscessed tooth, sore muscles, and a sprained ankle. Reckless, however, made it the entire way, carrying, for show, two empty artillery shell casings.[36]

Art Sickler remembered, "There [were] about 3,000 of us, and we marched down towards San Diego and we marched for two days and then we had a big beer bust. They came in with three semis of different beer. The Marine Corps always treated us real well that way.

"I didn't mind the marches because, being that I was the handler of Reckless, when I got tired I could put her in the trailer and drive along. That didn't set too good with the other troops, but that was the job and someone had to do it," Sickler said with a chuckle.

"A company commander told us…, 'You're not a Marine until you can go out the night before and get on a hell of a drunk, and get up the next morning at three and you go on a ten-mile hike and when you get back you have whiskey and bread for breakfast.' And that's the way we were treated, you know.

"Cpl B.C Evans gets out first aid kit to dress bruise on a hind leg of Fifth Marines famous horse S.Sgt Reckless, who had trouble on march." *Actual caption from* San Diego Union *picture, March 5, 1958, p. a-13. San Diego History Center*

"We had beer and just a day of rest on Wednesday and the camp looked pretty tough. And I remember Reckless, she was close to me all during this time and she would drink beer like crazy.

"And I got after these guys, and said, 'You know, she's going to colic on us. You stop that.' I was getting pretty upset with them doing that. She was eating everything…and we had chips and beer. About the only thing she wouldn't eat was the beefsteaks we had."

Sickler also said Reckless didn't like to fool around. "If she didn't like something, those ears got pinned right down. You could tell [she was thinking], 'Don't aggravate me. I'll do anything for you, but don't pester me.' She would pin her ears and you would show her respect!…I can still remember her asking for beer, and she was turned down and she would kind of pin her ears. She was just so great.

"…And so we marched back…And as bad as we looked on Wednesday, we were up the next morning at three o'clock and I had Reckless all ready to go; she walked a pretty straight line then, and then we marched back.

"And I remember that march so well because Colonel Schmuck was leading the march, and the troops were kind of complaining that we were strung out and we weren't able to stretch out and take bigger strides because the strides were so small, and we didn't understand what was going on.

"But I have the picture coming up to camp at the 5th Marines headquarters company, how we were strung out. And when we got up the hill, there goes an ambulance waiting for Colonel Schmuck.… He had a rupture and he was rushed to surgery, but he would not give up.

"It chokes me up even when I talk about it … he was just a tough guy, but he was fair. And I'll remember him like I remember Reckless," Sickler added.

PFC Sickler also remembers meeting a Marine sergeant who served in Korea with Reckless. "I don't remember the sergeant's name," Sickler recalled, "...but this sergeant had seen me handling Reckless, and I got to talking with him when I noticed he had a big scar out the back of his neck and in the front right by his Adam's apple."

Sickler asked about the twin scars, and the sergeant described a wartime patrol through an irrigation ditch muddied by drizzle. Rounding a turn in the ditch, the sergeant encountered an enemy soldier in the process of dozing off.

"And when he heard the sergeant come up on him, he got startled and jumped up and pulled his bayonet and he stabbed him right in the Adam's apple and it went through his neck. And the sergeant said he pulled his revolver ... and just unloaded it because he was

Various pictures of Reckless on the march. *Art Sickler, Clay Shanrock*

point blank right against him. And he said he had to unload that whole thing before he dropped.

"But then Reckless was there, she was back a little ways with some troops. In the bottom of that ditch, they placed the sergeant on her, and they got him back to sickbay for medical care. He [the sergeant] survived that—it missed everything, his jugular vein and stuff like that—so that was a miracle in itself, and just that that horse was there to take him out again, you know.

"That horse, the different things I heard, that horse saved so many lives over there that she's never had the credit…that she should have had. She probably saved more lives than a lot of medics did.

"She just won your heart because she was so obedient…like she understood you. You didn't have to say something, she just felt it, you know? And all the time I spent with her, she got to know me and we were just the best of buddies …

"I will never forget that horse as long as I live."[37]

Reckless's Duties

Life at Pendleton for Reckless was no free ride. The U.S. Marines required duties—especially public appearances.

On June 8, 1958, Reckless led the opening parade at the Navy Relief Rodeo and Carnival at Camp Pendleton before twenty-five thousand onlookers. She got to rub shoulders that day with TV western stars including *Gunsmoke*'s Amanda Blake ("Miss Kitty") and Milburn Stone ("Doc"), and Johnny Washbrook ("Ken McLaughlin"), the teenaged costar of *My Friend Flicka*.

Reckless also participated in military parades, mostly on base. Typical of these events was the 1st Marine Division Reunion in July 1958. That day, she was led to the parade grounds by Sergeant Lynn

Reckless proudly leads the opening parade at the Navy Relief Rodeo and Carnival. *Robert Hammershoy*

Mattocks, who positioned her to review the two-thousand-man procession that kicked off the festivities.

"My job in 1958," Sergeant Mattocks recalled, "was on special occasions when Sergeant Reckless was requested to make an appearance...I would walk her down the street and lead her...across the parade field. The folks at the Camp Pendleton base stables always had her groomed up and ready for me, and I would...make sure her mane and tail [were] very Marine Corps, in the proper place and such, and she'd be dressed in her best blanket with her ribbons and everything.

"And I'd just walk her along. That year, I led her in the Memorial Day Parade, Veterans Day Parade, Marine Corps [Birthday] Parade, the Christmas parade—you name it."[38]

Mattocks also led Reckless when she reviewed the troops during Changes of Command parades, which honored officers leaving for new assignments or generals receiving additional stars. A general departing for Marine Corps headquarters in Quantico, Virginia, would receive a formal ceremony and big parade on the great field at Pendleton. Reckless would be paraded out in full blanket and ribbons as part of the Change of Command, joined by the color guard and led by a Marine in full dress uniform.

Staff Sergeant James Wright recalled seeing Reckless in just such a capacity at his graduation parade at San Onofre, California. "When we graduated from the Infantry Training Regiment (ITR), we were then sent to a specialty. But for graduating ITR, we would have a parade and pass the reviewing stand where the officers were. And there was Reckless, standing right off to the side, watching us graduate. She was dressed in her best blanket and was treated just like every other Marine that bore her title. I will never forget that image."[39]

Reckless also was on hand for retirement ceremonies and made guest appearances on Armed Forces Day. The Marine Corps brass were thoughtful enough to give her a pass on public appearances when she was pregnant, but naturally she reviewed the troops when two of her colts joined the Marines.

What Reckless Shared with Gary Cooper

Gary Cooper was a reel war hero, winning a Best Actor Academy Award® in the title role of *Sergeant York*. Reckless was a real war heroine with the decorations to prove it. But the mare and the movie star also had something else in common: both could fall asleep anywhere, anytime.

Cooper often surprised film crews by effortlessly dropping off for naps between camera set-ups. And even in war-torn Korea, Reckless could fall asleep at will—in the tents of fellow Marines, for example, or as handlers brushed her down after a hard day.

But once she took up residence at Camp Pendleton, Reckless perfected the art of nodding off during parades and reviews. Sometimes after standing in place for long periods, she would get bored, cock her left hind leg (her lame leg), and, with the tip of her hoof

Reckless is a mascot for her Marines. *Camp Pendleton Archives*

touching the ground, drop her head slightly and go sound asleep. She even let out an occasional snore.

Reckless was the only Marine ever allowed to doze during a formation or parade—and for a good reason. At the time, no one realized she was doing it.

Keeping a Reckless Pace

Reckless kept her Camp Pendleton handlers on their toes. One in particular had trouble keeping up with his charge. Corporal Jesse J. Winters fed, exercised, and looked after Reckless's overall needs, including cleaning her stall.

"Because she was a war horse from Korea and carried ammo across no man's land to the troops on the front line," Winters recalled, "when she returned to the states, there were written orders that nothing would ever be placed on her back other than her blankets."

Winters asked how he was to exercise Reckless if he couldn't ride her. "That's when I learned that I was to run *alongside* until she got tired and wanted to go back to the stall. Lucky for me she knew the word *oats* and I could usually get her to cut her runs short."

Word around the base was that the young Marine was the best-conditioned leatherneck in the Corps because he had to run five miles a day next to her.

"There were times that some of the Marines, after a night on the town, would turn her out to run free, or, a number of times, take her into a barrack and tie her up to someone's bunk, or the first sergeant's door knob. As you may expect, I got little sleep those nights.

"On one occasion…she found her way to the flower garden of the wife of the base commander. I'm sure there were a lot of snickers about that, but let me tell you I was one PFC sweating bullets getting her out of there with the general standing in front of his house. I remember he was saying something—I don't think it was good. I do remember throwing him a salute as we took off at a trot up the trail."[40] Reckless was almost put on restriction for eating the commander's flowerbeds.

Marching toward Motherhood

Reckless was in a rather delicate condition for a second hundred-mile hike less than a year later, in January 1959. This time, the Marines hiked around Pendleton's perimeter and into part of the adjoining Cleveland National Forest (Twentynine Palms area). Twenty-five hundred 5th Marines took part in the five-day march, setting up overnight camp areas which included corrals for Reckless; otherwise, the rest of the camps were set up "'Civil War style,' with shelter tents lined up perfectly."[41]

Acting Gunnery Sergeant Frank D. Brady from Bridgewater, Massachusetts, was there that day. Brady worked for the disbursing office, which paid the Marines. "My office didn't have to go on the hike, but the captain and I flew up there and paid them," Brady recalled. "The kids would be out all day long getting in shape to go back to Pendleton. And she [Reckless] would go along. And she was at the end of the column and there was a jeep and a trailer pulling her, and she's riding. And the Marines were walking along and grumbling that, 'Here I'm walking and that damn horse is riding.'

"But at night when they got back to the area, they'd have a warm meal and had a portable kitchen, there'd be fifteen or twenty of them back there feeding her their apples and everything and petting her and making friends again…she never wanted for nothing."[42]

This hike was no walk in the park for Reckless. What the guys probably didn't know was at the time, Reckless was pregnant with her second foal. Seven weeks after the hike, on March 2, 1959, Reckless gave birth to her second colt, Dauntless. Again, newspaper headline writers behaved as if they had invented alliteration: "Marines' Famous Mare Becomes Mother Again" and "Marine Mare Mother."

Reckless Fans: The Next Generation

For the children of Marines, living on base had perks—especially if you were allowed to hang out at the stables.

"I was an enlisted kid, not an officer's kid," recalled Rebecca Meador of Hamilton, Ohio, "so I couldn't have my own horse. Therefore, I helped take care of Reckless. She had her own paddock at the end of the barn-stable area; there were pipe rails around it and it had a shelter, like a little cover, but there were plenty of trees in it. After she died, they had a plaque that talked about her being a Korean racing mare and that she had been injured twice in battle. I seem to remember one time they said she had been hit by a jeep."

It turns out that Reckless had acquired a friend around this time. "It was a flaxen mane chestnut Shetland pony named Sampson, and boy, was he a *stinker*." Meador recalled, smiling. "He would chase her around and nip and kick at her. He was really hairy, with a bushy, bushy mane. He was a stinker to the kids riding him and he was a stinker to everybody. He'd chase her and then she'd chase him. And then he'd get tired of it and then they'd stop and graze side-by-side again.

"Some kids got in real trouble when they got up on her bareback, because it was not allowed…you couldn't ride her. Not only because of her arthritis, but she had rank in the Marine Corps. And you didn't do that to her—you didn't treat her like that because of that rank. So, we'd mainly go over to her pen and groom her and stuff and watch Sampson be a pain."[43]

Denise Dwyer Reed from Commerce, Georgia, was ten when she first saw Reckless, at the base rodeo. "I remember kids at the rodeo feeding her popcorn and she would drink Coke. My best memory was seeing her with her colt, Chesty…. She was out in a large paddock with board fences and had a little run-in shed for shelter. Nothing fancy, but then you know the Marine Corps is pure simple function.

"One time when she was being led around in her paddock, I saw a private salute her as he went by. I've never forgotten that image after all these years."[44]

Cat Ballou and Mr. Ed

Debbie McCain, from Fallbrook, California, was nine when she posed with Reckless and Dauntless in 1959 at the base stables.

Her father, Captain G. M. "Jinx" McCain, had brought her to meet the famous Marine during a cookout at the stables. "It was somebody's birthday as I remember and one of the guys was having some food and Reckless ate a big plate of food and drank a bucket of beer. When she was done eating and drinking, she disappeared. And next thing you know, we looked over and she was leaning up against the stables taking a nap—and she just kind of stayed there for a long while. She didn't go anywhere."

Thinking back on it, Debbie laughed. "She looked just like the horse in the movie *Cat Ballou* leaning up against the side of the building. That image just stuck with me."

(Among the best-remembered images from the 1965 comic western was that of a drunken Lee Marvin passed out astride his equally inebriated equine, who's leaning against the side of a building, legs crossed during its own sodden repose.)

Debbie agreed with the prevailing opinion that Reckless marched to a different drummer. "She would come out and find a soft place in the sun and just lay down in the middle of where all the horses were. And she'd just lay there until she got finished sunning, and we just let her alone and she'd get up and wander off and do her own little thing."

And when it came to food—watch out!

"Down at the base stables, as kids you're always back there and you're always eating something," Debbie said. "And if she knew that you had food, she would hunt you down. And she wouldn't take no for an answer. And she was really pushy when she found out you had something to eat.

"So you just…knew that *she* knew that you had food, so you might as well just give it to her because she was going to follow you around and push you or nudge you or whatever until you gave it to her.

"So she turned into a big bully when it came to food. And not necessarily horse food, but she liked hot dogs and potato chips and

Young Debbie McCain poses with Reckless and Dauntless. *Debbie McCain*

sandwiches and cookies and candy bars—anything that you fed her, she would eat. And I'm sure it was because the Marines taught her to eat all this stuff; they spoiled her rotten."

Evidently the sins of the mother were passed to the boys. "All three of her sons would eat anything. Just like her. They had an appetite for food."

But loving junk food wasn't the only thing Debbie remembered about Reckless.

"She was the first horse I think I ever saw drool. I mean, she would just salivate if you had food and she saw you eating. She was like Mr. Ed with the lips—she would just mouth it and you gave it to her."[45]

At one point, the Marines put up a sign that read, "Please don't feed Sergeant Reckless"; so many visitors brought carrots that she put on weight, and there was real concern so many vegetable sugars could cause medical problems.[46]

Reckless's Final Promotion
to Staff Sergeant (E-6)

Around this time, the Corps changed its rank structure, adding two new pay grades, E-8 and E-9. Reckless's ranking of staff sergeant was level E-5, but with the new structure, her status was revised to acting staff sergeant, so she qualified for another promotion. It was also time for Dauntless to follow family tradition and join the Marines. As summer faded, on August 31, 1959, Reckless received her final promotion, to staff sergeant (E-6).

What was delightful about the promotions was how they reflected genuine respect the Marines held for Reckless; the stripes carried real weight.

"I was not permitted to lead her in the parade," Corporal Winters recalled, "because she outranked me and I could not give her orders. So they found a ranking NCO for that duty."[47]

Bestowing the honors this time was the Commandant of the Marine Corps, General Randolph McCall Pate himself, "the nation's number one Marine...during an impressive full-scale parade and review at the Base Parade Field."[48]

At the same ceremony, Dauntless enlisted as a private, which the *San Diego Union* previewed with the headline, "It'll be Pvt Dauntless: Sgt Reckless to See Son Enter Marines."

Reckless received a 19-gun salute as 1,700 Marines marched in formation. "A horse who really knows her oats," reported the base newspaper. "SSgt Reckless stood quietly amid all the pomp and ceremony as the division's Drum and Bugle Corps and combat-clad 5th Marine Regiment passed in review."[49]

The *San Diego Union* quoted Commandant Pate as declaring Reckless, "one of the greatest woman Marines we ever had." He also noted Reckless was in better shape for the ceremony than the

"THAT AIN'T HAY—ASSGT 'Reckless' looks at the chevrons of a staff sergeant (E-6) which she will receive from General Randolph McCall Pate, commandant of the Marine Corps Aug 31 during a combat parade and review by the Fifth Marines at the 24 Area parade field." *Original photo caption from* Pendleton Scout, *August 27, 1959, p. 7. Photo courtesy of USMC History Division, Quantico, VA*

last time he saw her—in Korea, when he promoted her to sergeant. "She had a hangover [back then]," he told the reporter. "You know, she likes beer."[50]

Her two sons, Private First Class Fearless and Private Dauntless, looked on, along with the Pendleton base commander and the commanders of the 1st and 5th Marine Regiments.

Also on hand were 125 other well-wishers in crisp green uniforms—Girl Scouts from the Pendleton area, "of which troop, Reckless last month was made an honorary member."[51]

A letter that accompanied Reckless's promotion warrant noted that "during the period since your last promotion, you have demonstrated exceptional, noteworthy and commendatory performance

"Private First Class Winford C McCracken, Headquarters Company 5th Marines stands by Reckless as General Randolph McC Pate, Commandant of the Marine Corps tacks on the chevrons on Staff Sergeant Reckless' blanket." *Original photo caption. USMC History Division, Quantico, VA*

on unusual assignments. You participated in two 100-mile hikes with the 5th Marines; a distinguishing observation in the January hike was the fact you completed the event without the aid of shoes—all other participants wore field boots."[52]

The letter closed by saying that "Reckless' performance of duty clearly reflects an ability or qualification exceptional to the degree that it merits accelerated promotion over other qualified Marines in the same occupational field."[53] So great was the Marines' respect for Reckless that it was made a court-martial offense to put anything heavier than a blanket on her back without orders to do so.

"In my career I have seen many animals that have been adopted by Marines," wrote General Pate, "but never in all my experience have I seen one which won the hearts of so many as did this lovely little lady known as Reckless."[54]

General Pate congratulates the newest Private First Class, Dauntless, as Reckless proudly watches. *Nancy Latham Parkin*

One typically moving tribute came from PFC Fred E. "Dutch" White of Foxtrot Company, Second Battalion, 5th Marines, who described what he saw that day Reckless was promoted:

"We marched from Camp Santa Margarita over to the large grass parade field at the end of the Camp Pendleton airfield (just across the road from the commanding general's ranch house). The reason for our marching over there was so that we could participate in Staff Sergeant Reckless's promotional ceremony and parade.

"We must've stood there for about two hours, waiting for the ceremony to finally begin. It was hotter than hell and we were all decked out in utilities, marching packs, helmets, and our T/O weapons....

"There was a whole lot of griping going on all up and down the ranks about having to stand out there in the hot sun all this time, 'because some damn horse was about to get promoted,' and

'What kind of sh*t is this?' and et cetera, et cetera, et cetera, as we all stood there sweating.

"When things finally did kick off, we went through all the normal, standard, regular parade proceedings, with all the normal, standard, regular 1ˢᵗ Marine Division Band music playing—just like we had done it a number of times before....

"But when the person on the microphone started giving the audience, and we Marine grunts, the background information on Staff Sergeant Reckless's heroic career in our Marine Corps during the Korean War, all of our attitudes turned around about 180 degrees.

"All of a sudden, we all stood a whole lot straighter in ranks. All of a sudden, we were very, very proud to be in the presence of such a true Marine Corps hero. What a magnificent Marine she was. What a great honor to be able to participate in her promotional ceremony and parade.

"I will never forget that day," White recalled so many years later, "for as long as I live."[55]

The Reckless Handicap

Jack Murphy's sports column in the *San Diego Union* on September 6, 1959, was devoted to the ninth running of the Del Mar Debutante at Del Mar Racetrack, thirty miles south of Pendleton, where the "Debs" had to share top billing with Reckless ("Top Del Mar Fillies Share Stage With Korean Plater") since the race was temporarily renamed "The Reckless Handicap."

A crowd of 17,905 watched as Reckless was paraded around the track before the race with jockeys warned to keep a "discreet distance" because, as one of her handlers advised a Del Mar executive, "Nobody rides Reckless.... It's a court-martial offense."

Darling June beat Fair Maggie by three-and-a-half lengths and ran the fastest six furlongs of any two-year-old filly in America at that time (1:09 1-5), earning a record $33,600 (with a record gross purse of $52,410).

Having grown up at a racetrack, it would seem natural Reckless would bask in and soak up the cheers and atmosphere of the scenic seaside track located "where the turf meets the surf."

And Murphy even remarked about how Reckless really seemed to enjoy the special attention: "In fact, she's such a showboat it seemed likely she might fluff out her skirts and curtsy when the crowd gave her a noisy ovation."[56] Reckless always knew how to command an audience.

Reckless: Coming to a Theater Near You?

In December 1959, United Press International reported—in what likely was just a rewritten studio press release—that United Artists soon would begin production on *Reckless: Pride of the Marines*, based on Andy Geer's book.[57]

Ten months later, Hollywood gossip columnist Hedda Hopper reported the picture would begin filming on location in Korea the following month. She added that World War II hero Guy Gabaldon would play a Marine in the film. (Gabaldon's own biopic, *Hell to Eternity*, with Jeffrey Hunter as Gabaldon, had just been released a month earlier.) On October 8, 1960, Hopper was reporting that an early November start date was planned.[58] November came and went. In January 1961, the *Long Beach Independent Press-Telegram* reported no decision had yet been made on whether Reckless would play herself. In the end, though, the project was abandoned for no readily apparent reason.

Staff Sergeant Reckless Retires to a Busy Life

On November 10, 1960—six years to the day her hooves first touched American soil—Staff Sergeant Reckless retired from the United States Marine Corps. PFC Fearless and Private Dauntless stood by as their staff sergeant mother, resplendent in dress blanket with battle ribbons and fourragère, was relieved of marching and parade duties amidst full military honors at a 5th Marine parade.

Acting Gunnery Sergeant Frank D. Brady of the 5th Marines disbursing office was her handler that day. "That was the only day I had anything to do with Reckless and I was more than pleased and proud

"MARINES HONOR BATTLE-SCARRED MARE—Sergeant Reckless, battle-scarred former Korean racehorse, stands at attention with G/Sgt FR Brady on the parade field at Camp Pendleton during ceremonies yesterday honoring retiring mare. Reckless was drafted into the Marines during the bitter fighting in October, 1952. She served her adopted country by making many solo trips through battlefields to carry ammunition to outlying gun placements. Reckless, who has lived a life of luxury with the First Marine Division at Camp Pendleton since 1954, will live out the rest of her life on a camp pasture." *Original photo caption. Frank Brady.* San Diego Union, *November 11, 1960, 22, San Diego, CA*

"AND THAT AIN'T HAY—SSgt Reckless receives the first installment of 'retirement pay' from LtCol N.P. Lengyel (r), 1st Div Disbursing Officer. The famed mare retired today with full honors during a 5th Marines parade. GySgt F.R. Brady assists with the payment." *Original photo caption from the* Pendleton Scout, *Nov 10, 1960, p. 3. Photo from the* Pendleton Scout

AGySgt. Frank Brady feeds Reckless a piece of birthday cake. *Frank Brady*

to do it," Brady recalled. "The base stables brought her over with two of her colts. They had a portable corral that they would use for her colts because whenever she went out anywhere on a parade or something, they always took those colts along. But some master sergeant brought her up there from the base stable all dolled up—her hooves all shined up and everything—and I just took her to the reviewing

stand. And after all of that, we 'trooped the line.' I led her and brought
her back and gave her a piece of birthday cake," he said with a laugh.

"I swear, as we trooped the line...and the whole regiment was
on line, all three battalions,... when we got to the end of the line she
looked back and whinnied like, 'I don't want to go.' Not real loud
and all...but like she didn't want to go."

Lieutenant Colonel Nicolas P. Lengyl was the 1st Division disbursing officer. So this final ceremony was, in essence, Reckless being
paid off for her duties as an Active Duty Marine. Now she was a
Retired Marine. "The last day of duty we paid her off just as we do
with every Marine," Brady recalled. "Every Marine, when they got
separated [retired], they came down and we paid them off and we'd
give them a check for their final settlement. For Reckless, it was that
big bag of oats in the picture."[59]

According to the *San Diego Union*, the ceremony "moved a few
veteran leathernecks to brush a sentimental tear from their eyes."
General Pate's successor as Marine Corps Commandant, General
David M. Shoup, issued the order: "Staff Sergeant Reckless will be
provided quarters and messing at the Camp Pendleton Stables in lieu
of retired pay."[60]

Winner's Circle: Reckless Returns to the Races

On July 28, 1962, the retired staff sergeant stepped before the
crowds on "Reckless Day" at Del Mar Racetrack. "The track has
chosen the first weekend to focus on the Armed Forces in general,"
the Camp Pendleton newspaper reported, "Camp Pendleton in particular, and Staff Sergeant Reckless most of all."[61] Reckless was
paraded before the stands prior to the featured Oceanic Handicap

and "stole the show...in an impressive ceremony conducted just before the sixth race."[62]

After the race, Reckless was led by her wartime pal Gunnery Sergeant Norman Mull to the winner's circle for a moment of silence honoring fallen American soldiers. Then, she stood humbly, "directing curious glances at the crowd" as her achievements were read aloud.

The sixth race was dubbed the "Staff Sergeant Reckless Purse," and its namesake watched quietly as Sergeant Mull crowned the winner, Harry Wragg, who ran the mile and one sixteenth in 1:41 2-5, winning by nearly a length and paying $5.40.[63]

1st Marine Division Reunion

In August 1962, a 1st Marine Division reunion honored famous leathernecks including the five-time Navy Cross recipient, Lieutenant General Lewis B. "Chesty" Puller, General Holland Smith ("the

Two great Marine Corps legends unite: Lieutenant General Lewis B. "Chesty" Puller and Reckless share a moment together at the 1st Marine Division reunion. *San Diego History Center*

father of modern amphibious warfare"), and Staff Sergeant Reckless.

As three thousand Marines paraded past in review, paced by the 1st Marine Division Band, Reckless stood at quiet attention through most of the parade, favoring her left hip. According to the *San Diego Union*, Reckless occasionally reared and showed the whites of her eyes, but, "when the Division's thirty red and gold battle colors filed by, she stopped breaking ranks and watched, ears cocked forward."[64]

Two More Blessed Events, One Tragedy

With little fanfare, Reckless expanded her family on December 6, 1964, when she gave birth to her third foal, a beautiful seal brown colt named "Chesty."

There was one last foal, a filly born in 1966, sired by a registered quarter horse stud. Like her mother, this little horse was a sorrel. Sadly, she died a month after birth; the cause of death was not reported.

A Vet's View of a Vet

"She was a pretty good horse to handle. She never got in much trouble, so we really didn't do much treatment for her," recalled Dr. Robert L. Miller, Reckless's veterinarian at Pendleton. "She was the queen over there. Had her own paddock and all her own attention and all the kids liked to go up and pet her, see her—and she had such a nice history behind her and they all wanted to go see Reckless."

Miller recalled the health problems that developed late in life. "She had severe arthritis in her older years. She was torn up pretty bad, which is common for what she did over in Korea.... It worked her joints pretty hard." But, according to Miller, that wasn't the worst of her problems.

"She was getting laminitis right at the end there. And that's an incurable situation. That's an inflammation of the coffin bone in the foot, and then the laminae are around it and there's just no way to treat it. You can ease it and make them comfortable for a while, but eventually it will take them. We had to put [Triple Crown winner] Secretariat down because of laminitis. They call it 'foundering.'"

Doc Miller remembered her fondly as "just a good ol' horse who stood her ground. She was a tough ol' gal."[65]

Last Years: An Understanding Friend

While the last years of Reckless's life were quiet, they were not without meaning and purpose. Despite pain from various conditions including arthritis and laminitis, she continued serving the Marines. Not in any formal or sanctioned way, but as a sounding board and therapist of sorts for combat veterans.

Postcard of Reckless after retirement.

"Old timers would come down to feed her," recalled Sergeant Art DiGrazia, one of Reckless's handlers. "They'd be dressed in civilian clothes and say to me, 'I served with her. I want to see her.'"[66]

"I think a lot of people overlook the role that Sergeant Reckless played in so many Marines' lives," said Sergeant Lynn Mattocks, "and that is that solitude of being able to go down and sit there and just reminisce, or talk to her, or whatever. And it was rehabilitation, you know. Therapy. And not only for Korean veterans, but from Vietnam.

"And it was the other thing [she did]. How she could also help people who just had deployments. Or the troops going to Hawaii, or the Philippines, or Japan. And family separation. No one will ever know the number of dependents that were left behind—wives, children. Or like me, I went out there when…I was going through terrible things and it was great to have that therapy.

"I spent a lot of time just going by and saying, 'Hi.' How many [Marines] got solitude and relief from Sergeant Reckless? She took their minds away from it all.

"I'm speaking first-hand what Sergeant Reckless did for me. And I know from earlier days— which really didn't dawn on me until later on—some of the guys who had been with her when they would go down there and just sit down there and drink a Coke and whatever. And would just sit there, and talked to her and give her a carrot, you know? It was just solitude. It was genuinely a giving back.

"She didn't quit serving the Marines when she came back from Korea and retired at Camp Pendleton. She always continued to serve."[67]

Staff Sergeant Reckless continued to serve the Marines she loved, and who loved her more than she could know, until May 13, 1968, when she passed away, at the age of twenty.

CHAPTER 12

RECKLESS'S FOALS

FEARLESS, DAUNTLESS, AND CHESTY

Frenzy over First Foal Fearless

When the media learned about the arrival of Reckless's first foal, they went crazy with coverage.

But the story of Fearless's conception and birth has never been told any better than by an eyewitness to the excitement. Decades after he served with the Marines in Korea, the late Roy "Boots" Reynolds now is a popular western artist, cartoonist, and humorist. The following account was originally published in *Chicken Soup for the Horse Lover's Soul* and is excerpted here with

Reckless stands proudly next to her newborn colt, Fearless. *USMC History Division, Quantico, VA*

permission. It shows what can happen when officers know everything and enlisted men nothing.

Sergeant Reckless, a Mighty Marine
by Boots Reynolds

I figured they'd at least offer me a blindfold or maybe a cigarette. My commanding officer marched back and forth in front of me and I could hear the crowd outside growing restless.

"You know why you're in here, don't you? I'm saving your life. You've ruined hers. You've destroyed her reputation along with that of the baby."

"It's a foal, sir. It's a foal, not a baby horse," I replied meekly.

"I don't care what the technical term is. The fact remains you have ruined its life, its mother's reputation and, in all probability, made a laughingstock of the Marine Corps!" he growled. "Now, sit yourself down and think about the consequences of your actions while I go out there and see what I can do to straighten out this mess!"

So this was how it was going to end. I had survived the war only to face a firing squad stateside for telling the truth. I was only doing my job....

Now, unbeknownst to Reckless, some high-ranking public relations officers decided it would be a great idea to arrange a "marriage" between her and some famous thoroughbred racehorse sire. The plan called for their offspring to be entered in and, no doubt, win the Kentucky Derby, thereby propelling Reckless and the Marine Corps even further into the limelight.

After the consummation of this marriage, Reckless was taken back to the base stable and turned out for daily frolics with the stable horses. At night, she was led back to her private stall and paddock, where she was queen of the stable and she knew it.

Before going any further, I must explain that in the armed forces, officers know everything. The enlisted men do not. That's just the military way, which means that most officers find it unnecessary to inform the enlisted ranks of their plans. This is exactly what happened with Reckless and her Derby-winning colt. We knew nothing about the officers' plans and most of the enlisted men would be discharged or transferred before the foal's birth.

It was at this time that Reckless and I crossed paths. After my "Korean vacation," I'd been transferred to special services and assigned to the base stable. One of my jobs was to help promote the annual Navy Relief Rodeo by being a trick roper and rodeo clown. Our base commander at the time was a strong supporter of the rodeo and through his efforts we received some bucking horses and bulls for the sailors and Marines to practice on.

One of the young bucking horses had gotten kicked in the chest and needed stitches. After a visit to the veterinarian, he was turned out with the stable horses so it would be easier to catch him when it came time to take out the stitches. The next morning when Reckless was turned out the crew gathered to see her put this new guy in his place. To their surprise, they discovered first that he was a stallion and second that Reckless was in love. By the time they got her back to her paddock and the young stallion into a corral, Cupid had shot all his arrows.

"You can probably brush off most of those scuff marks and comb out her ruffed-up mane," I explained. "But I don't know how you're going to get that smirk off her face." We all agreed not to tell anybody about this and swore an oath of secrecy.

Apparently the arranged marriage had failed and no one had informed the powers that be to check her in twenty-eight days to see if the ink had dried on the license. All was forgotten until one day I looked up and saw a staff car and veterinarian's truck parked outside Reckless's paddock. After the vet had checked her over, the staff car pulled up to the office where I was and the officers unloaded with big smiles on their faces. One proudly announced that Reckless was going to have a baby.

It was at this point that I became very confused. Why were they so excited about her being in foal with a common bucking horse? I didn't know about the earlier marriage with the champion stallion, and they didn't know about her affair with the rodeo bronc. I was fully expecting to be blamed for her condition while quietly wondering who'd let the cat out of the bag. Instead I was being ordered to make a big sign to put along the main base highway that ran by her paddock. They explained that they wanted everybody to be aware of the expected arrival and its gender once it got here.

The sign was to say, "It's a …," and then the appropriate sign of "Boy" or "Girl" was to be put up when the foal was born. Also, whoever was on duty at the time of the blessed event was to call the special services officer immediately and he would notify the press.

Well, it seems the foal came about a month later than expected and you can guess who was on duty the night it happened. Actually, it was about daylight when I looked out and saw her cleaning him off. So as instructed I hung the "Boy" sign, made the phone call and started my morning chores. Suddenly the driveway filled with staff cars and news media.

They were driving Reckless nuts. She was frantically trying to maneuver between the colt and the flashing cameras. I told the news people to step outside the paddock and I'd lead her past them so they could get the shots they wanted. The officers beamed with pride as the cameras clicked. When they were finished, I turned Reckless loose and she scurried to the backside of her paddock with her wobbly-legged offspring in tow.

While heading back to the barns, I heard one of the officers mention the Kentucky Derby. As I stopped to listen more closely, one of the reporters turned to me and asked in a very loud voice, "What is the name again of that famous sire that's the daddy of this colt?"

I proudly answered, "Well, sir, he ain't very famous, but he's one of our best bareback broncs. You know, a buckin' horse."

You could have cut the silence with a knife. My CO grabbed my arm and invited me immediately into the office for a "debriefing" while the other officers and the news media were left in a very disgruntled and confused state. During my meeting with the CO the entire story of the Corps' plans for Reckless was brought to my attention. I learned all about the tremendous amount of time and energy devoted to developing a PR strategy to keep her name in the spotlight and to make her even more famous.

In just a few seconds I had managed to dishonor the reputation of a war heroine and destroy a huge public relations campaign for the Marines.

My enlistment was up shortly after Reckless had her colt. After recent research, I discovered that she fell in love two more times. None of those offspring were Derby winners either.[1]

Foaling Around with the Facts: The Pendleton Paternity Plot

Fearless was foaled on April 5, 1957, at 10:00 p.m. and, not surprisingly, official records from the Camp Pendleton base stables maintain his sire was not the low-brow bronc Boots Reynolds described, but *a registered bay thoroughbred*.

Five days after the birth, the *San Diego Union* reported on Fearless's arrival under the headline, "Marines become Godfathers: 'Sarge' Reckless Bears Offspring." Without definitive proof of a cover-up, the *Union* could only insinuate the "Godfathers" were less than candid about the identity of Fearless's father. After describing how calmly Reckless had become a mother, the *Union* cut as close to the truth as possible, given the few available facts:

Reckless and Fearless in the mare-ternity ward. *USMC History Division, Quantico, VA*

Her masters, however, weren't so calm…they weren't too sure of the colt's sire. It seems that record keeping on Sergeant Reckless has been slim because of a succession of commanding officers in the regiment.

"We do know Reckless was bred to an Arabian stallion," one officer said. "But we're not too sure which one it was.

"The sarge [Reckless] wasn't saying anything. But she surely looked proud."[2]

The Name Game

Like most newborns, Fearless arrived nameless. So the 5th Marines held a "Name the Colt" contest. "Favorite names," reported the *Pendleton Scout*, "were Chosin, Pvt Diamond, Star Spangled…and a Corps favorite, Semper Fi."[3] None of the many entries satisfied Colonel Richard Rothwell, commander of the 5th Marines.

"I had the contest in the regiment," the colonel recalled, "and when no suitable name came after quite a long period of time, I got all the battalion commanders together and we tried to get the word out that there was this contest and a reward would be, as I remember—now I can't be too sure of this—but maybe a weekend of liberty or something like that. Just a symbolic thing.

"Well, I was very disappointed in the results. The battalion commanders probably sifted out the best names from the whole regiment—and I looked at those, and none of them fit the legacy of Reckless. They just didn't do it.

"They were good names but I decided that his name was going to be Fearless," Rothwell said. "And I was very, very disappointed that I had to do that—I didn't want to do that—but it was better

"NAME FOR FAMOUS SON—'Fearless,' two-week-old son of the 1stMarDiv's famed war-horse, Sergeant Reckless, takes his first quizzical look at the card bearing his new name. PFC Robert E Gibbs, the card holder, won the colt-naming contest held in the 5th Marines with which Reckless served during the Korean War. If the friendly nuzzle is an indication, 'Fearless' seems to approve his new name. Both mother and son will continue to live at Camp Pendleton, home of the 1stMarDiv." *Original photo caption from* Pendleton Scout, *April 25, 1957. Photo courtesy of USMC History Division, Quantico, VA*

than having him tagged with something that was inappropriate. So grudgingly, I had to take that route."

Today, the name Fearless seems a great choice, a perfect fit for Reckless's first-born.

The 1st Marine Division Association in Washington, D.C., gave the name final approval. Colonel Rothwell decided the prize for naming the Colt should still go to someone, so he randomly selected PFC Robert E. Gibbs, one of many who had submitted losing entries, as the designated contest winner.

Movin' on Up

On June 15, 1957, at the tender age of eight weeks and one day—about a year old to a human—Fearless was promoted to private first class. The proudest witness at the formal ceremony was his doting mother, herself promoted to staff sergeant the same day. Colonel Rothwell pinned the new chevrons on Fearless, who stood at attention as the full-scale regimental parade passed in review.

Taking a Different Path

Fearless soon joined his mother in making ceremonial appearances. After his brother Dauntless was born, Fearless became a trail horse for the base stables, reviewing troop parade marches alongside

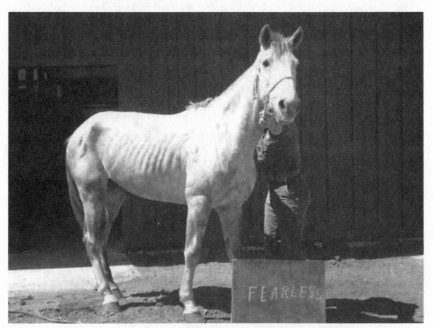

Fearless stands outside the base stables as he's being groomed. *Debbie McCain*

Dauntless, Reckless, and Fearless in one of the last pictures taken of Fearless.
Command Museum, Marine Corps Recruit Depot, San Diego

his mother when four-month-old Dauntless entered the Marines as
a private on July 1, 1959.

But Fearless's life took a decidedly different path from that of his
mother. He was sold and went to work at a ranch near the base
stables, although no record apparently exists as to who purchased
him or what his life was like as a ranch horse.

Captain Eric Pedersen secured rights to the foal when he sold
Reckless to the 1st Marine Division Association for a dollar, yet he
never exercised those rights.

Fearless survived his famous mother by only a year. He died in
1969—there's no record of the cause—and is buried at the Camp
Pendleton rodeo grounds.

Dauntless

Dauntless was foaled at 4:00 a.m. on March 2, 1959, at the base stables. This time, paternity of the steel-gray colt was not disputed. His sire was a registered gray Arabian named Mayr Nasr, who "boasted a long line of registered Egyptian folk"[4] and was owned by Maurita Brown of Santa Barbara, California. Mayr's own sire, Radban Lel Azrak, and dam, Nasr, were from Egypt. Dauntless's grand sire was a horse named Prince Mohammed Ali of Egypt.

Another Colt, Another Contest

As with Fearless, the Corps had a contest to name the new colt; unfortunately, none of the names passed muster with the sole judge, Marine Corps Commandant Randolph Pate. So he chose a name himself, dubbing the newborn "Dauntless." Unlike the last time, no one was chosen to receive a prize or pose for a picture in the *Pendleton Scout*. That the Commandant of the entire Corps took it upon himself to name the colt shows how much Reckless and her offspring were loved and highly regarded by the Marines.

Private Dauntless, Public Figure

Dauntless's enlistment at the age of four months was helped along by a friendly, PR-focused Corps eager to build on Reckless's feel-good story, which now was a tale of multi-generational loyalty to the Marines. Six days before the Pendleton enlistment ceremony—authorized by General Pate and featuring a parade and review—there was an interesting bit of back-story detailed in *The Pendleton Scout*:

"The enlistment of Dauntless was authorized in a letter from Marine Corps Headquarters on May 5, which solemnly stated that, 'after deliberation of a board of officers gladly convened for the

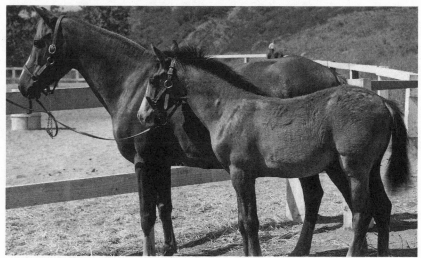

Reckless and Dauntless. *Command Museum, Marine Corps Recruit Depot, San Diego*

purpose, the normal enlistment requirements would be waived in the case of Dauntless.' It further assigned the young four-legged enlistee to the 5th Marine Regiment 'for recruit training as deemed appropriate by the commanding officer.'"

The base paper noted that Pate's letter authorizing the enlistment ceremony included an addendum by Major General E. W. Snedeker, the 1st Marine Division's commanding general, who was among those expected to join the reviewing party on the big day:

"He wrote, in part, 'Members of the Corps both past and present—as well as every officer and man of the 1st Marine Division—enthusiastically welcome aboard the son of a distinguished combat veteran whose heroic exploits have achieved a permanent niche in the proud history of country and our Corps.'"[5]

On July 1, 1959, Dauntless stood quietly as more than five hundred well-wishers watched the full-scale regimental parade and review. The formal oath was administered by Colonel Tolson A. Smoak, commander of the 5th Regiment. He was also the 1st Marine

Sgt. Tommie Mack Turvey Sr. poses with his favorite rodeo horse, Dauntless.
Tommie Mack Turvey Sr.

Division Association representative overseeing "the general welfare of Reckless and her colts."

Colonel Smoak's administering of the oath to Dauntless, which turned the colt over to the 5th Marine Regiment for "hoof training," concluded: "...*having fulfilled all prerequisites for enlistment, including an oath in horse language, I do hereby enlist him, Dauntless, a private in the United States Marine Corps.*"

The Pendleton newspaper noted: "After receiving 'recruit train-ing' with the 5th Marines, Dauntless will be transferred to the Camp Pendleton Base Stables where he will carry out his duties in company with his mother and brother."[6]

Rodeo Marine Dauntless was more than a trail guide. He also worked in the Marine Corps rodeo and was the favorite horse of Sergeant Tommie Mack Turvey Sr., who ran the rodeo grounds for three years.

"I used to ride Dauntless in the Grand Entry. At the rodeo, it's the first entrance when everybody who's in the rodeo, all the rid-ers—except the rough stock riders because they're back getting their horses and bulls ready—parade out into the arena. I led the Grand Entry on Dauntless.

"I kinda hogged that horse for myself because I liked him so much," Turvey said, smiling. "I controlled what saddles went on what horses, and who rode what horses at the rodeo grounds, so I just always used Dauntless because I liked him so well."

Dauntless was used as a "bull dogging" horse. In bull dogging, a steer bolting from a stall is flanked on both sides by riders on horseback. As the steer runs between them, one rider leaps from his horse onto the steer, to "bull dog," or wrestle him. "The bull dogger will be the rider on the left side. He's the one that actually gets off the horse and the horse has to run by; he can't stop, it's got to run by and drop you off on that steer's head."

Turvey remembered Dauntless as an outstanding bull dogger. "Once they open the chute, you have to give the steer about an eight-foot head start. Your horse has to pause a beat or two, and then boom—he has to go catch that steer and run by him. Daunt-less could put you on that steer from zero to thirty miles per hour in three seconds. And when he'd pass a steer, and you'd get off, he wouldn't quit on you and leave you hanging in mid-air. Every time we'd put Dauntless in the chute, he would always score."

Dauntless was also used as a "hazer," or guide horse. "The hazer is the guy on the other side," Turvey said, "and he'll push the steer straight so the bull dogger can get off.... Dauntless could go on either side, but mostly for three years I used him for my doggin' horse because he was so good and I would haze for everybody else on him."

Dauntless (L) and Chesty (R) attend memorial dedication ceremony.
Debbie McCain

Another of Dauntless's jobs was to rescue cowboys thrown from bucking horses. When a cowboy fell off, a rider astride a "pick up" horse would race to the bucking horse, yank the flank strap off, and bring the fallen cowboy to safety.

"That horse did it all. He just did it all," Turvey said. "I was real choosy over who I let ride that horse. He was actually one of the best horses for anybody. But he just had the looks and the muscles; everything was where it should be. He was the perfect build for a horse to do anything. And he had the perfect temperament.

"I could put a halter on him and ride him and he wouldn't take off on me. I could put a kid on him. I could take him in the Grand Entry. I could pick up bucking horses on him and he was fast enough to bull dog and win. He was something else, that's for sure."[7]

Memorial for Mom

On November 20, 1971, the 1st Marine Division unveiled a memorial headstone for Reckless at the entrance of the base stables.

Dauntless and his brother, Chesty, were in attendance for the tribute to their mother.

It's unclear when Dauntless died; records vary. In 1983, however, the Corps reported in a press release that Dauntless survived both Fearless and Chesty and added, "Dauntless is living out his old age in retirement at the base stables. While it's unknown if Dauntless is actually the last of Reckless's line, the 25-year-old gelding is the only relation left at Camp Pendleton. Sadly, a proud tradition appears to be nearing its end."[8]

When he died of natural causes, Dauntless was buried alongside both brothers at the Camp Pendleton Rodeo Grounds, an appropriate place for a horse who loved the rodeo so much.

Chesty

Chesty was foaled on Sunday, December 6, 1964, at 10:30 a.m. His sire was a registered bay thoroughbred—the same sire listed for Fearless in Camp records. Chesty's color was seal brown.

Chesty is introduced to his new name. *Camp Pendleton Archives*

Breaking with Tradition:
No "Less" on Chesty

Chesty was named for Lewis "Chesty" Puller, the most decorated Marine in Corps history, who retired as a lieutenant general in 1955. There was even a rumor that Puller had ridden Reckless while in Korea.

The winning entry in the contest to name him came from Staff Sergeant Philip T. Poe, a wire chief with the 2nd Battalion, 5th Marines. Poe's prize: a card redeemable for fifteen rides at the base stables.

Don't Mess with Chesty

Chesty was much bigger in size than his two brothers because his sire was a thoroughbred. Because of this, he was used mostly as a trail guide horse. "Chesty was just an exceptional horse," recalled Tom Fant, Chesty's main handler for several years at the base stables. "I loved that horse. He was great. We'd go out on trails and do brush poppin' and stuff, just having a great time. That horse was special."

Chesty was incredibly picky about who he would allow onto his back. Fant remembered when the base stables manager, Sergeant Major William Stepp[9] "let some boy come there who said he could ride anything with hair on it. Mr. Stepp called for Chesty to come up. And they never made it out of the paddock area. He was thrown right there in the dirt. Chesty also put one of my friends out of the Marine Corps because he rolled over on him and messed up his knee. He was trying to ride him one day and Chesty didn't like other people riding him." Even though Fant was among Chesty's favorite mounts, he still was thrown eighteen times and rolled over on three times.

Fant recalled the time several young girls who worked at the stable got a big straw hat and cut holes for the ears and plopped that

Tom Fant up on the back of his favorite horse, Chesty. *Debbie McCain*

hat on Chesty's head. Unlike his mother with the Australian hat, Chesty loved this one. "We'd put that hat over his ears and he'd stand underneath the shade tree on three legs with this big ol' hat on and fall asleep. He was so funny-looking. The hat made him look like a donkey, but he didn't care.

"And there would be times when guys would come out to ride and brag about their skills, so here they come leading Chesty out there with that hat on and the guys all thought this horse looked stupid and was no match for them. And then all of a sudden they'd get up there on his back and he'd throw them right there in the dirt and then he'd go back and stand under the shade tree, drop his ol' head and fall asleep on three legs.

"He was an exceptional horse because nobody could ride him except me and I was stupid enough to get out there and *do it!* He and I had a great time together."

Fant wanted to buy Chesty. "I loved that horse. I really wanted to keep him and I offered $500 for him. But Mr. Stepp said he couldn't sell him."[10]

Chesty Leaves Home

Fant must have been frustrated when, a few years later, the stables ended up giving Chesty to Sergeant Lynn Mattocks, Chesty's former rodeo rider.

"When Chesty became old enough to start breaking and schooled, we took him to the rodeo grounds, and he was a big dark thoroughbred horse. And so these guys who got sent down to the stables for sixty to ninety days to help clean up poop and stuff, they didn't know anything about horses. But the people who were assigned at the stables permanently were screened and selected. And Chuck Dacus worked at the stables, and he was quite a horseman. So Colonel Ace Bowen[11]—who was quite a cowboy, knew I was a professional cowboy before I came in—so it was Chuck and I who had the knowledge to do it. So we were given these horses to break.

"Well, Chesty came around, a really, really good horse, but you gotta remember that we were professional horsemen, so to speak— I'd been breaking colts since I was 14 years old—and here I am up in my twenties now and we had him working really good.

"So they decided, 'Hey, why do we only use him at the rodeo grounds four months out of the year? Let's send him over to the stables and let him pay for his keep.'

"Well, he was still pretty young, and they sent him over there. And of course, he's with Marines that are there [for] sixty to ninety days of temporary assigned duty; they're the ones that take the trail rides out. Well, they don't know how to ride and ninety percent of the people they had as trainers and riding instructors didn't know, either.

"So anyway, they just were too heavy-handed. This horse had a nice easy mouth, soft mouth, and he would work off the body and everything, and he was working real good as a young horse as long as we who knew what we were doing were riding them. And that's what they saw in the rodeo arena.

"So when the rodeo was over, they took him over to make him a trail guide horse. Well, these guys were holding up on him. They'd squeeze him and he'd take off because that's what he was trained to do. And then they'd jerk back on him and got him to rear up and flipping over backwards. Then he became a danger.

"And there was something in the [ownership] papers for Reckless that said that these horses could not be sold from the base. So what they did was, Colonel Ace Bowen and I think Colonel Jinx McCain—I believe he was the special services officer at the time—and I made a deal. They didn't sell the horse to me. But because he was deemed to be unsafe for the stables and I was deemed to be a professional cowboy horseman, the horse went to me, and I made a donation to the Navy [-Marine Corps] Relief Society. And so that way Chesty was never sold to me.

"And so in essence, he was given to me because he was a danger for the people over there at the stables who were not professional horse people.

"I brought Chesty home to my ranch in Murietta and I rode that horse all over that ranch. And one time I was riding up by Idyllwild, California. And I was up there getting cattle and this guy, he was in Korea in the 5th Marines and he knew Sergeant Reckless. And when he found out that I was riding Chesty...he just went spastic: 'I gotta have that horse. I've gotta have that horse.'

"And so I said, 'He's already seventeen or eighteen.'

"And he said, 'I don't care, I've gotta have that horse.'

"And so about a year later, I ran into him at the Swingin' Cafe in Temecula. And he said, 'You still got that Chesty horse?'

"And I said, 'Yessir, I do.'

"And he says, 'When can I come and get him?'

"And I looked at him and said, 'You're really serious, aren't you?'

"He says, 'I've been waiting for a year.'

"And I said, 'You know what, I'm going through a divorce. Bring the trailer.'

"He says, 'It's on the truck right now.' And so that's where Chesty went. And he told me later on, 'Oh, I love that horse. We can cover more miles across those pastures out there. Nobody can stay up with us.'"[12]

Chesty's last reported public appearance was the headstone dedication ceremony for Reckless at the base stables in the fall of 1971. Beyond the recollections of Fant and Mattocks, there is precious little information on Chesty, even down to when he died. Camp Pendleton records indicate 1976, of natural causes. But Mattocks claims Chesty died of old age sometime in the early 1980s.

Chesty is buried with his two brothers at the Camp Pendleton rodeo grounds.

Sadly, Fearless, Dauntless, and Chesty were all gelded; there were no offspring to carry on the bloodline of their heroic mother.

PART IV

IN MEMORIAM AND MORE

I am also sure that in the land of rewards that lies beyond, this chestnut mare with the handsome, blazed face and [three] white stockings is mingling even now among the men of the Corps. And when there's a load to be carried, when there's ammo to be rushed up to the front, she'll always be there to perform her tasks beyond the call of duty, in the spirit of "Semper Fidelis": Always Faithful.
—George Putnam, Los Angeles television news anchor

CHAPTER 13

"FAMED MARINE HORSE 'RECKLESS' DIES AT 20"

—PASADENA (CALIFORNIA) *STAR-NEWS* HEADLINE

Reckless's passing on May 13, 1968, came at age twenty—a respectable lifespan for any horse, much less one who had endured as much as she had. One final time, she was front-page news across the country.

Reckless had enjoyed a long, rich life with the Marines. In later years, however, she clearly suffered; the arthritis in her back and hip made it difficult to get around and her left rear leg was lame. Then there was the developing laminitis.

"We didn't talk too much about the laminitis," recalled Sergeant Art DiGrazia, who helped care for Reckless. "We knew what she had and just kept her comfortable. We gave her some Butazolidin [anti-inflammatory medicine] and that seemed to help her quite a bit. She got around okay on the 'Bute."[1]

Yet, Reckless's infirmities proved more than uncomfortable; they indirectly led to her death.

"She was out in the colonel's pasture," Eric Pedersen Jr. recounted. "When she didn't come in for her feed, they went out to look for her."

The Marines found Reckless severely injured, having fallen through a barbed wire fence into a ravine. "She wasn't in good shape. And right away we called Doc Miller," DiGrazia said.

They rushed Reckless into surgery, but her injuries were so severe that Miller felt compelled to make a veterinarian's ultimate medical decision: she had to be put down. "I haven't gotten over that yet," Pedersen painfully recalled forty years later.[2]

Reckless, whose war heroics and colorful postwar life were the stuff of legend, was buried quietly, without fanfare, in an unmarked grave behind the base stable office at Camp Pendleton. Today, unless you ask where the grave is, there's no way to identify it.

"At that time, we didn't know what they were going to do with the office there," DiGrazia recalled. "[Stables manager] Mr. Stepp, God bless his soul, said, 'We're just going to bury her next to the office,' and then he figured there would be a big memorial built for her there at some point in time. So we got the backhoe out there and that's where we did it.

"We wanted to get her underground as soon as possible. But the utmost care was taken to make sure that her resting place was in good shape—that even in death, she was really comfortable. And we made sure there wasn't a lot of public around when we did bury her."

It was a small, somber ceremony. "Everybody just stood there kind of very silently," DiGrazia reflected. "I think I said something like, 'God bless her for what she did,' but if anybody said anything, they said it to themselves."[3]

Memorial Erected in Reckless's Honor

On November 20, 1971, the 1st Marine Division Association dedicated a stone memorial at the stables' front gate, where some of her bones were re-interred after being exhumed from the gravesite behind the stable office building. Finally, Reckless received a burial with full military honors.

"The spirit of Reckless is embodied in the proud carriage of 'Dauntless' (l) and 'Chesty' (r) offspring of the 1st MarDiv's famous mascot, 'Reckless.' They are saddle horses at the Base stables where the 1st MarDiv Association will place a dedication marker at 10 am, Nov 20, in honor of the Mongolian mare which earned her position as Division mascot by carrying ammunition during combat in Korea. 'Reckless' lived out her remaining 19 years at Camp Pendleton's stables and was buried there in May 1968." *Original photo caption from* Pendleton Scout, *Nov 19, 1971, 10. Photo courtesy of Debbie McCain*

The black granite marker has a picture of Reckless wearing her parade blanket. A bronze plaque below it includes the following inscription:

In Memory of
R E C K L E S S
Pride of the Marines

KOREA

July 1949–May 1968

SSgt. U.S. Marine Corps, Recoilless Rifle Platoon, 5th Regiment

1ST MARINE DIVISION

The memorial headstone that sits at the entrance of the Stepp Stables at Camp Pendleton to this day. *Nancy Latham Parkin*

About 120 Marines and members of the association turned out for the ceremony. "This memorial that we dedicate today," said Major General George S. Bowman Jr., the base commanding general, "will insure that others will know that the Marines value courage and devotion to duty and by knowing what we value, they will know who we are."[4]

Moments later, he added, "She could have balked and refused to make those torturous trips up and down the hill.... A lesser animal would have done so."[5]

A Fitting Eulogy and Tribute

Longtime Los Angeles television news anchor George Putnam gave the eulogy at the dedication ceremony. Two nights later, he told his KTTV evening news audience about the truly unique American heroine:

> As a Marine and as a horseman, I am privileged to honor this magnificent mare.
>
> Whenever horsemen gather, the discussion usually turns to which was the greatest horse of all. You'll hear the names of Lexington, Man o' War, Count Fleet and Swaps, among the thoroughbred owners.
>
> And, if there's a Standardbred enthusiast present, he'll speak of Greyhound and Dan Patch.
>
> If you're an Army man, your horse served with the artillery—a wheel horse named Putnam.
>
> But, if you're a Marine and with the 1st Marine Division, then, for you, there's only one. She was Reckless—Pride of the Marines.
>
> She had the courage of a lion. She was shot through with determination. She was deep through the heart, as a good horse always is. And she took her name from the

weapon she served—the Recoilless 75 millimeter can-
non—the reckless rifle. . . .

And here it was, at these stables, that the magnificent
mare enjoyed the rewards of a combat-tested Marine
who's come home from the war. She was treated royally.
And her blazed face appeared at many public occasions.
And this always brought donations to the scholarship
fund.

Reckless produced four foals: Dauntless, Chesty—
named for Chesty Puller—Fearless and an unnamed filly.
So, she lives here today in these two fine offspring, Dauntless and Chesty.

Horsemen have a saying that a good horse should be
deep through the heart. In addition to being a point of
conformation, it provides stamina and courage. In every
sense of the word, the brave mare Reckless was deep
through the heart.

And so . . . we paid our respects to the gallant mare at
the base stables and you never saw so much brass as gathered there in tribute . . . and looking down upon this scene
from the pastures adjoining were broodmares and young
foals, keenly alert that something was in progress.

I am sure that all of us who are gathered here—members and friends of the Corps—held the same affection for
her as those who were privileged to fight beside her.

I am also sure that in the land of rewards that lies
beyond, this chestnut mare with the handsome, blazed
face and [three] white stockings, is mingling even now
among the men of the Corps. And when there's a load to
be carried—when there's ammo to be rushed up to the

front—she'll always be there to perform her tasks beyond the call of duty, in the spirit of 'Semper Fidelis': Always Faithful.

And now she is at rest. And where she is, the grass is tall and green. And the hillsides bright with flowers.

Sergeant Reckless—Pride of the Marines—is at rest.[6]

CHAPTER 14

A LEGACY
LIVES ON...

Except for an occasional article or acknowledgment, after her 1968 death Reckless all but disappeared from public consciousness. The world simply had moved on; she was a forgotten hero from a forgotten war.

But all that has started to change. Two generations later, Reckless once again is getting her due.

On November 10, 1989, the Marine Corps' 218th birthday, the first race at Aqueduct racetrack in New York was dubbed "The Sergeant Reckless," thanks to the efforts of Charlie Murphy, a former Marine who worked at the track, and Bruce Lombardi, secretary of the New York Racing Association.[1]

Picture that appeared in *Life* magazine of Lt. Eric Pedersen and a young admirer. *Nancy Latham Parkin and USMC History Division, Quantico, VA*

Life magazine's 1997 special collector's edition, "Celebrating Our Heroes," offered a brief account of Reckless's exploits and placed her in such heroic company as George Washington and Mother Teresa. Also in print, the July 2011 issue of *Cowboys & Indians* magazine, included a piece about Reckless by equestrian writer Elizabeth Kaye McCall.

Reckless began moseying her way back into the limelight. Thanks to the website www.SgtReckless.com and a dedicated Facebook page, Reckless is again receiving the appreciation she once enjoyed and rightfully continues to deserve.

Yet many modern Marines at Camp Pendleton still have not heard her story. Perhaps that will change with this book and other efforts to memorialize the greatest horse in the history of the Marine Corps.

A Model Horse

Breyer Animal Creations®, which makes and markets collectible models of celebrated equines, now is selling a beautiful, finely detailed, twelve-by-nine-inch rendering of Sergeant Reckless, clad in her red blanket, complete with staff sergeant chevrons, medals, and the prestigious French fourragère. A portion of each sale is donated to the Sergeant Reckless Memorial Fund, to help underwrite the cost of monuments honoring Reckless.

An Uphill Battle

One such monument can now be found at the National Museum of the Marine Corps and Heritage Center in Triangle (Quantico), Virginia. On July 26, 2013, the Corps unveiled a stunning bronze sculpture of the remarkable horse, titled "An Uphill Battle," created by the artist Jocelyn Russell.

The dedication drew the Corps' top brass, including the Commandant, General James Amos, and the Marines' highest-ranking non-commissioned officer, Sergeant Major Micheal Barrett. "The President's Own" Marine Corps Brass Band Quintet provided the music as the U.S. Marine Corps Color Guard marched into position carrying the Corps' battle colors and the National Anthem was performed.

General Amos turned to an aging but hale veteran in full military dress, a soldier who had known Reckless better than most Marines all those years ago. "Sergeant Wadley, will you give the command to unveil Staff Sergeant Reckless?"

Harold Wadley cut quite a figure. Nearly eighty, he appeared fit and strong, apparently the result of working his Idaho ranch for years after leaving the Corps following service in the Vietnam War. Wadley had retained his military buzz cut, although now his hair was understandably thinner and grayer.

"Aye aye, Sir," Wadley said, turning to address two waiting Marines. "Unveil the Reckless statue."

As thousands watched, the two soldiers lowered the camouflage netting hiding the monument. Onlookers gasped when they saw her standing there. One remarked about the striking sculpture, "I swear, I just saw her *move*."

Sentries stand guard as the Young Marines look on in the background. *Mark Tenally*

Coinciding with the outdoor dedication was an exhibit inside the museum devoted to Reckless. "Thirty-seven hundred people came through the doors of the museum this day," observed museum director Lin Ezell, "three thousand of them we attribute to Reckless."[2] The media also turned out in impressive numbers, filling the national news that day with stories recounting the unique Marine veteran's adventures.

Perhaps the most important guests that day were those surviving Marines who had actually served with Reckless throughout her career in the Corps. Wadley was joined by Bob "Doc" Rogers, John Newsom, Mike Mason, Bill Janzen, Chuck Batherson, Paul Hammersley, Art Sickler, Art DiGrazia, Ken Riley, Fred "Dutch" White, Ken Latham, Guy Wagoner, and Nick D'Amber. Also in attendance were Larry and John Meyers, representing their father John Meyers Sr., who was too ill to make the trip himself, and Mary Alice Gehrdes and John Riley, representing their father, Bill Riley, who had recently passed away.

As if the emotional event needed any more natural drama, the July 26 date was selected because it was a single day before the sixtieth anniversary of the armistice that officially ended the Korean War.

Reckless and a few of her men who made the trip to honor her. Left to right: Paul Hammersley, John Newsom, Bill Janzen, Chuck Batherson, Nick D'Ambra, Kenny Latham. *Mark Tenally*

As such, the monument instantly seemed to honor all American heroes—so many of them forgotten—who'd served in Korea.

A second monument will be placed at Camp Pendleton in 2014, along with a long-overdue bronze marker on Reckless's unmarked grave, still located out of harm's (and attention's) way behind Pendleton's Stepp Stables office building.

But statues and markers lack the human element so important to keeping history alive for future generations. Sergeant Chuck Batherson put it this way: "Whenever I get together with Marines, I

Reckless in her glory. *Rick Burroughs*

always ask them, 'Do you remember Reckless?' If they say 'No,' I pull up a chair and say, 'Well, let me tell you about this incredible horse….' And the story lives on."

"There will be a full moon coming up over the ridge," Sergeant Harold Wadley reflected, so many years after he saw Reckless amid the chaos of war, "and there will be one of my horses standing in the corral, and I don't know why, but that image of Reckless comes right with that first full moonlight through the trees.

"It's an image you can't get rid of….

"I tell everybody I know that loves horses that here it is—here's an incredible story and here's something that you'll never ever see again. You just can't beat this story."

"I'll finish with this thought," a reflective Sergeant Mike Mason said following the dedication in Virginia. "Reckless was and still is a highly respected animal. She had done more during her tenure in the Korean War than most Marines would have ever thought could be done.

"She had nerves of steel; firmly dedicated to the mission for which she was trained; a Marine who has earned the respect and admiration of everyone. She earned every award and rank bestowed upon her and certainly earned her place in history. The legacy of Staff Sergeant Reckless will live on forever."

Perhaps Navy Corpsman Bob "Doc" Rogers said it best: "When you get right down to it, she's a national hero and her story needs to be preserved." In a letter, he wrote, "May her memory live as long as we have the Marine Corps."

Amen to that. I like to think it will.

To Reckless: Long live your memory.

Semper Fidelis—Always Faithful—Staff Sergeant Reckless

Korean War "Certificate of Appreciation" from the Secretary of Defense, Chuck Hagel, honoring SSgt. Reckless's service

"OPERATION: RECKLESS"

I have made it my mission in life to make Sgt. Reckless as famous as the other two acclaimed "S" horses, Secretariat and Seabiscuit. When I first learned of Reckless's story in 2006, I felt a biography, documentary, and screenplay were certainly in order. But something was missing, something more tangible. Why not a *national monument* to honor this uniquely American heroine?

When I began researching this book, maybe the first person I tracked down was Navy Corpsman Bob Rogers from Coffeyville, Kansas. I discovered Bob when I googled "Sgt. Reckless" back in 2006. Bob suggested a statue. I agreed and asked his help to make it happen. A few years passed before I could take on that task, since I was deep into writing the book and screenplay.

In 2009, I had just finished the screenplay when I picked up the trade paper *Variety* and read Steven Spielberg was going to direct a film adaptation of *War Horse*. I could hardly breathe and began pacing around my office.

I felt ill.

I soon discovered it was a different war horse—based on Michael Morpurgo's wonderful children's book.

But because one of the greatest directors in the world was making a war horse picture, no one in Hollywood would touch my script. I couldn't get a meeting.

So I shelved the script until *War Horse* came and went, hoping Hollywood would come around to appreciate the glory of my own war horse tale which, unlike the Spielberg film, was true.

By August 2009, the time seemed right. I set up the California 501(c)(3) tax-exempt, non-profit corporation Angels Without Wings, Inc. to raise money for the tax-deductible project. In February 2010, the IRS approved the application. Woo hoo! We could start raising money!

Next, I set up a DBA for the Sgt Reckless Memorial Fund that was specific to monument fundraising because Angels Without Wings, Inc. had a broader scope than just the monuments. I began registering in all fifty states so we could accept donations from across the country.

In late 2010, I turned to Bob for help in finding a sculptor. An artist himself, Bob's beautiful portrait of Reckless still hangs above my desk. He offered up four names, with Jocelyn Russell's at the top of the list.

Bob had known Jocelyn for more than twenty years. She was innovative, self-taught, and brilliant. Best of all, Jocelyn was a horse lover herself. She was just what we needed—and Team Reckless was formed!

Ride 'em Cowboy

Elizabeth Kaye McCall's landmark article in the June 2011 issue of *Cowboys & Indians* reintroduced Reckless and included pictures I'd happily provided. Word of Reckless's story began to spread.

The *Cowboys & Indians* article also helped bring Team Reckless member number four. What Sgt. Harold Wadley brought was invaluable: moving, first-hand accounts of life with Reckless. Even better, Harold, a published author on horsemanship,[1] knew just how Reckless's packsaddle was lashed with the canisters. His technical advice to Jocelyn was priceless during the design phase.

Picking a Site

With the team assembled, our next step was selecting a site for the monument. Or should I say, monuments. We wanted one at Camp Pendleton, where Reckless spent her final, fruitful years and was buried, plus one in the nation's capital, near America's other great monuments.

My friend Rebecca Rothwell, whose husband promoted Reckless to staff sergeant, strongly suggested the National Museum of the Marine Corps in Triangle, Virginia. I wasn't very familiar with the museum but loved the idea of Reckless being with her Marines. However, having always lived according to the phrase "Go big or go home," I had my heart set on the National Korean War Memorial on the National Mall. In my early research, it appeared we'd need nothing short of an Act of Congress to get the monument placed there—which could take years.

At Harold's suggestion, on August 1, 2011, I wrote of our plans to Marine Corps Commandant James Amos and Sgt. Maj. Micheal Barrett, the Corps' highest ranking non-commissioned officer. Included were supporting letters from Harold, Bob Rogers, John Newsom, Dutch White and Col. Richard Rothwell. We also sent word to Camp Pendleton.

I also started on the political side. My own senator from California, Dianne Feinstein, was an avid horse lover and had supported legislation against horse slaughter. Her aide, Molly O'Brien, agreed to a meeting in late September. Jocelyn flew in from Washington state for it, and we used her presence as a reasonable excuse to visit Camp Pendleton, to scout locations and meet the powers that be.

Let the Meetings Begin

On September 28, Jocelyn and I drove south to Pendleton, where Capt. Andrew Wallace of the Judge Advocate's Office couldn't have been more supportive. But due to the huge cost of installing the monument there, we'd need approval all the way up the chain of command—to the Secretary of the Navy himself. This could take months.

Capt. Wallace said something that warmed our hearts: "I'm looking forward to one day, maybe ten years or so from now, bringing my kids to the base and showing them this monument and saying, "Kids, your dad had something to do with this."

We left the meeting stoked. "He's already bringing his kids!" We squealed like schoolgirls.

Next morning with Molly O'Brien, the light went on when she realized we weren't looking for money—we wanted to *donate the monument*. She promised to personally contact people in Congress and a friend at the Smithsonian Institution about getting the monument situated on the National Mall.

Alas, I soon learned the National Mall was off-limits for new monuments. And a nice gentleman from the National Capital Regional Office said animals weren't honored this way.

I cleverly countered with, "She wasn't a horse—she was a *Marine*!" I argued that while the memorial didn't fall under 8903 (b) Military Commemorative Works, maybe it could qualify under 8903 (c)—Works Commemorating Events, Individuals, or Groups.

It was a no-go. I was beating a dead horse.

Ironically, that rejection was the BEST thing that could have happened to us because it opened a window on Plan B—the National Museum of the Marine Corps in Triangle, Virginia.

What an amazing place and incredible opportunity to have Reckless showcased. The museum was just finishing the adjacent Semper Fidelis Park, a mile walk through beautiful woods with Marine Corps memorials along the way.

It was the ideal site.

Sorry ... Wrong Number!

I still hadn't heard from the Commandant's office about my monument material. I didn't have his number, so I googled the Commandant's phone number at the Pentagon. It came up!

"Hi, I'd like to speak to the Commandant's aide, please," I said in my most professional voice.

"Ma'am?" replied the nice-sounding sergeant manning the phone. "You what?"

"I'd like to speak to the Commandant's aide. I'm following up on a letter I sent to the Commandant about a horse."

"One moment please, Ma'am." He put me on hold.

"Ma'am? Where are you calling from, ma'am?"

"Camarillo, California."

"Ma'am. One moment please, ma'am." He put me on hold again, this time for a good minute. Silly me. I realized he wasn't asking me for my location, but my company.

"Ma'am. You're calling about a horse, ma'am?"

"Yes, a horse. Sgt. Reckless, the Korean War horse. Ever hear of her?"

"No, ma'am. One moment please, m'am." As I waited some more, it occurred to me he might be tracing my call. Helicopters could be hovering overhead any minute. He put me on hold a few more times until it dawned on me what number I'd called.

"Sir," I began nervously, "I'm very sorry but—is this the ... *War Room*?"

Long pause. "Ma'am, yes ma'am."

My cool demeanor collapsed. "Oh, my God. I am so sorry! I didn't mean to call the War Room."

I started to blather. I must have sounded like a complete idiot.

"Ma'am, that's okay, ma'am."

Finally, he transferred me to the right number.

We Found a Home!

On March 7, 2012, our proposal for the monument and exhibit at the National Museum of the Marine Corps was approved. On

June 1, much of Team Reckless made the journey to Triangle, Virginia, to pick a site. Director Lin Ezell led us down a winding path to a lovely pastoral area surrounded by trees. There was no other site like it in Semper Fidelis Park and we jumped at it and started planning the ceremony.

For the dedication date, we wanted July 27, 2013, the sixtieth anniversary of the end of the Korean War. But the Department of Defense's 60th Commemorative Committee (KW60) had already reserved that date for the big national celebration featuring President Obama. Here's where I met Maj Guillermo (Billy) Canedo who was coordinating everything for the KW60—and thankfully his duties included helping us with the Reckless monument. Maj Canedo convinced us to move our dedication up one day, to Friday, July 26, so that instead of competing with the national celebration, we'd complement it and other events.

So, we had the site and the date. Now all we needed to get Reckless to the starting gate ... was money.

Playing Beat the Clock

I had a year to raise the $165,000 for the monument and dedication ceremony. And I had to do it in a disastrous economy. But with such a great story, I knew I could get this done. I didn't know how—I simply believed it was going to happen.

I snagged a list of supporters of the Marine Corps Heritage Foundation and began cold-calling. I also turned to friends, family, the internet—anyone who could help—including celebrities.

We worked out a tax-deductible fundraising plan for donations ranging up to $25,000—where with a certain gift level you would receive the bronze model of the monument as our gift.

But we were fighting the clock. In particular, Jocelyn hadn't yet finished her initial design and I needed funds to cover every step of the process. Amazingly, whenever another bill would come in, so would the money to cover it. The first to come in was none other than PFC Johnny Newsom—who will always be my Number One.

Funds came in from the website and the store, while the Sgt. Reckless Fan Club on Facebook was tremendously supportive.

A Horse of Blue

On December 14, I made the trek up to Jozzy's studio in Friday Harbor, Washington state to get my fingernails dirty working on the statue and to carve my initials into the base. What an amazing weekend and best of all—I did the tail! Actually, I covered it in clay and tried to add a sense of fluidity and motion. But it still seemed heavy; Jocelyn must've fixed the tail after I left. But when historians come calling, I'll stick to my story: I did the tail!

So there. Jozzy will cover for me.

I wanted to carve my initials into the base, but where? I considered the tail, where I'd worked so diligently. Jocelyn's husband, Michael, suggested, "What about putting them on the base, because *you are* the foundation of this monument."

Through tears of gratitude—prodded on, I think, by plum wine Harold had sent—I agreed. Ultimately, I etched my initials under her right rear leg—a moment that will stay with me always.

People Start Responding

Around Christmas time, I sent queries to horse-loving celebrities. Betty White and William Shatner responded immediately. I was truly touched. It's hard reaching out to well-known people because they're always being hit up for cash. That I quickly received checks from both stars was incredible.

Again I tried reaching Arthur Allen of ASG Software in Naples, Florida. For months, I'd left messages, after sending him photos of Reckless posing with Gen. Chesty Puller, whose monument at the Marine Corps museum Art had generously supported. But this time, Art answered the phone. When I introduced myself, he admitted somewhat sheepishly, "I owe you a phone call." I laughed and we talked. He was gracious and kind but said he could only make a pledge and needed a year to fulfill it because of other commitments.

"I can work with that!" I burst out, giddy and grateful for his generosity.

At 6 the following morning I nearly fell out of bed when my phone rang. Like most people, a call at that hour sends my mind racing in fears of an emergency. But when I recognized the churning sound of my noisy fax machine, I shrugged and drifted back to sleep.

Later, I wandered into my home office without my glasses and could only make out a completed, faxed pledge form from Art.

I thought, "That was sweet, he pledged $5,000." I was so grateful—until I finally put on my glasses and saw it said *$25,000!* I trembled so much, I thought I might faint.

A few weeks later, a pledge came in from Watts and Sally Humphrey, who bred Genuine Risk, the chestnut filly who won the 1980 Kentucky Derby. Sally was so excited about the Reckless project that she even referred us to friends who were potential donors. Sally said both she and Watts found their bronze model of the monument so moving that when they received it, they wept.

"The President's Own" to the Rescue

I rushed invitations out to people. Maj Canedo provided his Department of Defense mailing list of a bazillion VIPs. I also sent a personal invitation to the Commandant, Gen. Amos and Sgt. Maj. Barrett.

I received word that the Quantico Marine Corps Band, which I so desperately wanted for the dedication, had another engagement that day.

Now what?

I tracked down "The President's Own" Marine Corps Band at Marine Corps Barracks and called the scheduler. After all, these guys play for the president of the United States.

I wasn't above cajoling, pleading, or simple, abject begging. And wouldn't you know it—by the grace of God they said yes. Plus, we received special permission to play echo taps at the end of the program.

Friends to the Rescue

Fred Smith, the founder and chairman of FedEx, was next up. A retired, highly-decorated Marine captain, Fred served two tours of duty in Vietnam. And like Art Allen, he also was an ardent, longtime supporter of the Corps' museum. I'd met Fred years earlier through my dear friend, filmmaker Tom ("Billy Jack") Laughlin. Fred and his lovely wife, Dianne, were incredibly gracious and generous. Fred found Reckless's story poignant and felt the monument would be important to the museum.

Also gratifying was the loyalty of friends. Over dinner one night, my former college roommate Karen Storms said she wanted to donate because she knew how hard I'd worked on the project. Sisterhood forever.

Breaking Ground

At last, in June we broke ground for the site. I flew to Washington for the photo op of me putting foot to shovel and slinging dirt. I was excited but anxious—I still hadn't raised nearly enough money.

Rick Burroughs of Kline Memorials in Manassas, Virginia, was our monument installer. Rick was at the groundbreaking with his son, Nick, to mark off exactly where we wanted the plaza built and what we hoped to do.

When it was time, I could not for the life of me get that shovel into the ground. In my defense, it was a flat head tool, not a pointed spade and wouldn't penetrate earth, even when I jumped on it. I felt like such a chippy. Finally, Rick got the shovel started and I scooped and tossed. Mission accomplished.

Regnery Publishing

God winked so many times throughout this journey, you might think He had an eye twitch. That Divine tic showed up again in Washington at the groundbreaking. I was staying with a lifelong friend, Cheryl Shaw Barnes, who illustrates children's books and whose day job is with Regnery Publishing. After Cheryl briefed Alex Novak, who runs the company's history imprint, Alex asked for a meeting.

Alex loved the story and I admired what he was doing with their history books. So I submitted my book proposal to Regnery History. They offered a generous publishing deal—quite a thrill for a first-time author. Even better, they understood how I wanted the book presented and they felt the same way.

Help Is on the Way!

Another person I heard from, Rosary Bovello, was a member of the fan club. Rosary and her family wanted to help with the event, since they lived nearby in Maryland.

"Do you know a good local printer?" I asked. "I need to get five hundred programs printed and I don't want to have to ship them from LA."

Her response blew me away. "My husband manages a print shop. We would love to print the programs and donate them to you."

The July deadline was closing in, I remained far short of our financing goal and bills were piling up. I had a great main event planned—with Gen. Amos and Sgt. Maj. Barrett, the top two Marines on the planet, now on board. I also had a dozen Marines who'd served with Reckless (and their families) coming to pay respects.

In total, more than five hundred people were committed to attending, including Rep. Ander Crenshaw, the Florida congressman whose daughter, Alex, has been a devoted supporter of the fan club for years.

So it was unthinkable that the celebration could be staged without the guest of honor. I just had to get the statue there. But I had no idea where to find the rest of the money—until my Guardian Angel stepped up to the plate to offer a loan.

It was Alda Vandling. My mom.

She and my brother, Michael Holzbeierlein, both knew the stress I was under. They were proud of what I'd done and believed once people saw this beautiful monument, they'd step up to help pay it off.

I also think they didn't want to see me publicly humiliated if I failed to deliver the star of the show. I've never been more grateful for anything in my life.

The Installation

We were scheduled to install the monument just a week before its dedication. Dave Thompson, media relations director for the Commemorative Committee, suggested a "Where is Reckless now?" media campaign tracking her cross country trek from the foundry to our installer in Manassas, Virginia.

FedEx was the only shipper we trusted. I contacted Fred Smith and not only was the promotional tracking campaign implemented on our fan club site but FedEx shipped the monument *for free*. Only FedEx broke their sacred promise to deliver Reckless on time.

Instead, they got her there *three days early*.

We were so very grateful for FedEx's incredible act of generosity and support for this great heroine.

The installation was July 18, 2013. That morning, Lt. Gen. Robert Blackman, president and CEO of the Marine Corps Heritage Foundation and I walked down together to oversee the installation and address news media covering the event. Rounding the curved sidewalk, I saw workmen already had uncrated her and that Reckless, so mischievous in life, seemed alive and vital again, peeking out across the field.

My heart raced. I burst into tears. I got the pony to the show.

I went up and touched the saddle straps; they looked so real. Then, Gen. Blackman provided one of my favorite moments of the trip. He continued up the sidewalk for a look from a different angle, bowing his head as if paying silent tribute to this heroic Marine. The moment is frozen in my mind's eye and tattooed on my heart.

When museum director Lin Ezell arrived to see Reckless, I asked what she thought. "I expect her to move," Lin said, grinning.

As they lowered her onto the pedestal, I slipped some tail hair from the real Reckless into the base. There's a little piece of Reckless inside the monument, thanks to Debbie McCain, who collected the hair when she was a young girl at the Camp Pendleton stables.

It's Show Time!

The big three-day weekend finally arrived. Thursday night was a special Evening Parade for Korean War vets and their families, hosted by the Commandant and Mrs. Amos at Marine Corps Barracks in Washington; Friday was the dedication—our main event; and Saturday was the big show at the National Korean War Memorial when President Obama would speak.

The Evening Parade was amazing for its patriotic pageantry. It was hard not to feel proud to be an American.

On Friday—D-Day, as in Dedication—I was up at dawn. Actually, I'd hardly slept, worrying about heat and rain. But it was an absolutely perfect day.

First was the 10:30 a.m. unveiling of the indoor exhibit about Staff Sergeant Reckless. Only a few family and friends attended because it was a small area.

Lin Ezell led the way through the museum to the display, where the lead quote on the wall had been culled from one of Lt. Bill Riley's letters: "During the time of attack she hauled quite a bit of ammo up the hills and earned her feed." Riley's daughter, Mary Alice Gehrdes, and son John Riley were as moved as I was.

The exhibit included Reckless's original shoe; a halter tag on loan from the Marine Corps Recruit Depot Museum in San Diego; a bronze model of the monument; and a life-sized, three-dimensional cutout of Reckless with hands painted up the side so children could measure how many hands high they stood compared to Reckless.

Lin handed me scissors to snip a bowed ribbon she'd strung across the exhibit. A beautiful commemorative museum challenge coin was attached to a card as a keepsake. What a wonderful way to launch Reckless Day.

Working with both the Marine Corps Heritage Foundation and museum personnel was delightful. Everything was done with such precision; they even had golf carts shuttling people back and forth to the site because of the heat and the distance to the monument.

Robin Hutton cuts the ribbon opening the exhibit as Debbie McCain (R) and Mary Alice Gehrdes (L) watch. *Mark Tenally*

Joe Bles of The Young Marines—a national group comparable to the Boy and Girl Scouts organizations—brought more than a hundred youngsters to help out. They came from across the country to pitch in by handing out programs, seating guests, pushing wheelchairs to the site in the woods, and offering water bottles.

At last, it was show time.

Emceeing was GySgt. Allyson Fagga, a Young Marine from West Virginia. The bright, articulate girl had received the script only that morning, but recited beautifully, right in front of the Commandant and sergeant-major of the Marine Corps. Pretty heady stuff for a seventeen-year-old.

When the gunnery sergeant called for the entrance of the Official Party, Lt. Gen. Blackman, myself, Jocelyn Russell, and Harold Wadley strode to our seats. I was heartbroken that Team Reckless's own Bob Rogers couldn't be part of the speeches. But because of time constraints, the program had to be on the short side. At one point, they nearly cut me out of the program. At least Bob was in the front row cheering us on.

Then came the March on Colors by the Commandant's Official Color Guard. When the band played the national anthem, I got goosebumps.

When Lt. Gen. Blackman addressed the crowd, a cell phone in the audience began to ring. But it wasn't just anyone's phone. It was *mine*, stashed in my purse on the ground beside Karen Storms, just two rows back from the Commandant. Karen tried discreetly kicking it under the chair in front of her—the chaplain's chair—as the Commandant looked around for the source of that annoying ringtone.

I chuckled to myself as Karen struggled to hide it.

I was up next, followed by Harold Wadley, whose majestic speech from the heart included mesmerizing first-hand accounts of Reckless. Besides the red Mongolian mare herself, the good sergeant was the undisputed star of the ceremony.

After Harold, the band played "Anchors Aweigh" and "The Marines' Hymn." By then, I wanted to be a Marine. We then adjourned to the site to unveil the monument.

Hundreds slowly worked their way down the pathway to the memorial. Reporters and camera crews pushed through to get primo spots from which to shoot the unveiling. We had more news coverage that day than any other museum event since the Iwo Jima Memorial dedication. The broadcast networks, C-SPAN, newspapers, and South Korean television all clamored for spots.

Reckless was shielded by a camouflage netting held by two Marines in dress blues. The Young Marines formed a backdrop behind the monument—standing at attention, so proud.

As we waited for everyone to arrive, I saw the Commandant give something to Sgt. Maj. Barrett, who then turned to me. "Looks like you're about to get a love letter."

"Wha—? From whom?" Before he could say, I got the signal to begin the ceremony.

I introduced Jocelyn, whose beautifully descriptive remarks culminated with the admission she'd sobbed when Reckless left in the FedEx truck and she turned back to see a suddenly empty studio.

General Amos came forward. Instead of ordering the unveiling, he asked *me* to step up. Which was when Sgt. Maj. Barrett read a certificate of appreciation from the Veterans of Foreign Wars. *For me!*

As I stood there, I got the shakes. I tried to hold back tears. The Commandant wrapped an arm around me, steadying me during the pronouncement.

When the sergeant-major finished, he handed the citation to the Commandant, who presented it to me. This was nothing short of an out-of-body experience. So afterward, how did I thank the VFW?

Call it a Jim Thorpe Olympics moment. In 1912, Sweden's Gustav V told the double gold medal–winning American, "Sir, you are the greatest athlete in the world."

To which the unsophisticated Thorpe casually remarked, "Thanks, King."

Only in my case, I blurted out, "This *ROCKS!*"

Seriously.

I'm still cringing.

The Commandant called Harold front and center. "Sgt. Wadley, will you give the command to unveil the Reckless statue?"

What a well-deserved moment for Harold! Our own Sgt. Wadley, standing straight and proud and with a vigorous, "Aye, aye, sir!" turned to the corpsmen poised and ready at the covered sculpture. "Unveil the Reckless statue!"

Robin Hutton proudly shows her VFW Certificate of Appreciation. From left to right: Gen. James Amos, Robin Hutton, Sgt. Michael Mason, Sgt. Maj. Micheal Barrett. *Kathy Reesey*

As the camouflage drape dropped, a collective gasp rose. There aren't words to describe those next moments. The hundreds looking on froze in a human tableau, taking in the image of a magnificent creature depicted scaling a hill, her tail waving in the breeze like Old Glory, the heavy ammo canisters strapped to her side unable to slow her pace, stunt her will, or diminish her grace.

An almost palpable wave of emotion swept through the crowd.

Gen. James Amos salutes as Echo Taps is being played to honor Reckless and the other fallen heroes of the Korean War. Robin Hutton (L) and artist Jocelyn Russell stand proudly. *Official USMC Photo by Kathy Reesey*

The benediction, by Chaplain Hodges, was the prelude to my favorite moment of the eventful day. The Commandant called Jocelyn and I up to share a moment of silence, followed by the playing of echo taps. Hearing it and watching the onlookers crowded together was something I will never forget.

A Final Push

A temporary plaque adorned the monument with just the names of donors to date. I knew more gifts would come, once people caught news coverage of the monument.

That's just what happened. Joanne Pearson of Santa Barbara sent a check, then enlisted her daughter and son-in-law's support, Jill and Alan Rappaport. Joanne's late husband, Andrall Pearson, had been CEO of Pepsi.

Mike Mason, my VFW friend who'd served with Reckless in Korea, and his wife Reva also contributed. Mike had such a great time at the dedication that he just wanted to be a part of the monument.

Sadly, Art Allen couldn't make the ceremony, so I sent him pictures of his name on the temporary plaque and a link to C-SPAN's coverage of the dedication. I mentioned that the plaque was temporary because I'd borrowed money to deliver the sculpture, so new names would be added as I paid off the loan. He responded to say he wanted to help with the loan. I thought he meant he wanted to pay his pledge now instead of the following February.

"No," Art corrected me. "I want to give you $50,000 to help pay your loan." I screamed loud enough to rattle windows in Seoul. Not only was he sending his pledge immediately, but *he'd effectively doubled it*. I.was.stunned. What an amazingly generous man!

With Art's incredible largesse, all my pledges coming through and new donors popping up—including many smaller donations not reflected on the plaque—the monument at the National Museum of the Marine Corps was paid in full by December 1, 2013.

But our work wasn't quite finished yet.

An Update on Camp Pendleton

The Sgt Reckless Memorial Fund has joined with the Camp Pendleton Historical Society to raise funds for Reckless's monument and grave marker at Camp Pendleton. Our projected dedication date is November 10, 2014, the sixtieth anniversary of the day Reckless first clopped onto American soil. There's still time to be part of this unique piece of history!

Kids Say the Darndest Things

In November 2013, the museum and I were co-hosting a booth at the Equine Extravaganza in Doswell, Virginia. Museum docents helped at the event, where children could pose for pictures beside a life-sized pop-up drawing of Reckless.

An energetic docent named Sam absolutely nailed every question and presentation he gave on Reckless. And every time he'd hear a new tidbit from me, he'd add it to his repertoire. I was impressed and told him so.

"Thanks," Sam replied, "but did you hear how I got schooled by an eight-year-old?"

Turns out it was Adam, whom we'd met a week earlier at another event. Adam fell in love with and became an expert on Reckless.

At one point Adam was listening to Sam describe how, " ... the horse did this, and the horse did that ... "

Suddenly, Adam was tugging on Sam's arm, protesting, "She wasn't a horse!"

Sam looked at him, then turned back to the audience. Again, Adam interrupted. "No," the lad insisted, "she wasn't a horse!"

Finally, an exasperated Sam looked at Adam. "Son, what do you mean she wasn't a horse?"

Adam ran to the table, retrieved a flyer, pointed to the cover blurb and read aloud: "She wasn't a horse—she was a *Marine!*"

Smart kid.

And the legend lives on...

WITH THANKS AND GRATITUDE

Reckless was an amazing horse, a valiant warrior, and an incredible hero. It's been an honor, a privilege, and a blessing getting to know her. I hope you feel the same.

I have met some wonderful people on my journey with Reckless—individuals who never would have crossed my path were it not for that remarkable horse. Some served with her, some educated me on the horrors of the Korean War—especially the Outpost battles of March 1953—and others knew her only in her retirement or only by legend.

I don't know where to begin, so let's start with TEAM RECKLESS:

Debbie McCain, for becoming such a good friend and for so generously sharing some of Reckless's tail hair and her hind shoe;

Bob "Doc" Rogers, for his great stories, the beautiful painting of Reckless he sent, for helping with the memorial statues, and especially for recommending our amazingly talented artist, Jocelyn Russell;

Jocelyn Russell, for becoming a forever friend, for her magnificent design of the monuments for Reckless, and especially for letting me work on the monument and leaving my handprint on her;

Harold Wadley, for his remarkable stories of wartime heroics. They made me cry and helped get the wheels rolling for the monument;

The late Colonel Richard Rothwell and his lovely wife, Rebecca, who had my back;

And Private John Newsom, for helping track down as many people who knew Reckless as possible and for being my Number One.

With a team like this, no wonder it's been such a great ride.

I especially want to thank:

Nancy Latham Parkin for trusting me with the Reckless memorabilia collected by her late father, Joe Latham;

Both the late Bill Riley for sharing his memories, and his daughter, Mary Alice Gehrdes, for being his messenger and sharing her father's priceless letters home from Korea;

Eric Pedersen Jr. for sharing his father's stories and his own memories;

Faye Jonason of the Camp Pendleton Archives and Museum, for so much hard work in helping me and for her dedication to building the Reckless archives;

Boots Reynolds for allowing me to reprint part of his wonderful story, the tale that started me on this incredible adventure;

The late George Putnam and his partner, Sallilee Conlon, for sharing his experiences and eulogy;

So many others …

Nancy Hoffman and Walt Ford of *Leatherneck* Magazine. Walt, thanks so much for giving this civilian a crash course in the Marine Corps protocol and lingo. But most especially for personally proof reading my manuscript and making sure it was by the book and accurate for Marine Corps standards. I am forever indebted to you for this incredible act of kindness and support—and making me look good! Ooh rah! You rock!

To Ray Berry, Chuck Batherson; Chuck Dacus; Nick D'Ambra; Art DiGrazia; Milton Drummond; Paul Hammersley; William Janzen; Ken Latham; Ken Lunt; Lynn Mattocks; John Meyers; Bob Purcell; Bud Ralls; Ken Riley; Quentin Seidel; Ralph Sherman, Art Sickler; Ronald Stowers; Guy Wagoner; Fred "Dutch" White; and J. R. Willcut—just some of the many Marines who enlightened me about this horse and the horrors of the Korean War.

I am eternally grateful to you—you all are such heroes to me!

If there's anything I missed, anyone who knew Reckless that I didn't reach or pictures that people would like to share with the world, I will be posting updates on her website: www.SgtReckless. com. You can also join us on Facebook at the Official Sergeant Reckless Fan Club page.

I also have a special thanks to my family, especially my mom, Alda Vandling, and my sister, Layne Wilson—who read draft after draft and kept me on the right path, especially at the end; as well as my dear friend, Suzanne Finstad, whose never-ending support included the recommendation of my two great editors.

They are Melissa Blazek, who made sure my i's were dotted and my t's crossed; and Barry Grey—especially Barry—who made this book what it is and did an outstanding job in making my prose pop in a way

I never could have imagined. God bless you, Barry, for making my manuscript sing! I am eternally grateful—you are an amazing editor!

Thanks also go out to the late Jim Taggart, Andrew Geer's nephew, for permission to use his uncle's book on Reckless, as well as Geer's articles and pictures from the *Saturday Evening Post*, and the wonderful pictures and stories about Andy that he shared;

Tom and Mary Geer, for sharing biographical materials about their Uncle Andy;

And to Linda Sword Johnson, the great niece of Kay Pedersen, who so generously shared her amazing research and old newspaper clippings—I should be so organized!

Without any of you, I don't know where this book would be. Or *if* this book would be.

Very special thanks to Elizabeth Kaye McCall, whose wonderful article in the July 2011 issue of *Cowboys & Indians* kick-started the restoration of Reckless's place in history in a way I never could have imagined. Elizabeth also helped restructure the manuscript. Reckless and I can never repay you for your generous efforts. And to my gifted cartographer, Jay Karamales, whose gorgeous maps let us see where everyone was going—great job! Thank you so much!

A big thank you goes to TEAM REGNERY—my incredible publishing house! First to Cheryl Shaw Barnes, my oldest friend who sent me to Alex Novak, my fantastic publisher, in the first place! Life comes full circle my dear friend! To Marjory Ross; my editors, Harry Crocker and Maria Ruhl; and the wonderfully creative promotion and sales force of Mark Bloomfield, Patricia Jackson, Lindsey Reinstrom, and Nicole Yeatman, who had my back and fought for Reckless beyond the pale to make this the amazing book that it is…you all will never know the bounds of my gratitude.

I want to take a moment here to acknowledge the huge debt owed to Lieutenant Colonel Andrew Geer. Were it not for his breathtaking perseverance in bringing Reckless to America, who knows what would have happened to this one-of-a-kind heroine? Andy Geer was there every step of the way, acting purely out of love and respect for Reckless. I hope, somehow, Andy knows that I say thank you, sir. Thank you for all that you did for this incredible, heroic horse. I am eternally grateful.

• • •

And lastly, a special thanks to everyone who made the dedication ceremony of the monument at the National Museum of the Marine Corps such an amazing success with their hard work and dedication to our very special event, especially Gen. James and Bonnie Amos and Sgt. Maj. Micheal Barrett; Maj. Billy Canedo at the DOD 60th Commemorative Committee; Joe Bles and the Young Marines; Rick Burroughs and Kline Memorials; and everyone at the Marine Corps Heritage Foundation and National Museum of the Marine Corps, especially Lt. Gen. Robert Blackman, Lin Ezell, Mark Joyce, Jennifer Vanderveld, Sarah Maguire, Gwen Adams, Dennis Hofstetter, Mary Carpenter, Pam Dodson, Susan Hodges, and Gretchen Campbell. You guys were awesome!

• • •

I also dedicate this book to my dearest friend, the late Tom "Billy Jack" Laughlin, who not only taught me the nine ingredients in writing but also believed in me and this project every step of the way. He saw the writer in me long before I ever knew she was in there. For that, I always will be grateful. I miss you, my dear friend.

In closing, I want to thank God for allowing me to be His instrument in getting this incredible story told. I am so very blessed—and lucky.

And, last but not least, as I said in my closing remarks at the dedication ceremony, "Finally, I need to thank Reckless, for just being Reckless … Reckless, as you look down upon us here today, I hope you know how grateful we are for the comfort you have given us, the love of friendship you have led us to, and the journey you have taken us on. For me, personally, you have forever changed my life. There are no words to adequately express the emotions and gratitude that I feel. I'm sure everyone here feels the same. I love you. Semper Fidelis—Always Faithful—Staff Sergeant Reckless."

—Robin L. Hutton

FACTS AND FIGURES
AT A GLANCE

BORN: Unknown, but believed to be 1948

DIED: May 13, 1968, at Camp Pendleton, Oceanside, California, from injuries suffered in a fall through a barbed wire fence; buried there with full military honors.

HEIGHT: About 13 hands high[1]

WEIGHT: About 700 lbs., although other reports range as high as 900 lbs.

RANK: Staff Sergeant, U.S. Marines 1st Marine Division, 5th Marines

MILITARY DECORATIONS:
Two Purple Hearts;
Marine Corps Good Conduct Medal;
Presidential Unit Citation with Star;
Navy Unit Citation;
National Defense Service Medal;

MILITARY DECORATIONS: (CONT.)
United Nations Service Medal;
Korean Service Medal;
Republic of Korea Presidential Unit Citation;
French fourragère;
Staff Sergeant chevrons, all displayed proudly on her red
and gold blanket

OFFSPRING: Fearless (male, 1957); Dauntless (male,
1959); Chesty (male, 1964); unnamed (female, 1966, died
at one month of undetermined causes)

LIKES: Beer, coke, cake, flowers, candy, peanut butter,
scrambled eggs (with salt, no pepper), milk, and coffee—
in fact, almost anything edible, except the chow of a stock-
feed company seeking her endorsement

DISLIKES: Dogs and goats—the latter because they
reminded her of dogs

NOTES

PART ONE: KOREA

CHAPTER ONE

1. Andrew Geer, *Reckless: Pride of the Marines* (New York: E. P. Dutton, 1955), 13.

2. Ibid., 14.

3. According to the *International Encyclopedia of Horse Breeds*, these ponies resemble both the Arabian and Mongolian breeds. Their predominant colors are chestnut, bay, and black, but occasionally could be gray, black, white, cream-colored (cremello), or even spotted like a pinto.

    Cheju ponies, reports the *International Encyclopedia*, possess a "nicely shaped head with a straight profile, large eyes and small ears. The jaw is deep, tapering to a small muzzle. The neck is short and well muscled; the back short and straight; the croup (highest point of the hindquarters to the top of the tail) is gently sloped but the tail is set fairly high; the shoulder is often quite straight; the legs are strong and well muscled with clearly defined joints and tendons."

In an effort to save the breed, in 1987 South Korea declared the Cheju pony the country's 347th National Treasure. To maintain the status, the South Koreans race them at Jeju Racecourse Park, where as many as five hundred ponies are stabled at any one time. Unlike thoroughbreds and quarter horses, there is no registry for Cheju ponies. But all the ponies registered to race at the Jeju Racecourse are pure domestic. The top race of the year for the Cheju pony is the Hallaibo Cup. Cheju Island also is home to the majority of Korean thoroughbred horse breeders.

CHAPTER TWO

1. Andrew Geer, *Reckless: Pride of the Marines* (New York: E. P. Dutton, 1955), 122.
2. Personal letter Lieutentant Bill Riley wrote to his then sweetheart, Patty O'Leary, on May 17, 1953, after he joined the platoon in March 1953.
3. A private interview with Private John Newsom.
4. Personal interview with Sgt. Ray Berry.
5. Ibid.
6. Ibid.
7. Personal correspondence with Colonel Walt Ford.
8. Personal interview with Sgt. Ray Berry.
9. Ibid.
10. Personal letter to Lt. J. C. McCamic from J. H. Rinyak.
11. Personal interview and correspondence with Lt. J. C. McCamic.
12. Personal interview with Sgt. Ray Berry.
13. Ibid.

14. Pedersen buys his horse at the racetrack, Kim says goodbye. Geer, *Reckless: Pride of the Marines*, 119, 132–33.

CHAPTER THREE

1. Personal interview with Scout Sgt. Ray Berry.
2. Personal interview with Sgt. Chuck Batherson.
3. Personal interview with Sgt. Ralph Sherman.
4. Personal interview with Sgt. Ray Berry.
5. Andrew Geer, *Reckless: Pride of the Marines* (New York: E. P. Dutton, 1955), 134.
6. Personal interview with Julian Kitral.
7. Personal interview with Sgt. Chuck Batherson.
8. Geer, *Reckless: Pride of the Marines*, 138.
9. Sgt. Tom Griggs, "The Little Sorrel Mare," (n. p.). A similar article, "One Lady Who Saw Lots of Combat," in *Navy Times* (June 28, 1976), 28, referenced the line but did not quote Latham.
10. Geer, *Reckless: Pride of the Marines*, 138.
11. Personal interview with Sgt. Harold Wadley.
12. Personal interview with Sgt. Ray Berry.
13. Geer, *Reckless: Pride of the Marines*, 139.
14. Personal interview with Sgt. Ray Berry.
15. Personal interview with Dr. Robert M. Miller, DVM, Thousand Oaks, CA.
16. Geer, *Reckless: Pride of the Marines*, 139.
17. Notes from Nancy Hoffman's interview with Joe Latham for *Leatherneck* Magazine article, 1992.
18. Personal interview with Sgt. Ray Berry.
19. Nancy Lee White Hoffman, "Sgt Reckless: Combat Veteran," *Leatherneck* (November 1992), 78.
20. Geer, *Reckless: Pride of the Marines*, 139.
21. Interview notes, Nancy Hoffman.
22. Ibid.

23. Sgt. Tom Griggs, "The Little Sorrel Mare." (n. p.). A similar article, "One Lady Who Saw Lots of Combat," in *Navy Times* (June 28, 1976).

24. Hoffman, "Sgt Reckless: Combat Veteran," *Leatherneck*, 78.

25. Personal interview with Sgt. Ray Berry.

26. Personal interview with Sgt. Ralph Sherman.

27. Interview notes, Nancy Hoffman.

28. Hoffman, "Sgt Reckless: Combat Veteran," *Leatherneck*, 79.

29. Geer, *Reckless: Pride of the Marines*, 140–41.

30. Ibid., plus an article by John Springer, "San Diegan Figures in Story of Korean War's Hero Horse," *San Diego Union* (October 31, 1954), 21. See also Nancy Hoffman's interview with Kay Pedersen for a *Leatherneck* Magazine article, 1992.

31. Personal interview with Sgt. Harold Wadley.

32. Ibid.

33. From the personal papers of Joe Latham.

34. Andrew Geer, "Reckless, Pride of the Marines," *Saturday Evening Post* (April 17, 1954), 185–86 (*SEP #1*).

35. Geer, *Reckless: Pride of the Marines*, 145.

36. Personal interview with Sgt. Harold Wadley.

37. Personal interview with Sgt. Ralph Sherman.

38. Geer, *Reckless: Pride of the Marines*, 144–47.

CHAPTER FOUR

1. Andrew Geer, *Reckless: Pride of the Marines* (New York: E. P. Dutton, 1955), 148.

2. Ibid., 152–53.

3. Ibid.

4. Ibid., 10.

5. Personal interview with Sgt. Ralph Sherman.

6. David Dempsey, "The Horse Marine," *New York Times Book Review* (October 16, 1955).

7. Interview notes, Nancy Hoffman.
8. Geer, *Reckless: Pride of the Marines*, 156–58.
9. Ibid., 159.
10. Poker game summarized. Geer, *Reckless: Pride of the Marines*, 159–60.
11. Ibid., 160.

CHAPTER FIVE

1. Personal letter from Sergeant Ken Lunt.
2. James J. Fisher, "In Harsh Winter, War Lives," *Kansas City Times*, December 25, 1989.
3. Andrew Geer, *Reckless: Pride of the Marines* (New York: E. P. Dutton, 1955), 166.
4. Command Diary for Anti-Tank Company, Recoilless Rifle Platoon, January 1953, 1–3.
5. Geer, *Reckless: Pride of the Marines*, 164.
6. Command Diary for Anti-Tank Company, 3.
7. Geer, *Reckless: Pride of the Marines*, 168; Command Diary for Anti-Tank Company, Recoilless Rifle Platoon, February 1953, and March 2, 1953, 6.
8. Geer, *Reckless: Pride of the Marines*, 168.
9. Ballenger, *The Final Crucible: U.S. Marines in Korea, Vol. 2: 1953*, 84.
10. "Special Action Report of 25 February 1953, Raid on Enemy Hill," Command Diaries, 3.
11. Personal interview with Sgt. Ken Latham.
12. Personal letter from Lt. Bill Riley to Patty O'Leary, March 21, 1953, Mary Alice Gehrdes Collection.
13. Personal interview with Bill Riley.
14. Riley personal letter home, March 21, 1953.
15. Geer, *Reckless: Pride of the Marines*, 170.

CHAPTER SIX

1. Andrew Geer, "Reckless, Pride of the Marines," *Saturday Evening Post*, April 17, 1954, 186.
2. Geer, *Reckless: Pride of the Marines* (New York: E. P. Dutton, 1955), 171.
3. Taken from Sergeant William Janzen's paper, "The Reno Block," 1–2, given to author and published in Herbert G. Renner, *Letters of War: An Anthology of the Korean War Era* (n.p.: Publish America, 2007), 180.
4. Personal interview with George Johannes.
5. Personal interview with Harold Wadley.
6. Personal papers and interview with George Johannes.
7. Ballenger, *The Final Crucible*, 126.
8. Ibid.
9. Geer, *Reckless: Pride of the Marines*, 172.
10. Personal interview with John Melvin.
11. Personal interview with Harold Wadley.
12. Bill Daum, *Pendleton Fetes "Reckless," Old Korea Pal of Local Pair*, Mascots, Historical Reference Branch, Marine Corps History Division (Quantico, VA: USMC, 1954).
13. Personal interview with Harold Wadley.
14. Geer, *Reckless: Pride of the Marines*, 178.
15. John Burrus, "A Little Brown Mare: Marines to Note 'Reckless' Deeds," *San Diego Union*, November 16, 1971.
16. Geer, *Reckless: Pride of the Marines*, 180–81.
17. Personal interview with Chuck Batherson.
18. Personal interview with JC McCamic.
19. Personal interview with Harold Wadley.
20. Ibid.
21. Ibid.
22. Elizabeth Kaye McCall, "Sgt Reckless," *Cowboys & Indians*, July 2011, 94. Plus personal interview with Wadley.

23. Boots Reynolds, "Sgt Reckless, Mighty Marine," *Chicken Soup for the Horse Lover's Soul* (Cos Cob, CT: Chicken Soup for the Soul, 2012), 104.

24. Geer, *Reckless: Pride of the Marines*, 182.

25. *Operations in West Korea: U.S. Marine Operations in Korea, Vol. 5: 1950–1953* (Quantico, VA: USMC Historical Branch, 1972), 292–93.

26. Personal correspondence and interview with Harold Wadley. Also includes comments from Canadian radio interview with Harold Wadley, *The Drive with Karen Black*, CJOB/680, January 13, 2012.

27. George Johannes interview.

28. "Marines Recapture Vegas Hill," *Leatherneck*, March 28, 1953.

29. Geer, *Reckless: Pride of the Marines*," 184.

30. Ibid., 185.

31. Ibid.

32. Beaven, *The Battle of Vegas*, 59.

33. Because China was (and remains) the world's largest garlic producer—garlic is a staple of most Chinese recipes— the pungent herb can bring a powerful "garlicky" smell to human perspiration. As such, Chinese soldiers were said to "smell like garlic." This is caused by allyl methyl sulfide, a gas absorbed into the bloodstream when garlic is metabolized in the body. From there it enters the lungs, then the mouth (creating bad breath), and to the skin, where it emanates from the pores.

34. Beaven, *The Battle of Vegas*, 59.

35. Ibid.

36. Personal interview with Bill Riley.

37. Personal interview with Harold Wadley.

38. Personal interview Harold Wadley. For a more complete account of Sergeant Wadley's experience on Vegas, see Appendix 2.

39. Ed Sullivan, "Reckless: Pony is Marines' Mascot and Hero," *Omaha World Herald*, November 14, 1954, 92.

40. 1st Marine Division Command Diaries, March 1953, 3.
41. Meid and Yingling, *Operations in West Korea*, 307.
42. Bill Riley personal letter, dated April 5, 1953.
43. Riley personal letter, dated April 20, 1953.

CHAPTER SEVEN

1. Personal letter from Bill Riley, April 12, 1953.
2. Personal interview with Bill Riley.
3. Personal interview with Bill Riley.
4. Bill Riley personal letter, April 29, 1953.
5. An earlier amphibious training exercise, MARLEX-XX, was staged April 13–17, 1953, and included the 2nd Battalion and units of the 5th Marine Regiment. However, the Recoilless Rifle Platoon was not a part of it. Rather, the amphibious exercise one section of the RR Platoon did participate in was MAR RCT LEX I, on May 7–17, 1953.
6. Personal interview with Bill Riley.
7. In his article published in the April 17, 1954, in the *Saturday Evening Post*, Geer stated the ship was "LSU Landing Ship, Utility-527." However, in *Reckless: Pride of the Marines*, he referred to it as LST-527. Further research indicates that if the ship number was indeed 527, it most likely would have been the LST-527, renamed USS *Cassia County* following the Korean War. The vessel was among those used in the pivotal D-Day invasion of Normandy. It earned one battle star in WWII and two for Korean War service. However, what further complicates this research is that the Battalion Operation Plan 26-53 for MAR RCT LEX 1 states the ships used were LST 1096 (USS *St. Clair County*), LST 1084 (USS *Polk County*), and APA 208 (*Talladega*). So while it appears an LST was used in the landing, precisely which LST remains a mystery.

8. Battalion Operation Plan, Appendix J to Annex Baker to OPN Plan 26-53.

9. Eagle Trader is identified only by his rank and name in Andrew Geer's book *Reckless: Pride of the Marines*, but he was, presumably, an American Indian thoroughly acquainted with horses.

10. Letter from Bill Riley, May 7, 1953

11. Andrew Geer, "Reckless, Pride of the Marines," *Saturday Evening Post*, April 17, 1954, 31.

12. Geer, *Reckless: Pride of the Marines* (New York: E. P. Dutton, 1955), 189–90.

13. Command Diary May 1953, 2nd Battalion, 5th Mar Regiment, 5.

14. Geer, *Reckless: Pride of the Marines*, 191.

15. Ibid.

16. May 17, 1953, letter from Bill Riley.

17. Personal interview with Bill Riley.

18. May 27, 1953, letter from Bill Riley.

19. *Pacific Stars & Stripes*, June 9, 1953, 7.

20. Undated article from unidentified newspaper in St. Petersburg, Florida; among print articles collected by Joe Latham.

21. Ibid.

22. Sources vary concerning the number of rounds to be carried. The June 9, 1953, *Pacific Stars & Stripes* reported the handicap as, "half a load of 75-mm shells," while Geer's *Reckless: Pride of the Marines* stated the handicap was "eight rounds of 75 mm ammunition (192 pounds)."

23. *Pacific Stars & Stripes*, June 9, 1953, 7.

24. Geer, *Reckless: Pride of the Marines*, 7–8.

25. Ibid., 193–94.

26. Personal interview with Harold Wadley.

27. From a personal conversation with Don Menzies.

28. Charles R. Smith, ed., *U.S. Marines in the Korean War* (Washington, D.C.: USMC Historical Branch, 2007), 587.

CHAPTER EIGHT

1.   Andrew Geer, *Reckless: Pride of the Marines* (New York: E. P. Dutton, 1955), 13.
2.   Ibid.
3.   Interview notes, Nancy Hoffman.
4.   Geer, *Reckless: Pride of the Marines*, 197.
5.   Ibid.
6.   Ibid., 198.
7.   Interview with Private Newsom.
8.   Personal interview with Corporal Paul Hammersley.
9.   From a personal interview with Corporal Seidel.
10. Hammersley personal interview.
11. From a personal interview with Bob Rogers.
12. From a personal interview with Private Newsom.
13. Personal interview with Bob Rogers.
14. From a personal interview with John Meyers.
15. Personal interview with Michael Mason.
16. Ibid.
17. Hammersley personal interview.
18. Geer, "Red Carpet for Sergeant Reckless," *Saturday Evening Post*, October 22, 1955, 48.
19. Personal interview with Robert Pontius.
20. Geer, *Reckless: Pride of the Marines*, 8.
21. Ibid., 199.
22. R. R. Sims, "New Ammo Diet Gives 'Reckless' Loose Denture," *First Word*, March 31, 1954, 2.
23. Personal interview with Robert Pontius.
24. Ibid.
25. Sims, "New Ammo Diet Gives 'Reckless' Loose Denture," 2.
26. Geer, *Reckless: Pride of the Marines*, 200.
27. Interview with Bob Rogers.
28. A red and green braid with a metal tip, reflecting French recognition of the Marines in WWI. Worn on the left shoulder of

service uniforms (not field/utility uniforms) of Marines serving in the 5th and 6th Regiments. Since Reckless was attached to a unit of the 5th Marine Regiment, she rated the fourragère; when Marines transfer out of the 5th or 6th Marines, they can no longer wear the fourragère.

29. For a description of each medal, *see Glossary*.

CHAPTER NINE

1. Personal letter of Bill Riley, May 2, 1954.
2. Andrew Geer, "Red Carpet for Sergeant Reckless," *Saturday Evening Post*, October 22, 1955, 48.
3. Geer, *Reckless: Pride of the Marines*, (New York: E. P. Dutton, 1955), 203.
4. Geer, "Red Carpet for Sergeant Reckless," 48.
5. Ibid.
6. Ibid.
7. Geer, *Reckless: Pride of the Marines*, 206–7.
8. Geer, "Red Carpet for Sergeant Reckless," 52.
9. Geer, *Reckless: Pride of the Marines*, 207–9.
10. Ibid., 209.

PART II: A HERO'S JOURNEY

CHAPTER TEN

1. Andrew Geer, "Red Carpet for Sergeant Reckless," *Saturday Evening Post*, October 22, 1955, 55.
2. Geer, *Reckless: Pride of the Marines* (New York: E. P. Dutton, 1955), 211.
3. Bob Considine, "Heroic Horse Coming to U.S.," *San Antonio Light*, October 25, 1954, 8.
4. Parsons, Louella, "Louella Parsons on Hollywood," *Rockford Morning Star*, Oct. 28, 1954, p. 33.

5.   Geer, *Reckless: Pride of the Marines*, 212–13.

6.   Ibid., 213.

7.   Geer, "Red Carpet for Sergeant Reckless," 55.

8.   Ibid., 56.

9.   Geer, *Reckless: Pride of the Marines*, 216.

10. Ibid.

11. Ronald Johnson, "Marine Sgt. Reckless Lands Here—On All 4," *San Francisco Examiner*, November 11, 1954, 19.

12. Ibid.

13. www.marineclub.com, website of the Marines' Memorial Club and Hotel.

14. Marines' Memorial Association, *Crossroads of the Corps* 7 (November 1954).

15. Geer, *Reckless: Pride of the Marines*, 217.

16. *Crossroads of the Corps* 7.

17. Geer, "Red Carpet for Sergeant Reckless," 56.

18. This information, from one of three scripts used during the ceremonial cake cutting, is on the official Marine Corps website, www.marines.mil/Portals/59/Docs/CAKE_CUTTING_SCRIPT.pdf.

19. Ibid.

20. Marines' Memorial Association, *Crossroads of the Corps* 8, no. 1 (December 1954), 8.

21. Geer, *Reckless: Pride of the Marines*, 217.

22. Interview with James Taggart.

23. Interview notes, Nancy Hoffman.

PART III: LIFE AT CAMP PENDLETON
CHAPTER ELEVEN

1.   Andrew Geer, "Red Carpet for Sergeant Reckless," *Saturday Evening Post*, October 22, 1955, 56.

2.   Geer, *Reckless: Pride of the Marines* (New York: E. P. Dutton, 1955), 218–19.

3.   Ibid., 219.

4.   Ibid.

5.   Ibid., 220.

6.   Geer, "Red Carpet for Sergeant Reckless," 56.

7.   Geer, *Reckless: Pride of the Marines*, 222.

8.   Ibid.

9.   Ibid.

10. Geer, "Red Carpet for Sergeant Reckless," 56.

11. David Dempsey, "The Horse Marine," *New York Times*, October 16, 1955.

12. Lyle W. Nash, "Book Reviews," *Pasadena Independent Scene*, October 23, 1955.

13. Marine Corps Association Archives, February 1958, 13.

14. Geer, "Red Carpet for Sergeant Reckless," 56.

15. Ibid.

16. "Marine Association Buys Sgt Reckless," *Navy News*, December 1955.

17. Ibid.

18. "We Buy Reckless," *Old Breed News* 4, no. 10 (December 1955): 1.

19. Personal interview with Art Sickler.

20. Personal interview with Bill Riley.

21. Ibid.

22. Personal interview with PFC John Newsom.

23. "War Hero, Son Promoted during 5th Mar Ceremony," *Pendleton Scout* (June 20, 1957): 5.

24. Ibid.

25. Personal interview with Colonel Rothwell.

26. Personal interview with Art Sickler.

27. "War Hero, Son Promoted During 5th Mar Ceremony," 5.

28. Personal interview with James Taggart.

29. Neill C. Wilson, "Andy Geer: Great Marine, True Bohemian," *Bohemian Club Library Notes* 2.

30. Ibid.

31. "Best-Seller Author Andrew Geer Dies," *Marin Independent Journal* (December 23, 1957): 1.

32. Scott Vogel, "Convivial Pursuit: The Search for the Perfect Mai Tai Becomes a Labor of Love and Lore," *Honolulu Star Bulletin* (June 10, 2001).

33. S. A. Erickson, "Reckless Brings Back Memories," *San Diego Union* (July 31, 1966): 37.

34. Geer, "Red Carpet for Sergeant Reckless," 56.

35. "5th Mar Back Home after 110 Mile Hike," *Pendleton Scout* (March 13, 1958): 8.

36. "Marine Hikers Reach Camp Elliot Bivouac Area," *San Diego Union* (March 5, 1958): A-13.

37. Personal interview with PFC Art Sickler.

38. Personal interview with Sergeant Lynn Mattocks.

39. Personal interview with Jim Wright.

40. Personal interview with Jesse Winters.

41. "'All the Way' Fifth Marines Rest after Week Long 100 Mile Hike around Camp Pendleton," *Pendleton Scout*, no. 3 (January 22, 1959) 6.

42. Personal interview with Frank D. Brady.

43. Personal interview with Rebecca Meador.

44. Personal interview with Denise Dwyer Reed.

45. From a personal interview with Debbie McCain.

46. Personal interview with Sergeant Lynn Mattocks.

47. Personal interview with Corporal Jesse Winters.

48. "Commandant Promotes 'Reckless' to Staff Sgt," *Pendleton Scout*, no. 36 (September 3, 1959): 1.

49. Ibid.

50. Bill Parry, "Shoup Selection Defended by Pate," *San Diego Union* (September 1, 1959): 13.

51. "Commandant Promotes 'Reckless' to Staff Sgt," 1.

52. Ibid.

53. Ibid.

54. Geer, *Reckless: Pride of the Marines*, 8.

55. Private interview with Fred "Dutch" White.

56. Jack Murphy, "Top Del Mar Fillies Share Stage with Korean Plater," *San Diego Union* (September 6, 1959): 33.

57. Louis R. Guzzo, "Wave of War Movies Coming," *Seattle Daily Times* (July 18, 1960): 11.

58. "Horse Film Set," *Springfield Union* (October 8, 1960), 24.

59. Retirement ceremony comments from personal interview with Frank Brady.

60. "Sgt Reckless Transfers to FMCR; Subs & Quarters Provided for Life," *Pendleton Scout* (November 3, 1960): 5.

61. "Del Mar Honors SSgt Reckless," *Pendleton Scout* (July 27, 1962): 8.

62. Nelson Fisher, "Doc Jocoy Wins Del Mar Feature," *San Diego Union* (July 29, 1962): 147.

63. Ibid., 149.

64. Lester Bell, "Living Legends Meet at Review," *San Diego Union* (August 4, 1962): 15.

65. Personal interview with Dr. Robert L Miller, DVM.

66. Personal interview with Art DiGrazia.

67. Personal interview with Lynn Mattocks.

CHAPTER TWELVE

1. Boots Reynolds, "Sgt Reckless, a Mighty Marine," *Chicken Soup for the Horse Lover's Soul*, (Cos Cob, CT: Chicken Soup for the Soul, 2012), 102–8.

2. "Marines Become Godfathers: 'Sarge' Reckless Bears Offspring," *San Diego Union* (April 10, 1957), 9.

3. "1st Div Foal Name Test Undecided," *Pendleton Scout*, no. 16 (April 18, 1957), 1.

4. "Fifth Marines Massed to Watch Dauntless Take Oath of Enlistment," *Pendleton Scout* (July 9, 1959): 2.

5. "Latest Reckless Kin to Be Enlisted Next Wednesday—Public Invited," *Pendleton Scout* (June 25, 1959): 1.

6. "Fifth Marines Massed to Watch Dauntless Take Oath of Enlistment," 2.

7. Personal interview with Tommie Mack Turvey Sr.

8. Dennis Litalien, "Official Press Release No. 152-83," Joint Public Affairs Office, Camp Pendleton, May 24, 1983, 4.

9. Sergeant Major William F. Stepp, a Korean War veteran and Bronze Star with Combat "V" recipient, was Camp Pendleton's stables manager for twenty years. In 2003, the base stables were renamed in his honor.

10. Personal interview with Tom Fant.

11. Among other accomplishments, Marine Colonel A. C. "Ace" Bowen is remembered for developing and overseeing Camp Pendleton's rodeo grounds, which were renamed in his honor in 1982.

12. Personal interview with Sergeant Lynn Mattocks.

PART IV: IN MEMORIAM AND MORE

CHAPTER THIRTEEN

1. Interview with Art DiGrazia.

2. Interview with Eric Pedersen.

3. Interview with Art DiGrazia.

4. "Reckless Plaque Shown," *Pendleton Scout* 29, no. 47 (November 26, 1971): 1.

5. Ibid.

6. Excerpted from George Putnam's televised remarks, November 22, 1971, 10:00 p.m. news broadcast, KTTV Los Angeles, and his November 20, 1971, eulogy, reprinted with permission.

CHAPTER FOURTEEN

1. Nancy Lee White Hoffman, "Sgt Reckless: Combat Veteran," *Leatherneck* (November 1992): 85.
2. Personal conversation with Lin Ezell.

EPILOGUE

1. Harold Wadley, *Spirit Blending Foals Before and After Birth, An Old Way Continued* (Indianapolis: Trafford Publishing, 2003).

FACTS AND FIGURES

1. On p. 12 of Lt. Eric Pedersen's declassified April 7, 1953 Security Information Report on the Anti-Tank Company's actions for the previous month, he offers the following vital statistics on Reckless: "Age: five years (approximately); Weight: 550–600 lbs.; Height: seven hands; Characteristics: Four-legged, hoofed, vegetarian; Disposition: Docile." This was her height and weight in Korea, as best as Pedersen could estimate on the battlefield. Yet in photographs, Reckless appears noticeably larger than seven hands high. Camp Pendleton personnel and others also differed from Pedersen's estimates. Some claimed she was eleven hands high and about 700 lbs.; others insisted she was 14.1 hands high and about 900 lbs. Harold Wadley felt Reckless was between twelve-and-a-half and thirteen-point-two hands high and between 500 and 600 pounds. Her true measurements are lost to history.

BIBLIOGRAPHY

Books and Articles

"1st Div Foal Name Test Undecided." *Pendleton Scout*, no. 16, (April 18, 1957).

"5thMar Back Home after 110 Mile Hike." *Pendleton Scout*, March 13, 1958.

"'All the Way' Fifth Marines Rest after Week Long 100 Mile Hike around Camp Pendleton." *Pendleton Scout*, no. 3, January 22, 1959.

"Author of the Week: An Equine Heroine of the Korean War." *Council Bluffs (IA) Daily Nonpareil*, October 23, 1955.

Ballenger, Lee. *US Marines in Korea*. Vol. 2, *The Final Crucible, 1953*. Washington, DC: Brassey's, 2001.

Beaven, William E. "The Battle of Vegas," *Leatherneck*, March 1973.

Bell, Lester. "Living Legends Meet at Review," *San Diego Union*, August 4, 1962.

Berry, Henry. *Hey, Mac, Where Ya Been?* New York: St. Martin's Press, 1988.

"Best-Seller Author Andrew Geer Dies." *Marin Independent Journal*, December 23, 1957.

Bevilacqua, Allan C. "Korea: The Third Year of War," *Leatherneck*, July 2002.

———. "The Nevada Outposts." *Leatherneck*, March 2003.

———. "The Nevada Outposts: Counterattack." *Leatherneck*, April 2003.

Blair, Clay. *The Forgotten War: America in Korea, 1950–1953*. New York: Anchor Books, Doubleday, 1987.

Burrus, John. "A Little Brown Mare: Marines to Note 'Reckless' Deeds." *San Diego Union*, November 16, 1971.

Campbell, Jim. *War in the Land of the Morning Calm*. Alpharetta, GA: BookLogix, 2012.

Coleman, James F. "Un-Gok." *Leatherneck*, July 1953.

"Commandant Promotes 'Reckless' to Staff Sgt." *Pendleton Scout* 17, no. 36 (September 3, 1959).

Command Diaries and Special Action Reports. U.S. Marine Corps. USMC Archives, Korean War CDs, nos. 21, 22.

   1st Battalion, 5th Marines, Command Diaries, January 1953–December 1953.

   2nd Battalion, 5th Marines, Command Diaries, January 1953–December 1953.

Anti-Tank Company, Recoilless Rifle Platoon, 5th Marines, Command Diaries, October 1952–April 1953.

Battalion Operation Plan 26-53, MAR RCT LEX-1, Shore-Based Training Operation, May 1953.

Considine, Bob. "Heroic Horse Coming to U.S." *San Antonio Light*, October 25, 1954.

———. "Stateside … for Pride of the Marines." *Omaha World Herald*, October 25, 1954.

Cox, Lillian. "Four-Legged Marine Hero Retired to Camp Pendleton." *San Diego Union-Tribune*, November 14, 2004.

Cumings, Bruce. *The Korean War: A History*. New York: Modern Library, 2011.

Daum, Bill. "Pendleton Fetes 'Reckless,' Old Korea Pal of Local Pair." Files: Mascots. Historical Reference Branch, Marine Corps History Division, Marine Corps Base, Quantico, VA [November 1954?].

"Del Mar Honors 'SSgt Reckless.'" *Pendleton Scout*, July 27, 1962.

Dempsy, David. "The Horse Marine." *New York Times*, October 16, 1955.

Erickson, S. A. "Reckless Brings Back Memories." *San Diego Union*, July 31, 1966.

Fehrenbach, T. R. *This Kind of War*. New York: MacMillan, 1963.

"Fifth Marines Massed to Watch Dauntless Take Oath of Enlistment." *Pendleton Scout* 17, no. 28, July 9, 1959.

Fisher, James J. "In Harsh Winter, War Lives." *Kansas City Times*, December 25, 1989.

Fisher, Nelson. "Doc Jocoy Wins Del Mar Feature." *San Diego Union*, July 29, 1962.

Fugate, Robert T. "Vegas, Reno and Carson." *Leatherneck*, July 1953.

Gartz, Spence R. "Staging Regiment." *Leatherneck*, January 1953.

Geer, Andrew. "Reckless." *Leatherneck*, May 1955.

———. *Reckless, Pride of the Marines*. New York: E. P. Dutton, 1955.

———. "Reckless, Pride of the Marines." *Saturday Evening Post*, April 17, 1954.

———. "Red Carpet for Sergeant Reckless." *Saturday Evening Post*, October 22, 1955.

Griggs, Tom. "One Lady Who Saw Lots of Combat." *Navy Times*, June 28, 1976.

Guzzo, Louis R. "Wave of War Movies Coming," *Seattle Daily Times*. Julu 18, 1960.

Hemingway, Al. "'Highest Damn Beachhead in Korea': At Reno, Carson and Vegas—Dubbed the Nevada Cities—Marines Once Again Defeated the Chinese in March 1953." *VFW Magazine*, March 1, 2003.

Hendricks, Bonnie. *International Encyclopedia of Horse Breeds*. Norman: University of Oklahoma Press, October 1995.

Hoffman, Nancy Lee White. "Sgt Reckless: Combat Veteran." *Leatherneck*, November 1992.

"Horse Film Set." *Springfield Union*, October 8, 1960.

"It'll Be PVT Dauntless: Sgt Reckless to See 'Son' Enter Marines." *San Diego Union*, June 27, 1959.

Janzen, William H. "A Bad Night at Reno Block." *Leatherneck*, March 1998.

———. "The Reno Block." Published manuscript.

Johnson, Ronald. "Marine Sgt Reckless Lands Here—On All 4," *San Francisco Examiner*, November 11, 1954.

"Latest Reckless Kin to Be Enlisted Next Wednesday—Public Invited." *Pendleton Scout* 17, no. 26 (June 25, 1959).

Litalien, Dennis. "Memories of Reckless." *Enterprise*, April 26, 1984.

————. "'Reckless' Earns Place in Marine Corps History." Official Press Release no. 152-83. Joint Public Affairs Office, Marine Corps Base, Camp Pendleton, CA: May 24, 1983.

————. "Reckless—Pride of the Corps." *Western Horseman*, September 1983.

Marcus, Steven. "Sgt Reckless, Bless Her Soul, Makes News with a Reckless Foal." Files: Mascots. Historical Reference Branch, Marine Corps History Division, Marine Corps Base, Quantico, VA [April 1957?].

"Marine Association Buys Sgt Reckless." *Navy News*, December 1955.

Marine Corps Association. *Guidebook for Marines*. Quantico, VA: 2001.

Marine Corps Association Archives. February 1958.

"Marine Hikers Reach Camp Elliot Bivouac Area." *San Diego Union*, March 5, 1958.

"Marine, Mare, Mother." *Trenton Sunday Times Advertiser*, May 17, 1959.

"Marines Become Godfathers: 'Sarge' Reckless Bears Offspring." *San Diego Union*, April 10, 1957.

"Marines Recapture Vegas Hill." *Leatherneck* Magazine, March 28, 1953.

Mason, Janet, and Seth Goddard. "Man's Very Best Friends." *Life*, collector's edition, "Celebrating Our Heroes," May 5, 1997.

Matthias, Howard. *The Korean War: Reflections of a Young Combat Platoon Leader*. Tallahassee: Father and Son Publishing, 1995.

McCall, Elizabeth Kaye. "Sgt. Reckless." *Cowboys & Indians* 19, no. 5, July 2011.

McCamic, Jeremy C. *Korea Revisited*. Wheeling, WV: Taylormade Printing Services, 2006.

McConnell, John P., ed. "Dateline … Korea: The Challenge." *Leatherneck*, August 1953.

McLeod, A. C. "Marine Hero to Movie Star." *Long Beach Independent Press-Telegram*, January 22, 1961.

Meid, Pat, and James M. Yingling. *U.S. Marine Operations in Korea, 1950–1953*. Vol. 5, *Operations in West Korea*. Washington, D.C.: Historical Division, Headquarters U.S. Marine Corps, 1972.

Middleton, Alastair. "JeJu Racecourse Park." *Horse Racing in Korea* (blog). Korearacing.wordpress.com/jeju-racecourse-park.

Murphy, Jack, "Top Del Mar Fillies Share Stage with Korean Plater." *San Diego Union*, September 6, 1959.

Nalty, Bernard C. *Outpost War: U.S. Marines from the Nevada Battles to the Armistice*. Washington, D.C.: U.S. Marine Corps Historical Center, 2002.

Nash, Lyle W. "Book Reviews." *Pasadena Independent Scene*, October 23, 1955.

"'Night-Mare' in Shape: Marine Mare Dares Dancer." *Pacific Stars & Stripes*, June 9, 1953.

Parry, Bill. "Shoup Selection Defended by Pate." *San Diego Union*, September 1, 1959.

Parsons, Louella. "Louella Parsons on Hollywood: 'Joe McBeth' to Be Filmed." *Rockford (IL) Morning Star*, October 28, 1954.

Pontius, George. *Grace over the Long Run*. Bloomington, IN: iUniverse, 2010.

Putnam, George. "In Memory of Staff Sergeant Reckless." KTTV Los Angeles, November 22, 1971, 10:00 p.m. news broadcast. Reprinted with permission.

———. "Reckless." Eulogy, November 20, 1971. Reprinted with permission.

"Reckless Plaque Shown." *Pendleton Scout* 29, no. 47 (November 26, 1971).

Renner, Herbert, G. *Letters of War: An Anthology of the Korean War Era*. Baltimore: PublishAmerica, LLLP, 2007.

Reynolds, Boots. "Sgt Reckless, Mighty Marine." In *Chicken Soup for the Horse Lover's Soul*. Deerfield Beach, FL: Health Communications, 2003.

Ridgway and Clark Report. *Pictorial History of the Korean War, 1950–1953*. Veterans of Foreign Wars Memorial Edition, 1954.

Rothwell, Richard B. "New Era New Wars." In *Semper Fi*. Nashville, TN: Hammock Publishing, November/December 2007.

Russ, Martin. *The Last Parallel: A Marine's War Journal*. New York: Rinehart, 1957.

Sims, R. R. "New Ammo Diet Gives 'Reckless' Loose Denture." *First Word*, March 31, 1954.

Smith, Charles R. *U.S. Marines in the Korean War*. Washington, D.C.: History Division, United States Marine Corps, 2007.

Springer, John. "Reckless Had Local Saddle: San Diegan Figures in Story of Korean War's Hero Horse." *San Diego Union*, October 31, 1954.

"SSgt Reckless Transfers to FMCR; Subs & Quarters Provided for Life." *Pendleton Scout*, November 3, 1960.

Suhosky, Robert A. "Books Reviewed: Reckless—Pride of the Marines." *Leatherneck*, October 1955.

Sullivan, Ed. "Reckless: Pony Is Marines' Mascot and Hero." *Omaha World Herald*, November 14, 1954.

———. "Saga of Korea Race Horse That Became Marine Hero." *New York Daily News*, November 7, 1954.

Vogel, Scott. "Convivial Pursuit—the Search for the Perfect Mai Tai Becomes a Labor of Love and Lore." *Honolulu Star Bulletin* 6, no. 149 (June 10, 2001).

"War Hero, Son Promoted during 5thMar Ceremony." *Pendleton Scout*, June 20, 1957.

"We Buy Reckless." *Old Breed News: The Official Publication of the 1st Marine Division Association* 4, no. 10 (December 1955).

Wilson, Neill C. "Andy Geer—Great Marine, True Bohemian." *Bohemian Club Library Notes*, no. 2 (February 1959).

Wood, Ralph C. "Pickel Meadows." *Marine Corps Gazette*, October 1952.

"Writers Conference to Feature Panel Sessions." *Oakland Tribune*, April 8, 1956.

Personal Interviews and Letters
Special Thanks to Everyone
Who Added to This Story

Sgt. Chuck Batherson

Doug Bell

Sgt. Ray Berry

Lt. Col. Frank D. Brady

Lt. Tom Bulger

James Campbell

Nick D'Amber

Chuck Dacus

Cpl. Jake Dearing

Donald Denny

Sgt. Art DiGrazzio

Gunther Dohse

Cpl. Larry Donovan

Lt. Col. Milton Drummond

Tom Fant

Col. Walt Ford

Cpl. Paul Hammersley

Robert Hammershoy

John Henson

Nancy Hoffman

Sgt. William H. Janzen

Linda Johnson

Jim Johnston

Sgt. George Johannes

Roland O. Johnson

Cpl. Julian "Pete" Kitral

Pvt. James Larkin

Sgt. Ken Latham

Sgt. Kenneth D. Lunt

Sgt. Michael Mason

Sgt. Lynn Mattocks

Lt. Jeremy C McCamick

Debbie McCain

Rebecca Meador

Capt. John Melvin

Donald Menzies

Sgt. John Meyers

Robert L. Miller, DVM

Robert M. Miller, DVM

PFC Myron "Mad Mike" Mudurian

PFC John Newsom

Nancy Latham Parkin

Eric Pedersen Jr.

Navy Corpsman Robert Pontius

Lt. Col. Robert Purcell

George Putnam

Roland "Bud" Ralls

Denise Dwyer Reed

Herbert G. Renner Jr.

Boots Reynolds

Ken "Buzz" Riley

2nd Lt. William Riley

Navy Corpsman Bob "Doc" Rogers

Col. Richard Rothwell

Col. Richard B. Rothwell

Sgt. Robert Clay Shanrock

Cpl. Quentin Seidel

PFC Stanley Shafer

Sgt. Ralph Sherman

PFC Art Sickler

Sgt. Ronald Stowers

Mary Joe Streit (PFC Robert F. Dabb)

James Taggert

Sgt. Tommie Mack Turvey Sr.

Mary Tillery

Sgt. Harold Wadley

PFC Guy Frank Waggoner

George Waselinko

PFC Fred "Dutch" White

Cpl. J. R. Willcut

Cpl. Jesse J. Winters

S.Sgt. James Wright

ARTICLES ABOUT RECKLESS AND/OR HER FOALS APPEARING IN *PENDLETON SCOUT*

MARINE CORPS BASE, CAMP PENDLETON, CA. ARRANGED ACCORDING TO DATE PUBLISHED

"Reckless—Heroic Horse Marine Coming to Pendleton Pastures." *Pendleton Scout*, October 29, 1954, 2.

"Korean 'Hero' Foals Aspirant for 'Derby.'" *Pendleton Scout* 15, no. 15 (April 11, 1957): 1.

"1st Div Foal Name Test Undecided." *Pendleton Scout*, no. 16 (April 18, 1957): 1.

"Name for Famous Son." *Pendleton Scout*, April 25, 1957, 1.

"War Hero, Son Promoted During 5thMar Ceremony." *Pendleton Scout*, June 20, 1957, 5.

"Commandant Makes the Acquaintance of PFC Fearless." *Pendleton Scout*, October 31, 1957, 6.

"Mare Meets Mule." *Pendleton Scout*, February 27, 1958, 2.

"5thMar Back Home after 110 Mile Hike." *Pendleton Scout*, March 13, 1958, 8.

"Last of the Horse Marines." *Pendleton Scout*, July 17, 1958, 6.

"Reunion Photo Highlights." *Pendleton Scout*, July 24, 1958, 4–5.

"'All the Way' Fifth Marines Rest after Week Long 100 Mile Hike around Camp Pendleton." *Pendleton Scout*, no. 3 (January 22, 1959): 1, 6.

"SSgt. Reckless Adds New Colt to Family." *Pendleton Scout*, March 5, 1959, 3.

"Tell Me about the War, Mom." *Pendleton Scout*, March 12, 1959, 10.

"Latest Reckless Kin to Be Enlisted Next Wednesday—Public Invited." *Pendleton Scout* 17, no. 26 (June 25, 1959): 1.

"Fifth Marines Massed to Watch Dauntless Take Oath of Enlistment." *Pendleton Scout* 17, no. 28 (July 9, 1959): 1–2.

"Commandant's Tour." *Pendleton Scout*, August 6, 1959, 7.

"Reckless Makes E-6." *Pendleton Scout*, August 27, 1959, 7.

"Commandant Promotes 'Reckless' to Staff Sgt." *Pendleton Scout* 17, no. 36 (September 3, 1959): 1.

"Introducing SSgt Reckless." *Pendleton Scout*, October 27, 1960.

"SSgt Reckless Transfers to FMCR; Subs & Quarters Provided for Life." *Pendleton Scout*, November 3, 1960, 5.

"And That Ain't Hay." *Pendleton Scout*, November 10, 1960, 3.

"Horse Enthusiasts." *Pendleton Scout*, November 18, 1960, 11.

"1st MarDiv Reunion Slated for August." *Pendleton Scout*, July 20, 1962, 9.

"Del Mar Honors 'SSgt Reckless.'" *Pendleton Scout*, July 27, 1962, 8.

"Div Reunion at San Diego Is Successful." *Pendleton Scout* 20, no. 32 (August 10, 1962): 1.

"Son of Famed SSgt Arrives without Name." *Pendleton Scout* 22, no. 50 (December 11, 1964): 1.

"Wanted, One Name." *Pendleton Scout*, December 18, 1964, 2 (entry form).

"Winning Entry." *Pendleton Scout* 23, no. 5 (February 5, 1965): 1.

LeValley, Vera. "Meet a Marine—SSgt Reckless." *Pendleton Scout*, December 15, 1967, 6.

"Famed Mare Dies Following Wire Mishap." *Pendleton Scout*, May 17, 1968, 3.

"The Spirit of Reckless." *Pendleton Scout*, November 19, 1971, 10.

"Reckless Plaque Shown." *Pendleton Scout* 29, no. 47 (November 26, 1971): 1.

INDEX

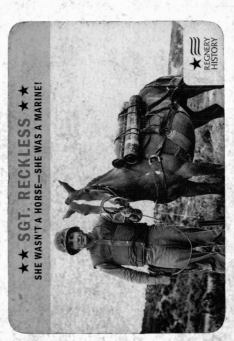

Card 1

USMC ★ ★ ★ ★ ★ ★ ★ ★ ★ ★
SGT. RECKLESS

1

SGT. RECKLESS STATS

Ht: 13 hands	
Wt: 900 lbs	
Drafted: 1952	
b. June 1948, Seoul, South Korea	
d. May 13, 1968, Camp Pendleton, CA	

CAREER HIGHLIGHTS

Award	No.
Purple Heart	2
Korean Service Medal	1

On October 26, 1952, Eric Pedersen, commander of the Recoilless Rifle Platoon, purchased the mare (for $250 from a young Korean man) as an ammunitions carrier for the Anti-Tank Division of the 5th Marines.

Card 2

USMC ★ ★ ★ ★ ★ ★ ★ ★ ★ ★
SGT. RECKLESS

2

SGT. RECKLESS STATS

Ht: 13 hands **Wt:** 900 lbs

Drafted: 1952

b. June 1948, Seoul, South Korea

d. May 13, 1968, Camp Pendleton, CA

CAREER HIGHLIGHTS

Award	No.
Navy Unit Citation	1
National Defense Service Medal	1

As a Marine, she was renamed "Reckless" for the gun she carried—the recoilless rifle—a weapon so dangerous it was nicknamed the "reckless" rifle. She also transported grenades, small arms ammunition, barbed wire, and communications wire, which unspooled from a pack on her back as she walked.

Card 3

USMC ★ ★ ★ ★ ★ ★ ★ ★ ★ ★
SGT. RECKLESS

3

SGT. RECKLESS STATS

Ht: 13 hands **Wt:** 900 lbs

Drafted: 1952

b. June 1948, Seoul, South Korea

d. May 13, 1968, Camp Pendleton, CA

CAREER HIGHLIGHTS

Award	No.
MC Good Conduct Medal	1
Republic of Korea Presidential Unit Citation	1

Amidst the terrifying sounds of exploding shells, Reckless carried five 150-pound loads of ammunition from the supply point to the firing site at the center of Jamestown Line—a series of defensive positions spanning thirty-five miles—in late November 1952, her first mission.

Card 4

USMC ★ ★ ★ ★ ★ ★ ★ ★ ★ ★
SGT. RECKLESS

4

SGT. RECKLESS STATS

Ht: 13 hands	
Wt: 900 lbs	
Drafted: 1952	
b. June 1948, Seoul, South Korea	
d. May 13, 1968, Camp Pendleton, CA	

CAREER HIGHLIGHTS

Award	No.
Presidential Unit Citation with Star	1
United Nations Service Medal	1

Reckless was used to eating whatever was on the menu in the officers' mess, ranging from scrambled eggs, coffee, Coke, and chocolate. Occasionally bartenders would pour the mare a few beers, which she happily slurped from a bucket.